EMIGRATI

MALYN NEWITT

Emigration and the Sea

*An Alternative History of Portugal
and the Portuguese*

OXFORD
UNIVERSITY PRESS

OXFORD

UNIVERSITY PRESS

Oxford University Press is a department of the
University of Oxford. It furthers the University's objective
of excellence in research, scholarship, and education
by publishing worldwide.

Oxford   New York
Auckland   Cape Town   Dar es Salaam   Hong Kong   Karachi
Kuala Lumpur   Madrid   Melbourne   Mexico City   Nairobi
New Delhi   Shanghai   Taipei   Toronto

With offices in
Argentina   Austria   Brazil   Chile   Czech Republic   France   Greece
Guatemala   Hungary   Italy   Japan   Poland   Portugal   Singapore
South Korea   Switzerland   Thailand   Turkey   Ukraine   Vietnam

Oxford is a registered trade mark of Oxford University Press
in the UK and certain other countries.

Published in the United States of America by
Oxford University Press
198 Madison Avenue, New York, NY 10016

Library of Congress Cataloging-in-Publication Data is available
Newitt, Malyn
Emigration and the Sea/An Alternative History of Portugal
and thePortuguese
ISBN 978-0-19-026393-5

Printed in India on acid-free paper

CONTENTS

LIST OF TABLES

GLOSSARY

asiento	Contract to supply the Spanish territories in America with slaves
azulejos	Decorative ceramic tiles
bandeirantes	Men who formed the *bandeiras*
bandeiras	Armed expeditions sent into the interior of Brazil
bidonvilles	Shanty towns on the outskirts of Paris
Brasileiro	An emigrant to Brazil who returned rich to Portugal
caixeiros	Sales person in a shop
cantineiro	Bar keeper
capela	Land endowment for the support of religious services
carreira da Índia	The voyage of Indiamen from Portugal to India
cartaz	License to trade, sold to Asian shipowners and merchants
Casa de Portugal	Name given to clubs or associations of expatriate Portuguese
casados	Portuguese soldiers given permission to leave the colours and marry
colonatos	Subsidised agricultural settlements in Africa in the 1950s and 1960s
compadrazgo	Godparentage
contias	Financial payments made for those serving the Portuguese Crown in a military capacity
conto	A thousand escudos

ix

conversos	Jews who converted to Christianity
cruzado	Portuguese silver coin worth 400 reis
degredados	Convicts
dotar	Institution for providing dowries for Jewish and New Christian girls in Amsterdam
encomienda	Grants of population made to Spanish conquerors in Moorish territory, the Canary Islands and America
engajadores	Labour recruiters
engenho	Sugar mill or plantation
estrangeirado	Someone who has settled abroad and been influenced by foreign culture
faiscador	Gold prospector
fajãs	Settlements on the island of São Jorge in the Azores formed on the edge of the sea by landslips or the estuaries of small streams
favelas	Shanty-town settlements around Rio de Janeiro
fazenda	Rural estate or plantation
fazendeiro	Owner of a plantation
feitoria	Trading factory
festa	Communal festival, often celebrating a saint's day
fidalgo	Nobleman by birth
Francês	Someone who has made money working in France
Gastarbeiter	Foreign migrant workers in Germany
grogue	rum distilled in Cape Verde
grumetes	African servants and clients of the Portuguese in West Africa
impérios	Chapels built in the Azores to celebrate the cult of the Holy Spirit
indígena	Native of the Portuguese African colonies subject to the *indigenato* labour code
indigenato	Laws governing the natives in the Portuguese African colonies
lançados	Renegades who lived on the African mainland outside Portuguese jurisdiction
lavradores da cana	Sugar growers
Lei das Sesmarias	Law of the wastelands. The law by which land was granted to settlers to farm

GLOSSARY

levadas	Irrigation channels in Madeira
limpeza	Cleanness; used especially by Old Christians to describe the idea of 'purity' of blood
Lingua Geral	A creole dialect of Portuguese and Tupi-Guaraní
manilhas	Bracelets or anklets usually made of brass and used as a trade item
marranos	Converted Jews who practised a religion mixing Jewish and Christian elements
milrei	Brazilian currency unit
Misericórdia	The Santa Casa da Misericórdia was a charitable organisation, membership of which conferred high social status
morgadios	Entailed property of a noble family
moradores	Portuguese settlers in the overseas territories
morna	Music and dance genre from Cape Verde
nação	Nation; used to describe Portuguese Jewish communities outside Portugal
Orfãs do Rei	Crown Orphans
padroado real	The royal patronage over the Catholic Church in Asia
palmatoadas	Beating the palms of the hand
palmatoria	'Paddle' for administering punishment on the palms of the hand
panos	Cotton cloth produced in the Cape Verde Islands
pardos	People of mixed race
pontas	Farms worked by Cape Verdeans in West Africa
povo	The ordinary people
prazos	Grants of land and population made to Portuguese in the Zambesi valley and the hinterland of Sofala and Quelimane
rancho	A musical group or party
recôncavo	Sugar-growing area of the northern Brazilian coast
reconquista	The reconquest of territory in the Iberian peninsula and North Africa from the Moors
regimentos	Official instructions drawn up for fortress commanders or ships' captains

retornados	Returning migrants, especially those returning from Africa after the independence of the colonies in 1975
ricos homens	A term commonly used in the Middle Ages for the noble class in Portugal
roças	Coffee and cocoa plantations in São Tomé and Príncipe
salinas	Salt pans
Senado da Câmara	Senate; governing body established in cities by royal charter
sertão	Backlands, the interior
serviçais	African contract labourers
tangomaos	Portuguese settlers on the African mainland who were more embedded in African culture
vínculos	Entails (of property)
vizinhos	Citizens (literally neighbours)

FOREWORD

In 2010 I published a book on Portuguese history entitled *Portugal in European and World History*. Its focus was on metropolitan Portugal, and in particular on the decisive importance which the port of Lisbon gave to what would otherwise have been an insignificant fragment of mountain and coastline to the west of the Iberian peninsula. However, as four chapters in the book made clear, the history of the Portuguese cannot be limited by a study of the small European state of Portugal, but has to include the communities planted by the Portuguese throughout the world and the networks constructed between these communities, whether in colonies formerly ruled from Lisbon or in other states where ethnic Portuguese or people who have assumed a Portuguese identity have established themselves. 'If America is a nation of immigrants,' wrote Caroline Brettell, 'Portugal is a nation of emigrants.'[1] It is the purpose of this book to examine the history of this greater Portugal, of the Portuguese communities which for various reasons became separated from the national territory of European Portugal. It is a history of the Portuguese rather than a history of Portugal.

1

EMIGRATIONS, DIASPORAS
AND PEOPLE ON THE MOVE

Understanding emigration

The history of all human communities is marked by the interaction of two apparently conflicting tendencies: the desire to remain securely in a single place and the desire to move in search of a more favourable environment and enhanced opportunities in life; in other words, the passion to put down roots and the passion to move to pastures new. As this book will demonstrate, these are not conflicting tendencies at all but aspects of human society that are complementary and mutually supporting.

At one time the term 'diaspora' was largely reserved for the story of the dispersal of the Jews, but it is now much more widely used. There are countless examples of individuals and whole communities dispersing over great distances, under various political, social and economic pressures, who continue to maintain a cultural identity rooted in the idea of a homeland or place of origin: the various *Völkerwanderungen* which dispersed Asian populations eastwards across the land bridge of the Bering Strait throughout the American continents or by sea through the Pacific Islands; the movement of Central Asian peoples westwards through the steppes to Russia, Poland and western Europe; the spread of Greeks throughout the Mediterranean and Black Sea regions; the dispersal of Scandinavians throughout the North Atlantic and down the

1

rivers of Russia; the migration of the Indian caste that came to form the distinctive Roma communities of Europe. The list is endless. With these migrations, languages, religions, social customs and economic practices were widely disseminated, merged with other cultures and evolved in a constant process of 'creolisation'. Most migrants do not seek to return to the place from which they migrated and are quickly assimilated into the communities where they settle. However, some migrating groups retain a strong attachment to a homeland, real or imagined, or seek to retain an identity, a cultural separateness, which keeps them from being fully absorbed into the society within which they are living. These communities are true diasporas.

In many cases lack of evidence means that the reasons for migrations, which were sometimes movements of individuals or small groups and sometimes of large communities, are little understood. Although it is self-evident that many people migrate in order to better their condition in some way, such a general assertion needs a greater degree of focus before it can mean very much. Migrations, for example, are not always voluntary and can arise from the forcible expulsion of individuals or groups from their place of settlement for political or cultural reasons or because of economic pressures (poverty, unemployment, land shortage, climate change, over-population). The exile of convicts, contract labour, slavery and the slave trade are also forms of migration—forced migration clearly, but frequently leading to the establishment of long-lived diasporic communities.

Voluntary migrations may be what are now called trade diasporas (traders who travel and settle outside their homeland in the pursuit of commercial opportunity). In a recent, highly acclaimed book on the slave trade, Toby Green uses the term diaspora to apply to 'trading communities characterized by the ability to retain distinctive original cultural features and [which] also adopt traits of the host culture'.[1] Migrations may also be migrations of elites (military leaders and soldiers of fortune, scions of ruling families seeking to establish new communities over which to rule) or migrations of members of the educated classes (scholars, *sharifs*, missionaries, artists and literati). Pilgrimages are a form of migration, the pilgrim leaving home in search of some spiritual destination. In the imagination of religious writers the whole of life becomes a pilgrimage, a migration from a point of origin to a distant goal of spiritual fulfilment. Many migrations share more than one of the above characteristics, and in most cases there are 'pull' factors as well as 'push' factors—certain destinations exert an attraction, which may exist only in the imagination, but which nevertheless provide a powerful incentive for people to move who might otherwise not have done so.

Migrations, therefore, whether of individuals or whole groups, usually present a complex mixture of motives, causes and historical contingencies. Recent studies have emphasised just how complex migrations can be. The commonest form of migration is internal migration, from one part of a country to another or from the countryside to the town—the history of almost all large towns is one of in-migration of very diverse groups from the surrounding rural areas or from further afield. William McNeill has stressed the importance of the high mortality in towns, which created a kind of demographic vacuum that sucked in population from rural areas.[2] Some migrations were only seasonal with regular return to the point of origin. Others were staged (single males who would later be joined by other family members). Then there were chain migrations and networks which linked people from extended families or neighbourhoods in migratory movements which, without such linkages, might never have taken place. It is no coincidence that many of the adventurers who enlisted with Pizarro for his expedition to Peru were from his own home town of Trujillo. There can also be onward migrations as people from migrant communities move on from their original first port of call to further destinations or decide to return to their original homeland. As the means of travel have become easier, so the to and fro of migration has become ever more complex. Recently the 'grey' migration of retired people heading for retirement locations in Florida or the Mediterranean has acquired the kind of volume typical of earlier migratory movements.

On the other hand, the ties which have bound people to a homeland and settled community have always been strong—some human communities revealing through their DNA an identity with a single place stretching back hundreds, even thousands, of years. Among the factors that attach communities to specific locations are the belief in the religious significance of special places (tombs of ancestors, religious shrines); the control of economic resources (land, water, minerals, rights over hunting and gathering); the importance of a support network of kin and community for survival; common language and customs; strong cultural identification with a particular environment; real or perceived difficulties presented by any move, and simple inertia. In

3

the case of true diasporas, a community may move or be displaced from its homeland but retain a deep attachment to the land, community and place which they have left behind. There will often be an attempt to recreate the homeland in the new place of settlement. James Sweet even entitled his study of the slave community in Brazil *Recreating Africa*.[3]

There are further issues that need clarification. Human migrations, it has been claimed, cannot be understood in general terms that are applicable to all eras of human history, but have to be seen as the result of specific circumstances related to specific times and places. Recent mass migrations, for example, cannot be explained by looking at historic patterns of migration but have to be placed in the context of the development of global capitalism. As Miriam Halpern Pereira put it,

although a phenomenon of ancient origin, [migration] came to acquire in the course of the nineteenth century new characteristics: it ceased to be predominantly integrated into an imperial project and became the result of distortions in the development of dependence capitalism.[4]

Joel Serrão made the same point when he wrote, 'it is becoming more clear, at least in our view, that the emigrations which took place in the socio-economic context of the Ancien Régime are structurally different ... from those which have taken place in the context of contemporary industrial capitalism'.[5] A strong case can be made for this distinction, but it requires that powerful elements of continuity between the different periods be discounted. Moreover, it is saying little more than that history never repeats itself exactly, despite the underlying structures that exist over the *longue durée*, just as no two landscapes are exactly similar despite the underlying similarities of their geology. Looking at six centuries of Portuguese migration, it is the similarities not the differences in the processes of emigration and the experiences of the emigrants that are most striking.

One reason for migrations, forced or otherwise, has always been the requirements of the global labour market and the imbalance in regional economies. For some economists this is reason enough. Before the sixteenth century most movements of labour were probably fairly small-scale: seasonal labour at harvest time, the use of slaves in domestic service, in mining, agriculture or the rowing of galleys. However, the sixteenth century saw the beginning of what grew into a transfer of very large numbers of human beings to satisfy a large and rapidly growing demand for labour. It was the development of plantation agriculture, first in the Atlantic islands and then in the New World, which required labour in unprecedented quantities. The demand was met in two ways: by the use of various bureaucratic measures to engage the poor or criminal classes in forms of time-limited apprenticeship, and the purchase of African slaves. In the nineteenth century slavery was gradually replaced by a return to the idea of time-limited work contracts for the poor. Most of this demand was met from India and China, but thousands of poor Europeans, among them many Portuguese, were also contracted in this way.

In the twentieth century contracted labour was largely replaced by freeing up the movement of voluntary labour, making it easy for people from underdeveloped economies to migrate to meet the demands of the developed world. There is no sign of such transfers coming to an end or even slowing. In the twenty-first century there is still a massive demand for labour in agriculture and construction, while the megacities of the world employ armies of cleaners, caterers and maintenance staff. Stand and look out over the cityscapes of London, Chicago, Dubai or Shanghai and ask, who cleans all these buildings, disposes of the rubbish, builds the skyscrapers and provides the food and services? The answer is a vast multitude of usually low-paid workers, mostly immigrants from poorer countries. These migrants are nearly invisible to the citizens and bureaucrats. They live and work beneath the radar of the law and the social services. They are not exactly slaves but they are removed only halfway from slavery. They usually have no rights and often no legal status or protection. They do not even have the advantage, which some contracted workers had in the past, of being able to look forward to the end of their servitude with a paid return passage or the right to settle and own land.

To understand modern mass migration it is always necessary to see how it fits into the demands for labour and the cycles of the world's economy. Even so, migration cannot be understood by abstract economic principles alone. Networks and chain migration are still important. Traditional areas of migration still count for more than simple demand in the labour market. Affinity of language between migrants and the host countries can be of crucial importance. Migration still remains an individual decision related to an individual's circumstances.[6]

Joel Serrão also makes a distinction between 'colonisation' and 'emigration'. The colonist, he says, is acting 'due to the initiative of the state or is integrated in some project within the national ambit'; the emigrant 'abandons his country exclusively for personal motives'.[7] This was an important distinction for those who sought to control and direct emigration, as the Portuguese governments frequently tried to do. In the eyes of the governing elite there were good and bad migrants, just as there were deserving and undeserving poor. However, when the causes and effects of migration are viewed in the long term, the colonist and the emigrant are frequently one and the same person. Nevertheless the recent history of European colonisation and decolonisation has, in many respects, added a new dimension to the story of emigration. The rapid expansion of European empires in the nineteenth century was accompanied by a great increase in the numbers of elite emigrants (colonial administrators, technicians, soldiers, teachers, scientific researchers) who had a profound cultural impact on the societies where they operated; but the equally rapid dismantling of these empires did not involve just repatriating these migrants. As John Darwin has pointed out, decolonisation had unexpected consequences in the great influx into the metropoles of peoples from the former empires who made full use of the networks that imperial rule had established and who were often slow to integrate with the host society.

If decolonisation had necessitated the fashioning of new national identities, it had also encouraged the cultural expression of innumerable 'subnational' ones. This cultural expression had to be portable; that is, it had to be accessible and comprehensible to outsiders—whether local or international—if the economic and political claims it embodied were to stand any chance.... Hence, vast numbers of people previously equipped only with a highly localised culture ... quickly acquired the basic techniques of preserving a distinct cultural identity in an alien environment....[8]

An important distinction is usually made between diasporas and other types of migration by focusing on the explicit desire of the diasporic community to retain ties with the real or imagined homeland and to preserve identities which create links with other diasporic communities. This characteristic can vary from the celebration of loose cultural identities to a desire to maintain a wholly separate, ghetto existence within the host society. This attachment of diasporic communities to a homeland, or the idea of a homeland, is sometimes expressed as a conscious desire to return: Jews still utter the words 'next year in Jerusalem' at the end of every Passover Seder; and in many cases the idea that one day you will return can help to assuage a number of psychological problems encountered in the process of migration and be the factor that reconciles the conflicting tendencies of wanting to remain rooted with the desire to better oneself by moving away.

However, by no means all diasporic communities actively seek a physical return to the homeland; rather more common is the attempt to recreate an idealised version of the homeland in the place where they have settled. This is particularly the case with elite emigrants who have aspired to form new polities which recreate their homeland and reassert its values. To illustrate this one might consider the Viking chieftains who settled in Iceland and Greenland, the Crusader lords who carved out kingdoms and counties in the Middle East, or the Islamic 'Swahili' elites in eastern Africa where over a period of many hundreds of years leading members of ruling families migrated to found new towns and settlements where they sought to recreate the traditional Islamic community they had left.

In contrast to the tendency of some diasporic communities to maintain distinct identities defined by the idea of a cultural homeland, it has been maintained that communities of migrants almost always undergo some form of creolisation; that is, they absorb elements of the culture of the host country without becoming totally absorbed by it. Sometimes this adoption of elements of the host culture is merely a device to enable the individual to operate successfully in the host society; sometimes it is a stage on the way to total absorption, as so often happened with emigrants to the United States. However, creolisation may also be the birth of a new ethnic identity. The study of creolisation is sometimes very narrowly focused on a few self-styled 'creole' societies who speak 'creole' languages, but creolisation itself is much more common in human history. It is the process by which all cultures grow and change—the English language, for example, is the result of a process of creolisation which merged Celtic, Latin and Germanic elements into a new language. Portuguese and Spanish are creolised forms of Latin, while Swahili is also a creole language derived from Arabic and Bantu elements. What is true of languages is also true of cultures, which are never static and evolve through interaction between groups. From this perspective, *métissage* is not the result of crossing distinct cultures but part of what is a very fluid process of interaction and change that is constantly taking place in all societies.

In the twenty-first century the demands of global capitalism, the ready flow of information and the relative ease of travel have turned migration into a massive phenomenon. Sometimes it seems as if the whole world is on the move, meeting the demands of a global labour market or seeking the grass that is always perceived as being greener across the sea. Virtually every ethnic group now has its diasporic community, and the ideological fictions that still attempt to confine ethnic groups to defined national territories are every year more difficult to defend.

In the twenty-first century there remains the assumption, stridently voiced in some political quarters, that it is somehow natural for people of a single ethnicity to inhabit a nation state and that this normal condition of society is threatened by the existence of diasporic communities. The assumption that nations inhabiting national territories were somehow a norm which has been undermined by globalisation, and that nation states represent some golden age ideal to which we all struggle to return, is totally to misunderstand history. The idea of the nation inhabiting a nation state was employed in comparatively recent times to legitimise certain power structures and deny legitimacy to others. Linda Colley, for example, has eloquently demonstrated just how recent a construct the idea of being 'British' really is.[9] Before the nineteenth century people were more flexible in their loyalties and identities and moved about with greater readiness than this view of history will permit. The large multi-ethnic states of the past, like the Mongol khanates, the Austro-Hungarian Empire, the Ottoman Empire or the Russian Empire always contained, on an extensive scale, what today would be called diasporas: Venetian communities were established in China under the Mongol khans, Tatar and German communities were to be found throughout imperial Russia, Greeks and Armenians had their own quarters in most Ottoman cities. In all these cases ethnic communities, while taking advantage of the relative freedom of movement within the overarching imperial state, retained a strong identity with their cultural homeland and sometimes negotiated separate privileges for themselves from the rulers. Edward Shils has argued that such multi-ethnic states are only possible if the ethnic minorities are content to remain somewhat detached from the centre and do not challenge the culture or power structure of the dominant elite.[10]

In many ways, therefore, the global migrations of the twenty-first century mark a return to a past when multi-ethnic, not national states were the norm, a past which historians and politicians embedded in the nationalist traditions are so reluctant to recognise. For this reason the study of diasporas should suggest ways in which the twenty-first century might think more positively about the immigrant communities brought about by globalisation. It has been pointed out that, although the separate identities that diasporic communities seek to maintain in their host country can lead to conflict and even to 'ethnic cleansing', the opposite can also be true. 'The strategy of being different to be equal or being special to belong has predominated in societies where cultural diversity is not only a valued feature but also a central characteristic of the social structure.'[11]

Yet it is one of the ironies of history that the diasporic communities tend to cultivate nationalist sentiment as much if not more than their compatriots who remain behind in the homeland. Ethnic or national consciousness is often essential for the cohesion of the diasporic community and for the preservation of its identity. Moreover the nationalism which it asserts is often an idealised construct built on distant and increasingly fictitious memories. This can make the diasporic communities appear conservative and out of touch with the social and cultural change that has been taking place in the homeland. It is a commonplace that English expatriate communities often were, and still are, the last guardians of an imagined English society and outdated English values that in England itself are long gone. The profound disillusionment of emigrants who return to the homeland they have idealised is, after all, a very common experience.

Characteristics of the Portuguese diaspora

Portuguese emigration, which first assumed a large dimension in the fifteenth century, was the earliest major migration of western European people beyond their own continent and beyond the Mediterranean basin. Many of those who left their Portuguese homeland over the course of the next six centuries were migrants who became absorbed into other communities, but others sought either to create a new Portugal overseas or held on to a Portuguese identity which set them apart from their host community. There are twists and turns in this story which make it exceptionally complex and difficult fully to describe.[12] Below are set out some of the characteristics that distinguish Portuguese emigration, none of them in themselves unique but, taken together, forming a remarkable story which is perhaps without parallel in history.

First, the migrations of the Portuguese were not concentrated in one short period but were continuous over six hundred years—the complaints of sixteenth-century writers that Portugal was being depopulated were echoed in exactly the same terms by writers in the nineteenth and twentieth centuries. In the fifteenth century Portuguese peopled the islands of the Atlantic; in the sixteenth century possibly as many as a quarter of a million Portuguese endured the harrowing journey to India; in the seventeenth and eighteenth centuries emigrant Portuguese settled Brazil, sometimes in such numbers that the Crown sought to control the outflow; in the nineteenth century tens of thousands left for the USA, the Caribbean and Brazil, reaching a peak in 1910–11; in the twentieth century emigrants left not in their thousands but in their hundreds of thousands for France, Germany and Switzerland but also for Canada, Venezuela, Argentina, Australia and South Africa. And in the twenty-first century emigration has begun once again, this time to Africa. Over the centuries the idea of emigration has become deeply embedded in Portuguese culture and the reality has profoundly influenced the political economy of Portugal itself.

Second, Portuguese emigration provides examples of all the main types of migrants and migrations. There were forced migrants—individual convicts, orphans and political exiles as well as whole groups like Jews, gypsies and black slaves; there were poverty-stricken and landless peasant families driven by economic hardship to seek to better their lives by seasonal migrations or by leaving permanently for distant lands; there were merchants who settled outside Portugal to carry on their business and members of the nobility—the military and political elite—who sought lucrative official positions in the empire or seigneurial landholdings in the colonies to maintain their status. There was also a steady emigration of the intelligentsia: missionaries bound for the East or South America and scholars and churchmen seeking preferment, appointments or patrons in other European states. The Portuguese who made their careers in foreign courts, salons and universities or who practised their professions abroad have a name. They are the *estrangeirados* who are to be found in most European countries from the sixteenth century to the present, among their descendants some of the greatest figures of western European civilisation, for Baruch Spinoza, Diego Velázquez and Benjamin Disraeli all descended from Portuguese living in exile from their homeland. Nor should one forget the soldiers of fortune heading for glory and wealth wherever there was war and the large number of women who left to join their husbands and families who had already left the homeland. It was the coming together of these very different elements that enabled the migrants to attempt to recreate a Portuguese homeland in so many parts of the world.

Third has been the fact that the migration of Portuguese has not consisted only of men and women departing from Portugal itself. The Portuguese communities established overseas have themselves generated further migrations. After the first wave of Portuguese emigrants had settled in the Atlantic islands, fresh migrations took place from these island homelands. Some left to search for other islands in the Atlantic, while others, intent on trade, left the sovereign territory of the Portuguese Crown and formed trading communities along the West African coast. This process would continue in the East where Portuguese left the officially established Portuguese cities of Goa or Malacca to migrate to new lands in South-East Asia, Bengal or the China Sea, or to seek their fortunes among the indigenous populations as traders, mercenaries, pirates or missionaries. In the nineteenth and twentieth centuries this process continued as migrants in increasing numbers left Goa to find careers in British India and East Africa, while Macaonese and Timorese, who held Portuguese nationality, went to Australia and Portuguese from Mozambique moved to South Africa. Meanwhile many Portuguese who had settled in Hawaii and Trinidad relocated to California and Illinois. The Portuguese story is not therefore one of departure from a single homeland, it is also the story of the dispersal of the emigrant communities themselves. Individual Portuguese, particularly in the early days, have been highly mobile. The Portuguese world was essentially, although not exclusively, a maritime one in which the coastal settlements from Brazil to China were connected by a network of sea routes. Along these pathways individual Portuguese would move in surprisingly varied ways, and the viability of this maritime empire depended on the facility with which people could move within it. John Russell-Wood called his study of the Portuguese empire *A World on the Move* to emphasise that the Portuguese who left their homeland were essentially a mobile migrant people.[13]

Fourth, in the 1490s the expulsion of Jews and their descendants from the Iberian peninsula began. Initially the policy had been to put pressure on the Jews to convert to Christianity, but those who did convert and came to form the *converso* (in Portugal called 'New

Christian') communities were soon seen as a Judaic fifth column within society. The Inquisition was established in Spain and later in Portugal to ensure their orthodoxy. Castile began the expulsion of unconverted Jews in a systematic way in 1492, and three years later Portugal was persuaded also to implement laws enforcing conversion or expulsion. Large numbers of Jews took the opportunity to emigrate—forced migrants who resettled initially around the shores of the Mediterranean and subsequently in northern Europe, western Africa and the New World. Over the next three centuries persecution of the 'New Christians', descendants of Jews who had converted, continued. These persecutions, sporadic as they were, nevertheless ensured that there was a steady and continuing emigration of 'New Christians' to join Jewish and *converso* communities outside Portugal, in the process forming the Sephardic branch of Judaism. The Jewish and New Christian diaspora never wholly merged with that of the other streams of Portuguese migrants though the two streams often ran through the same bed, mixing their waters along the way to such an extent that in the eyes of many host states no distinction was made between 'Portuguese', Jew or New Christian.

The dispersal of the Sephardic Jews must be considered a forced emigration, though many left voluntarily and once departed from Portugal were able to move freely to find a congenial community in which to settle. The same, however, could not be said for the third stream of migration which also began in the fifteenth century and merged with the other two to create new Portuguese communities throughout the Atlantic world. The slave trade from Africa was always a form of forced migration, though the settlements that resulted from it often assumed the status of free Portuguese communities. In the fifteenth century the Portuguese labour market was not elastic enough nor was the demographic surplus sufficient to secure the effective occupation of the newly discovered islands. So the Portuguese developed a slave trade to supplement the labour force at home and to provide additional labour resources for the island settlements. By the middle of the sixteenth century slaves brought into the Portuguese settlements were equalling and possibly exceeding the numbers of Christian and New Christian Portuguese, and slaves were also being landed in Portugal to replace the Portuguese who were leaving. It has been estimated that by the middle of the sixteenth century nearly 10 per cent of the population of Lisbon may have been slaves. The emigration of Portuguese was being matched by the immigration of Africans—a two-way movement of population, similar to that of the late twentieth century when Cape Verdeans were encouraged to come to Portugal to replace the large numbers of emigrants departing for northern Europe. The slaves supplied the labour needed by the Portuguese economy and by the new settlements overseas, but they also provided women to complement what was largely a male Portuguese migration. In this way the forced migration of African slaves merged with the Portuguese Christian and New Christian diasporas, and through their mulatto offspring the slave women gave rise to the free black Portuguese communities which grew up in the islands, along the African coast and in Brazil.

If these factors made the tapestry of the worldwide Portuguese diaspora a complex one, further complication was provided by the assimilation into the Portuguese communities of people who were not slaves and who had no direct link with a Portuguese homeland. In the fifteenth and sixteenth centuries, although national consciousness certainly existed enabling people to describe themselves as 'English' or 'Portuguese', people were first and foremost subjects of their overlords rather than citizens of a nation state. People of different ethnic origin who spoke different languages could find themselves subjects of the same monarch. As Portuguese expansion unfolded, first in the Atlantic and West Africa and then in Brazil and maritime Asia, very many people who had no personal or family origin in Portugal became subject to the Portuguese Crown, beginning with the French, Genoese and Flemish who helped people the Atlantic islands. In Africa, Asia and America many thousands, and eventually millions, of people acquired a Portuguese allegiance either directly through living in a Portuguese settlement or indirectly through becoming subject to the *padroado real*—the royal patronage over the church in the eastern half of the world—granted by the Papacy to the Portuguese Crown. The communities of the Portuguese diaspora also acquired clients, servants, wives and workers from local communities. Through adoption of the Christian religion and the use of the Portuguese language these groups became 'Lusitanised', adopting Portuguese names, religious practices, dress and other cultural symbols. Many of these people and their descendants in time identified themselves, or became identified by others, as 'Portuguese'. Moreover this process was not always limited to the lower orders of society and in many locations in Asia individuals from elite families assumed a Lusitanian identity. This Portuguese identity often involved a high degree of local adaptation which departed ever further from a recognised European norm. Stefan Halikowski-Smith has commented on the 'Portuguese' of Ayutthaya who 'appropriated certain items of Portuguese dress such as hats whilst neglecting others such as shoes'.[14]

Although emigrant Portuguese clung to their Portuguese identity, this did not prevent their Portuguese culture being radically altered by close association with slaves and with peoples native to the areas where they settled. The hybrid cultures that evolved can legitimately be called 'creole', and their most striking features were the Portuguese creole languages which evolved in Asia and in the Atlantic where they still flourish in the Cape Verde and Gulf of Guinea islands and in Guinea-Bissau. The thesis advanced by Toby Green is that creolisation was inextricably linked to the diaspora of Jews and New Christians—'the *lançados* [Portuguese settled in West Africa] were only able to operate with such success because of their cultural pre-disposition towards flexibility, which was a result of their New Christian origins and the recent history of the New Christians in Portugal'.[15] Elsewhere he suggests that 'Old Christians [had] an increasingly inflexible ideological outlook in which "intermarriage" was a positive slur on one's *limpeza*' which they were 'less able to countenance than New Christians'.[16] Whatever may have been the case in western Africa, this alleged reluctance of the Old Christians to countenance intermarriage was self-evidently not the case in the rest of the world where the willingness of Portuguese of all classes to marry or cohabit with local women began the process of creolisation wherever the Portuguese settled in the world.

There were also cases where a Portuguese creole culture took root in societies that were not under Portuguese rule at all and where Portuguese immigrants were few. The most notable example of this was the kingdom of Kongo in West Africa where the Mwissikongo aristocracy adopted Christianity along with Portuguese titles, names, styles of dress and material culture. This Kongolese elite can hardly be considered part of the Portuguese diaspora, but the creole culture that evolved in Kongo possessed many similarities with the creole cultures that evolved in areas of Portuguese settlement.

The establishment of Portuguese communities so widely dispersed across the world would not have been possible without an institutional cement to bind them to one another and to the homeland of Portugal from which they derived their identity, even if only at many times removed. This strong institutional underpinning is a marked characteristic of the Portuguese diaspora. The Catholic church has probably been the strongest bond tying together so many far-flung communities, and in many ways the Catholic church has been a national church for the Portuguese since Papal Bulls in the fifteenth and sixteenth centuries conferred on Portugal special rights over the church in Africa and Asia—rights which included making church appointments, regulating missions, authorising regional church councils and collecting ecclesiastical taxes. These rights covered all Christians and not just the immediate subjects of the Portuguese Crown. Through the existence of church courts, including the Inquisition which was established in Goa in 1560, this made all Christians subject in their spiritual life and in the organisation of their family and social affairs to the influence, if not always the direct jurisdiction, of the Portuguese Crown.

For Portuguese throughout the world it was not just belonging to the church that bound them together but celebrating specific festivals and venerating specific saints. Although many communities celebrated the protection of their local saints, it was Saint Anthony of Lisbon (and Padua) and Saint Elmo, patron saint of sailors, who were venerated throughout the Portuguese world. The annual feast of Corpus Christi was the highlight of the Christian Year for all Portuguese, while Azorean emigrants took with them wherever they went the special devotion to the Holy Spirit, a devotion which was traced back to the canonised Portuguese queen—Saint Isabel.

The larger cities of the Portuguese empire had a chartered town council—a Senado da Câmara—modelled on that of Lisbon. These councils that governed, among others, the communities of Funchal, Macao, Malacca, Goa, Luanda, São Tomé, Bahia and Rio were similar in their constitutions, their responsibilities and their *modus operandi*. They, more than any other institution, bound the communities of the Portuguese together into a mutually supporting worldwide community. Each Portuguese community also established religious brotherhoods and a Santa Casa da Misericórdia. The Misericórdia was a highly prestigious organisation, primarily of lay Portuguese, originally founded in Lisbon in 1498 by the dowager queen D. Leonor. It raised money and owned property, the income from which was dedicated to charitable causes—the care of the sick, the burial of the dead, the support or ransom of prisoners, the protection of widows and orphans. The Misericórdias also operated as banks and trustees for the property of orphans, widows or absentees.

Wherever a Portuguese travelled in the world he would find familiar religious brotherhoods and a Misericórdia, and could take part in the annual celebration of Corpus Christi or, in the twentieth century, pay his respects to Our Lady of Fatima. Take, for example, this description of the seasonal migration of Portuguese fishermen to the Grand Banks off Newfoundland.

> On 27 May [1955], four thousand Portuguese fishermen, clad in their colourful checkered shirts, walked fifteen to twenty abreast up the hilly streets of St John's to the Basilica of St John the Baptist, bearing the three-and-one-half-foot-high statue of Our Lady of Fatima, their gift of gratitude and friendship. Our Lady was to be a holy link between the two peoples.... The six thousand men and women who filled the cathedral, along with those who lined the streets, were part of "one of the most colourful, inspiring, and solemn events ever to take place in St John's".[17]

The church has remained important for Portuguese communities throughout the world, with the veneration of Our Lady of Fatima perhaps now more prominent than that of St Anthony or St Elmo. However, as befits a more secular age, the Misericórdias have been replaced by mutual aid societies, which from the nineteenth century have been funded by most Portuguese emigrant communities and which have survived in the better organised communities until the present. At first these were established to provide financial support for poor and struggling migrants, but as the twentieth century advanced and Portuguese communities became financially more stable they were often refounded as cultural organisations. In many diasporic communities there is now to be found a Casa de Portugal, which provides Portuguese language lessons, celebrates festivals, not all of them now religious, arranges visits to Portugal, supports Portuguese folklore and dance or Portuguese bands, and sponsors a range of social and cultural activities. Some of these Casas link with each other through regional conventions. It is not unknown for people with no personal or family ties to Portugal to join such an organisation and in this way to become part of the Portuguese diaspora, just as many Asians and Africans did in the past.[18]

Emigrant communities are not static. They evolve as the original migrant generation is succeeded by second, third and subsequent generations. The memories of the homeland fade and are replaced by new ideas of what it is to be Portuguese: '"Roots" and "Heritage"... become separated from "place".'[19] Frequently it happens that the 'Portuguese' community is largely absorbed by the more numerous local indigenous population and the old Portuguese identity lingers on only in Portuguese family names (still common in many parts of Asia), in Catholic observance or in isolated unconnected cultural survivals—faint ghostly remnants of the old diasporic community.

A final characteristic of the Portuguese diaspora has been its role in promoting 'globalisation'. The migrations of the Portuguese were the first that took a people from their homeland to settle in almost every part of the world (with the exception perhaps of Russia and Central Asia). In the process of creating their settlements in Asia, Africa and the Americas the Portuguese had a profound impact on the way that human communities have interacted in modern times. By the early seventeenth century the Portuguese were operating a global trading network in which silver mined in Spanish America and Japan was being employed as a global currency; and the spices, silks, cottons, drugs and luxury products of Asia were being traded in ever increasing quantities to Europe and the Americas, in the process bringing about a revolution in European tastes and ideas. The Portuguese were also redistributing food crops and animals around the world, taking maize, potatoes and tobacco from the Americas and introducing citrus, grapes, bananas, cattle and horses. A global redistribution of labour saw thousands of slaves moved in Portuguese ships from Africa to the Americas. Meanwhile Portuguese had become an international language of commerce from Japan and the Moluccas to West Africa and South America, while Christianity had become a world religion with a global reach. The Portuguese and Spanish had begun the process of modelling a world order based on European legal concepts and a scientific revolution, which involved the mapping of the world and the scientific description of its geography, its languages and its peoples, had begun. Although the Dutch, French and English were eventually to surpass the Portuguese in promoting this global revolution, the Portuguese were undoubtedly the pioneers who created the parameters within which so much of modern history has been played out.[20]

2

POINTS OF DEPARTURE

PORTUGAL FROM THE FIFTEENTH
TO THE NINETEENTH CENTURY

In all the villages nearby and in all the parishes in the vicinity, there was the
same aspiration to emigrate, to go in search of riches to far off continents. It
was a powerful dream, a profound ambition which dug deep into their souls
from infancy through to old age.

(Ferreira de Castro, *Emigrantes*)[1]

The military elite of Portugal seek their fortunes overseas

When migration from Portugal began on a large scale in the fifteenth
century, the peoples of western Europe had already been involved in
internal colonising enterprises for centuries. The pressure of population on land resources fluctuated with changes in demography and climate, but the twelfth and thirteenth centuries in particular saw the
rapid expansion of Christian Europe's frontiers and the movement of
population to colonise marginal land. At the same time the military elites
became active, carving out new lordships in the eastern Mediterranean
(the Crusades being the most obvious, but not the only example), on
the frontiers of Germany and Poland, and in the Celtic lands border-
ing the kingdom of England.

One major region of expansion and internal colonisation was the
Iberian peninsula where from the eleventh century to the thirteenth

constant warfare led to the Christian conquest and settlement of the whole peninsula except for the southern kingdom of Granada. This *reconquista* involved people of all classes. If the lead was taken by the rulers and the military elites (the Military Orders), an important part was played by foreign adventurers and merchants, by the church and by farmers, herdsmen and settlers. During the fourteenth century, however, the *reconquista* of the Iberian peninsula stalled and the pressures of population on the land, both in the peninsula and elsewhere in Europe, were temporarily eased by the Black Death. Moreover, Portugal and the Spanish kingdoms were sucked increasingly into the wider conflict of the Hundred Years War which absorbed the energies of the military class. North Africa was also an area which lured some Iberians away from their homeland, and during the periods of peace in the Iberian peninsula soldiers originating in Portugal were to be found in many north African armies, though these do not seem to have formed a permanent community, and for the most part those who survived the fighting converted to Islam and were absorbed into the Moorish population.

There were a number of economic developments that contributed to the great expansion of emigration that took place in the fifteenth century. In the thirteenth century Venetians and Genoese, who had begun to exploit economic opportunities in north Africa and northern Europe, established a commercial entrepôt in Lisbon, where they provided captains for the new fleet of royal galleys and stimulated the growth of Portuguese maritime activity. In the wake of the Italians, Portuguese merchant communities grew up in England and the Netherlands—forming the beginnings of a trading diaspora of the kind that was becoming increasingly common in maritime Europe and which gave rise to the institution of the factory (*feitoria* in Portuguese), the extraterritorial commercial community which enjoyed rights and privileges negotiated with the local sovereign power. This Portuguese merchant diaspora was probably on a small scale but, in the Netherlands at least, a *feitoria* of some permanence was established.

Once Portugal began to recover from the effects of the Black Death and once Portugal and Castile were able to extricate themselves from involvement in the Hundred Years War, the memories and ideologies of the *reconquista* began to be revived, first among the Portuguese and then, in the last quarter of the fifteenth century, among the Castilians. The institutions which had been developed as instruments of conquest and settlement, notably the *encomienda*, were put to use once again in the early phases of Portuguese and Castilian expansion in the Atlantic basin.

During the earlier phases of the *reconquista* soldiers and settlers had been attracted from many parts of Europe—famously the capture of Lisbon in 1147 had been accomplished by soldiers from England, Scotland, the Low Countries and Germany as well as by Portuguese, and Muslim lands and preferment in the church were granted to men of many different nationalities and allegiances. So, in the new phase of the *reconquista* in the Atlantic many people joined the enterprise from France, Italy, the Low Countries, Germany and Scandinavia while men from Portugal joined the expeditions and armies of the Castilians in the New World. The people who formed this first phase of the Portuguese diaspora, therefore, came from many different parts of Europe and were not all Portuguese. Their Portuguese identity came from their involvement in what was an enterprise, directed in its earliest phases by the Portuguese Crown and nobility.

The small size and poverty of Portugal had had a profound influence on the way its social structure had evolved ever since Afonso Henriques had declared Portugal to be an independent kingdom in 1139. As the *reconquista* had progressed, the lands newly conquered from the Moors had passed into the possession of the church, the Crown or the Military Orders of knights. To maintain their status the Portuguese nobility had become very dependent on grants of lands or commands which they obtained as members of the Military Orders or on retainers paid by the Crown, the most important of which were the *contias* or financial payments made for those serving the Crown in a military capacity.[2] Others sought to benefit from preferment within the church. Only a few of the noble families had landholdings large enough to be independent, and many of these had family ties outside Portugal with the Castilian nobility. From the late fourteenth century the Portuguese Crown systematically sought to control the wealth and patronage of the Military Orders by securing the masterships for close relatives; by the mid sixteenth century the Crown had taken control of all the Orders, and their wealth, including lands, towns and fortresses, had become part of the Crown's patrimony. The knights, *fidalgos* and lesser nobility were now even more dependent on the Crown and on the few large noble families and entered their service in various roles, as soldiers, as ship's captains and, as expansion in the Atlantic gathered pace, as the organisers of colonising expeditions. The prospect of obtaining land or lordships in the newly discovered Atlantic islands proved especially attractive to elements of the Portuguese upper classes who found patrons in the Infantes Dom Henrique (Henry the Navigator), who was governor of the Order of Christ, one of the two major Military Orders in Portugal, and Dom Pedro his brother, the second son of D. João I. It has been estimated that up to the death of the Infante Dom Henrique in 1460, 80 per cent of the captains of ships that traded to Africa were members of the prince's household.[3]

Dom Henrique was also an enthusiastic advocate of campaigning in Morocco, where the prospect of making fresh conquests attracted members of the nobility who had family and class memories of the rewards that had followed the conquest of Muslim territory in the twelfth and thirteenth centuries. The first campaign in Morocco was mounted in 1415 and led to the capture of the port-city of Ceuta. For the next hundred years the Portuguese extended their conquests, eventually securing control of ten Moroccan coastal towns and considerable swathes of their rural hinterland, providing in the process careers for the military class and opportunities for its enrichment. The captaincies of the Moroccan fortresses tended to become monopolised by individual noble families who made their tenure quasi-hereditary.[4]

Understanding the extent to which the military elite and the noble families of Portugal (the *fidalgos* and *ricos homens*) depended on service to the Crown is fundamental to any interpretation of Portuguese overseas expansion. In no other country of Europe were the nobility so dependent on enterprise overseas and so willing to uproot themselves to take part in what was soon to become a global migration. The assumption that status and advancement were to be sought in the service of the Crown overseas became deeply rooted in the cultural outlook of the Portuguese upper class. By the end of the fifteenth century a pattern had emerged of leading servants of the Crown moving from one overseas posting to another, a trend illustrated by the careers of Diogo de Azambuja and Duarte Pacheco Pereira. Azambuja was a knight of the Order of Avis and a member of the household of the Infante Dom Pedro. Having fought in the campaign that captured the Moroccan town of Alcacer Sequer in 1458 and in the war against Castile in 1476, he was selected in 1481 by Dom João II to command the armada that built the castle of São Jorge da Mina (Elmina) on the coast of modern Ghana. He was later to serve as captain of Mogador and Safi in Morocco, dying in 1518. Duarte Pacheco Pereira was a member of the king's household and his personal squire. Sent on a voyage to West Africa, he returned with Bartolomeu Dias in 1489. As a geographical expert he was part of the Portuguese delegation which negotiated the treaty of Tordesillas. He may have made a voyage to the coast of Brazil in 1498 and in 1503 commanded a ship in Afonso de Albuquerque's fleet bound for India. He commanded Portuguese forces at the siege of Cochin in 1504 and on his return to Portugal wrote the famous *Esmeraldo de Situ Orbis*, the first major Portuguese account of the discoveries in West Africa. In 1509 he was sent to track down and capture the French corsair Mondragon and in 1518 he was made governor of Elmina.

Military commanders expected to be rewarded by the Crown either with further commands or with the grant of lands in the possession of the Military Orders or with pensions paid by the Crown from its own revenues. It is well known that Fernão de Magalhães (Magellan) left Portugal and entered the service of Castile because he felt he had not been adequately rewarded by Dom Manuel. This pattern of service and reward continued throughout the history of Portuguese expansion. On the one hand it proved to be a way in which the aristocracy could live off the patrimony of the Crown and survive as a service nobility in the empire, while at the same time it provided a means for the Crown to control the aristocratic families and keep them subservient to its purposes.

With the members of the military aristocracy willing to take up commands and positions in Morocco and in the African fortresses, it was only natural that their squires, clients and retainers would accompany them. There was competition for the most prestigious commands between the members of the rival Military Orders (especially the Orders of Christ and Santiago), but for the most part these military clients of the Crown and the royal princes were not permanent migrants and always had the intention of returning to Portugal. This is made clear in a letter from the governor of the fortress town of Azamour in 1514. Writing to the king about the knights serving in the city, he says,

They all now openly say that they do not have to stay here to begin the war all over again ... and that Your Highness should send others who can be here for the same amount of time. And now Your Highness can recall how many times I begged and advised him that he would not engage any more *fidalgos* for the war except those who are satisfied to have some posting here.[5]

The Moroccan fortresses were close to Portugal, and the society that grew up behind their walls closely reflected that of Portugal itself. The Portuguese populations in Morocco, apart from the soldiers and convicts serving in the garrisons, were made up of family units and formed a fixed population. In 1500 a count of the Portuguese population in Alcacer Sequer revealed that women and children made up 39 per cent of the population.[6] All the men who resided in these towns were liable for military service, an obligation which characterised the early days of Portuguese overseas settlement and was repeated in the fortress towns established in the Indian Ocean. However, almost from the start this military elite took a major part in trade, at first principally the trade in slaves and captured cattle, which could be seen as the spoils of war, but soon commercial activity of all kinds so that the historian Vitorino Magalhães Godinho could describe the 'noble merchant' as the most dynamic element in Portuguese society.[7]

The Portuguese settlements in Morocco grew and to some extent prospered during the period 1470 to 1530, but permanent Portuguese populations never established themselves there. The fortresses became too expensive for the Crown to defend and one by one they were abandoned, beginning in 1541 with Santa Cruz de Guer (Agadir) until only Ceuta, Tangier and Mazagão remained. Ceuta remained in Spanish hands when Portugal declared its independence from Spain in 1640 and Tangier was surrendered to the English as part of the dowry of Catherine of Braganza. Mazagão was finally abandoned in 1769, the Portuguese population being evacuated to a new settlement in Brazil.

While the campaigns in Morocco and the settlement of the islands was under way, the Crown took the lead in exploiting the commercial potential of western Africa. This involved a system for licensing trading ships, and eventually the leasing of the trade on sectors of the coast to syndicates of merchants, wealthy individuals who paid for the privilege, or to foreign banks in return for loans. From the 1440s the trade with the Sahara was organised in this way from a *feitoria* at Arguim; the Guinea coast trade was leased between 1469 and 1474 to a Lisbon merchant, Fernão Gomes; and the trade of the Niger region went to the Florentine Marchioni Bank. The Crown meanwhile exploited, directly through it own factors, the trade of the Gold Coast and the Congo region and organised a number of exploratory voyages in search of a sea route to India. The *feitorias*, an extension of a practice that had been familiar to Mediterranean traders in the Middle Ages, became the focus for small communities of merchants whose settlements, although they were located within African territory, enjoyed a privileged and protected status.

As well as sending expeditions to the Canary Islands from around 1420, the Portuguese princes organised the occupation and settlement of the archipelagos of Madeira and the Azores, partly to pre-empt activity by the Castilians in these waters. The islands were to be granted to clients of the Infantes as quasi-feudal 'donatary captaincies', institutions which were to be hereditary and which laid an obligation on the captains to recruit settlers, undertake the distribution of land and organise the defence of their captaincies. In return for these services the captains had extensive fiscal and manorial rights and were allowed to acquire limited amounts of land for themselves. When the Cape Verde Islands were discovered in the 1450s and the Gulf of Guinea islands in the 1470s, captaincies were again granted as a means of securing their settlement and economic exploitation. The system of 'donatary captaincies' was as near as the fifteenth-century Portuguese monarchy came to organising overseas emigration.

With the setting up of the Estado da Índia in 1505, the opportunities provided by Crown service enormously expanded. To the command of ships and fortresses were added posts in the royal administration, diplomatic missions and church appointments, all of which carried with them opportunities for enrichment for oneself and one's followers. Captaincies of the royal trading ships and the fortresses were specially sought after and long waiting lists developed of men who had been promised the position of captain of one of the great fortresses like Mozambique or Ormuz. Throughout the period from the fifteenth to the eighteenth centuries, making grants of land and appointments to military commands and administrative offices in Portugal's overseas possessions provided the Crown with a substantial part of its patronage. Except during the period of the Union of the Crowns of Portugal and Spain (1580–1640), when the noble families of Portugal had access to high office in the Spanish kingdoms, the opportunities for wealth and advancement in Portugal itself were always limited. It was in the empire that the real opportunities lay, and it was the offices and commands that were in the king's power to grant that guaranteed the loyalty of the needy noble class. As the Frenchman François Pyrard observed, the short tenure of office in the fortresses in the Indian Ocean, which was normally only for three years, was intended by the king to 'enrich and satisfy his subjects'.[8] Debates among historians as to whether Portugal profited from its empire are often debates about entirely the wrong issue. Whatever the defence of this vast empire might cost, neither the Crown nor the class of *fidalgos* in general could dispense with the patronage on which the Crown depended to maintain its authority and on which the upper classes of Portugal depended to supplement their income and maintain their status.

Mainland Portugal as the source of mass emigration

Although the early emigrants who settled in the islands came from all districts of Portugal, the majority came from the populations north of the Tagus, and this was to remain true of Portuguese emigration throughout. With the exception of the river valleys, much of northern Portugal is mountainous and barren, and the tradition of smallholdings and partible inheritance made it difficult for families to survive through agriculture alone. In the centre and south of Portugal, which was less mountainous, the process of the *reconquista* had led to large estates accumulating in the hands of the church, the Military Orders and the aristocracy. The granting of lands as *morgadios* (entailed estates) secured the position of these elites but stifled access to the land for peasant farmers and hindered the process of internal recolonisation. Much land in this region lay uncultivated, and wasteland expanded as a result of the depopulation caused by the Black Death. Internal migration, therefore, was not an option for the overcrowded populations of the north, except for seasonal work during harvest time. In an attempt to remedy this, in 1375 the *Lei das Sesmarias* (the Law of the Wastelands) sought to bring abandoned land back into cultivation. Wasteland was to be granted to farmers on condition that it would be brought into full production within five years on pain of forfeiture. This law had only limited impact within Portugal itself, but was to provide the legislative framework for settling people on virgin land overseas.

In the late fourteenth and fifteenth centuries the population of Portugal barely exceeded one million, and throughout the first three centuries of overseas expansion it never rose above a million and a half. It was not, therefore, a buoyant and expanding population as such that was the cause of migration, but a landholding system and an economy that did not provide a subsistence for even the small population that existed. Unable to make a living directly from the land, men left their communities to work as seasonal labourers in the vineyards, wheatfields and olive groves of Leon and Castile, and there was an accelerated movement of population to the coastal regions where agriculture could be supplemented by various maritime activities. Coastal communities made their living through working salt pans (*salinas*), collecting seaweed as fertiliser, building boats and fishing, while in the south piracy, slave raiding and seal hunting in Moroccan waters offered tempting alternative opportunities. These maritime occupations fostered a mentality by which many individuals looked to make their living outside their immediate community and led to the expectation that they might be away at sea for months at a time.

The basic structure of the rural economy and society of northern Portugal remained remarkably unchanged. Many of the characteristics that describe fifteenth-century rural society could still be used to describe Portugal in the early twentieth century, and the structural causes of migration remained the same. In the twentieth century, as in the fifteenth, much of the rural population of Portugal lived by subsistence farming, supplemented by migrant labour or fishing. Alan Villiers, writing of the 1950s, described with deep admiration the hard life of the seasonal fishermen who went to Newfoundland and Greenland,[9] while Caroline Brettell, also writing of the twentieth century, explained how the household economy of the peasant community proved so long-lasting:

the peasants of northern Portugal survived by means of a rather efficient division of labour, whereby women, as producers of food and nurturers of offspring, reproduced a household to which male migrants contributed capital [in the form of remittances]—capital that was necessary for the continuation of a local economic unit.[10]

In the twentieth century the rural economy of Portugal continued to be based on the production of wine, olive oil, citrus, fish, cork and salt, which had been the staples five hundred years earlier. In 1937 wine, fish and cork still made up 55 per cent of all Portugal's exports.[11] Moreover, much of the rural population remained, as it had always been, illiterate and cut off from the developments taking place elsewhere in Europe. To a remarkable extent the economic, social and cultural development of Portugal in the five centuries after 1400, and the contribution made by Portuguese to European and world civilisation, would come from the overseas diasporic community, not from the relatively stagnant and unchanging society of Portugal itself.

In the fifteenth century, to the economic pressures which pushed men in the north to leave the land and to take up maritime occupations was now added the fact that the Portuguese Crown began actively to encourage emigration to the Atlantic islands. As the Crown and the military elite began to organise their settlement, the networks of communication encouraged migration, especially from the maritime communities, to the islands where fertile land was waiting to be exploited. It is likely that chain migration was a factor from the start as maritime activity was often organised on the basis of the extended family and it was from the coastal cities, where boats were built and seamen were recruited, that emigrants and merchants set out to the islands.

It was the northern ports with their rural hinterlands which came to dominate the story of Portuguese overseas expansion. By the seventeenth century Lisbon, Setúbal, Porto, Aveiro and Vianna do Castelo, the dominant ports of the north and centre, had become the principal points of departure for overseas. Lagos and the southern ports, important in the early days because of their proximity to Morocco, dwindled in significance. Instead the great Spanish port-city of Seville with its monopoly of trade with the New World dominated the regional economy and provided a magnetic pull for merchants, seamen and migrants from the southern regions of Portugal.

The Portuguese economy: a long view

Since the traditional economy of Portugal, based on fishing and the production of a limited range of 'Mediterranean' products, never supported the population beyond subsistence level, the development of industries might have provided a more profitable alternative, as it did, for example, in the Low Countries. In the sixteenth century there was some indication that this might happen. There was a range of artisan crafts, notably ceramics, which had produced a reservoir of skills, and overseas expansion had created a market for shipbuilding and the production of cannon. After the Union of the Crowns of Portugal and Spain in 1580, Lisbon became the principal port and naval arsenal for the Atlantic war fleet maintained by the Habsburgs.

However, the development of the Portuguese economy took a turn—familiar enough to economic historians—which placed a premium on emigration. In the sixteenth and seventeenth centuries the wealth generated by Portuguese overseas enterprise (the trade in gold, silver, diamonds, pepper, spices, slaves, sugar, tobacco and silk) enabled Portugal to buy abroad the goods to satisfy the consumer market. Increasingly armaments, ceramics, foodstuffs, textiles and consumer goods generally were bought more cheaply abroad than they could be produced in Portugal. The persecution of the New Christians by the Inquisition also created a flight of mercantile capital abroad, so that some of the most productive Portuguese enterprises were to be found not in Portugal itself but among the diasporic communities in Amsterdam, Hamburg and London.

Some attempt was made to reverse this trend between 1670 and 1690 when the Conde de Ericeira tried to promote import substitution and industrial development in imitation of the policy pursued by Colbert in France. Ericeira's experiments, however, failed partly through the opposition of the Inquisition but more significantly because in the late 1690s Portugal discovered a great new source of wealth overseas in Brazilian gold and diamonds.[12] The flow of wealth into Lisbon after 1700 once again enabled the Portuguese to import all that they needed from the industrialised countries of northern Europe. The change of direction was sealed by the Methuen Treaties of 1704 which tied Portugal economically and politically to Britain—exporting Portuguese wines in exchange for British woollens, and increasingly relying on the Royal Navy, which established a base for its operations in Lisbon, to look after the defence of Portugal and its empire. During much of the eighteenth century the flow of gold meant that the Portuguese currency was exceptionally strong—a strong currency usually having the effect of boosting imports at the expense of exports. The result was that Portugal almost always ran a deficit on the balance of trade, a deficit that was met by payments in gold. The historian A. H. de Oliveira Marques has estimated that remittances of bullion from Brazil during this period constituted around 9 per cent of royal income, a figure comparable to the benefits that Portugal was later to derive from the remittances of its emigrants in Brazil.[13]

During the ascendancy of the Marquês de Pombal (c.1750–77), Portugal once again embarked on an attempt to industrialise, securing for itself its colonial markets and protecting its industries from British competition. This policy had some success and by the early nineteenth century a cotton textile industry had become established in northern

Portugal. However, this burgeoning industrialisation was held back by the turmoil of the Napoleonic Wars, especially the devastation of northern Portugal by the French and British armies between 1808 and 1811, by the relocation of the centre of the monarchy to Rio de Janeiro (1807–21) and then by the civil wars. Once peace had been restored to Portugal after 1851, Portuguese manufacturers pressed for protection for their textiles and provided a powerful lobby advocating imperial expansion in Africa where they could enjoy a captive market.

So, from the sixteenth century onwards Portugal became dependent on the wealth that flowed from overseas, supporting the Crown, the aristocracy and the mercantile classes, and enabling the country year after year to finance a large deficit in its balance of trade. This wealth took a variety of forms: the profits of trade, the rewards of office-holding in the empire repatriated in the form of the personal wealth of noble families, the profits from landownership in Brazil, and the remittances of gold from Brazilian mines to the Crown. When these sources all dried up in the nineteenth century, the remittances of emigrant workers came to take their place.

Portuguese emigration, therefore, cannot be understood solely in terms of rural poverty but has to be seen as embedded in the long-term structure of the Portuguese economy. The remittances of emigrants from Brazil at the end of the nineteenth century replaced the remittances of gold that had come in the form of the royal fifth to the Crown in the heyday of the Brazilian gold rush, which, in turn, had replaced the fabulous wealth that the viceroys and others had brought back from the East during the golden years of the Estado da Índia.

The social structure of Portugal

The history of the Portuguese diaspora brings into sharp relief the fact that Portugal has lacked an active and influential middle class. Looking at the story of the diaspora there is no class of person, except perhaps the Sephardic Jews and New Christians, who obviously bridge the gulf between the elite nobles and *estrangeirados* and the poor and frequently illiterate peasants and workers who filled the emigrant ships. While in the twenty-first century the international community can easily recognise and acknowledge high-profile figures like José Manuel Barroso or José Mourinho, and while the cultural and financial moguls who run the Gulbenkian Foundation, the Fundação Oriente or the

Espirito Santo Bank can move freely in elite international circles, the mass of working people who make up the Portuguese diaspora can still be described as largely 'invisible', or as having a 'low profile' and existing 'beneath the radar'. The Portuguese diaspora lacks a middle, any discernible group who can bridge a gap that is not only one of wealth and social status but also one of communication.

There is no single explanation for this absence of a 'middle'. For much of the early modern period (sixteenth to eighteenth centuries) there was deep suspicion in Portugal of the New Christians who were prominent in commerce and finance. What can best be described as an alliance of the aristocracy and the *povo* (the common people) allowed the Inquisition to persecute the New Christians and in doing so to prevent the emergence of a dynamic indigenous middle class. It was in exile in Amsterdam, London and Hamburg that the Portuguese middle class of bankers, merchants and entrepreneurs became established—not in Lisbon or Porto. In Portugal the place of the New Christians was increasingly taken by the English who, by the mid eighteenth century, had come to dominate Portuguese commerce and much of the business sector of the Portuguese economy. The English were an unpopular and very much a foreign group which, it has often been maintained, treated Portugal as a colony, even as a conquered country, and maintained its influence well into the nineteenth century.

Portugal is a small and in many ways an intimate society, almost like a village, in which 'everyone knows everyone else'. The Portuguese elites have networks through which banking and business are linked with universities and politics—during the Salazar dictatorship 40 per cent of all ministerial appointments were of academics from the university sector.[14] It is comparatively easy for wealthy or successful people of the 'middle' to gain acceptance within this elite circle, but very difficult for anyone from lower in society. Whereas the Portuguese elites have a long tradition of establishing networks and careers for themselves outside Portugal—a tradition that goes back to the days of the close ties with Castile and the Castilian monarchy—the networks that ordinary people establish, the community solidarity that is so apparent in the story of the diaspora, are also factors that isolate them not only from the Portuguese upper classes but also to some extent from the societies of the host nations.

Emigration has had another consequence for Portuguese society. Exile and emigration have always been seen as a way of relieving social tensions and preventing political upheaval—and also of avoiding the necessity for social and economic reform. The expulsion of Jews and the persecution of the New Christians helped to externalise social tensions in the early modern period; and in the nineteenth and twentieth centuries mass emigration was seen by many as a way of defusing potential social conflict, and even of preventing revolution in Portugal—just as, in the Atlantic islands, it was seen as a solution to the problems of drought, famine and overcrowding. And at the beginning of the twenty-first century Portuguese of all classes are once again taking advantage of free movement within the European Union to escape the consequences of indebtedness and austerity at home through emigration rather than political action.

Finding manpower for the empire

In the first three centuries of Portuguese expansion the supply of voluntary migrants was never adequate and the Portuguese Crown, and the military and landowning elites to whom was entrusted the administration of the empire, had to resort to many expedients to meet the empire's manpower needs. Captains of ships and 'donatary captains' who were entrusted with the peopling of the islands, and later the Brazilian and Angolan mainlands, had to seek emigrants where they could find them: Italians and Germans were licensed to trade in Portuguese possessions, Flemings were encouraged to settle in the Azores, Germans were recruited as gunners and mercenaries, Jews, expelled from Portugal itself, were allowed to settle as colonists in the African fortresses and island settlements.[15] Slaves were also used to supplement manpower, being employed in every capacity—as crews of ships, builders, soldiers, labourers on plantations and sexual partners—so that in many parts of the Portuguese world they came to form a substantial part of the Portuguese community. In this way the 'Portuguese' diaspora became a diaspora of people of many different ethnic and religious origins.

The Portuguese Crown adopted other various expedients to obtain sufficient numbers of people to man ships, to garrison fortresses and to people overseas settlements. The full complement of soldiers and sailors to man the ships of the *carreira da Índia* were obtained by forced levies in the towns of Portugal, though, as Pyrard pointed out, 'when they are in the Indies all are free'.[16] Another solution was to rid

Portugal of people considered to be undesirable, and this kind of forced emigration was to remain a reality in some parts of the Portuguese world until nearly the end of Portugal's empire. Among the earliest 'forced migrants' were convicts, known in the Portuguese world as *degredados*. As early as the fifteenth century the Portuguese Crown was remitting the capital sentences of the courts to exile.[17] Timothy Coates, in his study of the Portuguese convict system, listed the serious crimes that might be punished by exile or deportation as 'blasphemy, murder, committing an injury, kidnapping, rape, witchcraft, attacking jailers, entering a convent with dishonourable intentions, committing damage for money, injuring someone in a procession, or harming a judge'.[18] Convicts were sent to people the Guinea islands and later Brazil and to help man the fortresses in Africa and the East. They were also chosen for dangerous missions overseas. Some were landed on remote coastlines with the idea that they would learn the languages spoken by the native inhabitants, explore the interior and familiarise themselves with local conditions. Others would be despatched from the fortresses on dangerous missions, men like António Fernandes who was sent between 1511 and 1513 from the fortress of Sofala in eastern Africa to undertake two exploratory journeys into the African interior.[19] Some *degredados* earned their freedom, others fled, either disappearing without trace or surviving as renegades, adding to the numbers of *lançados*, as those who settled away from authorised Portuguese settlements were sometimes called.

During the seventeenth and eighteenth centuries convicts continued to be enrolled as crews on ships, or sent as soldiers to garrison forts or as settlers to help populate difficult and dangerous frontier regions. Prisoners condemned either by the royal courts or by the Inquisition would be assembled in the Limoeiro prison in Lisbon to be sent aboard fleets bound for Brazil or India. On arrival they were free to move about within the district to which they had been sent and could take up any occupation, though they were debarred from holding official positions. The number of these exiles was never great—possibly 100 a year on average from Portugal and another 150 sentenced by the courts in Goa and Brazil. This would give a total of around 20,500 from Portugal over the period 1550–1755 and 50,000 for the whole empire.[20] These numbers constitute a very small percentage of those who left Portugal. Although convicts seldom proved satisfactory colonists, Portugal continued to send them to the colonies until 1934.

Forced emigration was not just a means of ridding Portugal itself of 'undesirable' elements. It was also employed to remove such people from one Portuguese settlement to another. Convicts might be sent from Portugal to Goa, while those convicted in the Goa high court might be sent to Mozambique, or from Brazil to Angola, or within Brazil from the coastal cities to the Amazon. Portuguese emigration was never a linear affair as both voluntary and involuntary migrants moved in many different directions within the Portuguese world, weaving in a way that was totally unplanned a dense network of contact and dependency.

To those convicted of serious crimes should be added whole groups such as gypsies, and those sentenced by the Inquisition for crimes against orthodox Catholic belief. The persecution of gypsies was sporadic but the law provided for sentencing men to the galleys and women to exile. Eventually so many gypsies were sent into exile in Brazil that a considerable gypsy community grew up there.[21] Victims of the Inquisition were also frequently sentenced to exile for a specific number of years or for life. Additionally among those sent into exile were political prisoners, and this category grew considerably as a result of the civil wars in Portugal between 1827 and 1851. During the early years of the Estado Novo political prisoners were deported to the notorious concentration camp at Tarrafal on Santiago island, and there were some notable individual cases of banishment as late as the 1960s—Mário Soares, the future president of Portugal, being exiled to São Tomé in 1968.

From time to time the Portuguese state tried its hand at organising settlement schemes, offering incentives to migrants as well as some pressure to obtain enough recruits. The 'donatary captaincy' system tried out in the Atlantic islands was employed with mixed success to mobilise private capital for the settlement of Brazil and Angola. This system had its drawbacks as the few captains who were successful in planting settlements frequently acted very independently as over mighty subjects whose freedom threatened the Crown's purposes. So the São Tomé captaincy was abolished in 1522 and that of Angola after the death of the first captain, Paulo Dias de Novais, in 1589. The Castilian Crown found the same problem with the *conquistadores* who were granted *encomiendas* in the New World and in the end had to fight a full-scale war to reduce the *encomenderos* of Peru to obedience. It is significant that the system of hereditary 'donatary captaincies' was never used in the Estado da Índia where Crown appointments, including the office of viceroy, were not hereditary and were almost never made for longer than three years.

There were two officially sponsored settlement schemes attempted in eastern Africa in the seventeenth century and some in Brazil in the eighteenth century: for example the attempt to move the Portuguese population of Mazagão in Morocco to Amazonia in 1769, when 340 families were resettled in an area called Nova Mazagan. The nineteenth century saw further settlement schemes attempted in both East and West Africa as well as a continuation of the policy of establishing convict settlements. These schemes are usually represented as failures, but the settlements on the coast at Mossamedes and in the Huila highlands in southern Angola were ultimately successful in establishing permanent Portuguese communities.

Emigration might also be used as the solution to pressing social problems. It was the solution offered to victims of famine, particularly in the Cape Verde Islands when periodic droughts reduced the population to the edge of starvation. Even in the twentieth century the Portuguese government's official attitude to famine and over-population was to encourage emigration, even if that was to the hostile environment of the São Tomé cocoa plantations.

In the seventeenth century reformed prostitutes were sometimes sent to the colonies, though their numbers were never great. Orphans might also be put on ships and sent to overseas Portuguese communities. Orphan boys would be enrolled in ship's crews or in the retinues of noblemen. François Pyrard describes 'the little boys brought out of Portugal, not grown enough to bear arms... their service only is to attend their masters, and to carry messages'.[22] Girls would be given dowries either by the Crown or by some charitable institution and sent overseas to find husbands. In Lisbon there was an orphanage, the Recolhimento do Castelo, which was intended especially to provide a refuge for orphans from respectable and even noble families who would be destined to be sent overseas. Some, known as *Orfãs do Rei* (Crown Orphans), were given the reversion of important offices and commands as their dowries, so that anyone marrying them would have a lucrative Crown appointment or some allocation of land or revenue along with his bride. The orphans were to be sent either to Brazil or to India. In Goa a special institution, the refuge of Nossa Senhora da Serra, was created at the end of the sixteenth century for the reception of orphan girls. It seems that this policy had little to do with any desire to boost emigration and has to be understood largely in the context of its charitable objectives. The numbers of orphan girls sent to the colonies was never great and contributed very little to the establishment of Portuguese communities overseas. The evidence suggests that Portuguese in the East were reluctant to marry these unfortunate girls, even with their dowries, and preferred to marry Indian women or cohabit with their African slaves. Many of the orphans, unable to find Portuguese husbands, were married locally to Indian men.[23]

In spite of its unsatisfied need for manpower, the Portuguese government was always ambivalent about voluntary emigration. Already in the sixteenth century voices were raised warning that emigration was depopulating the kingdom and pointing to the large import of black slaves needed to supplement the workforce. From time to time in the seventeenth century, when population numbers in Portugal probably went into decline, there were sporadic attempts to curb emigration. This was especially the case in the eighteenth century when regulations for the granting of passports were introduced to control the large numbers who departed for Brazil following the discoveries of gold and diamonds. However, the Portuguese Crown did not have the administrative capacity to control emigration either then or subsequently, and there were always voices raised in favour of the emigrant, pointing to the riches derived from the developing colonies and the success with which emigration relieved social tensions and extremes of poverty.

How many left Portugal?

For centuries no one tried to count in any systematic way the numbers who left Portugal; and, given the disorganised nature of the emigration, it would have been impossible to arrive at any figure that had much meaning. So many migrants were seasonal or temporary migrants and so many of those who left for the overseas territories, even the *degredados* condemned to exile, found opportunities to return that the numbers who left Portugal in any year and the net loss of population are quite different calculations.

The historian Vitorino Magalhães Godinho made an estimate for the numbers who left, which is probably as near to being accurate as any calculation, though it is not clear if he was including departures from the islands or only those who left from mainland Portugal.

POINTS OF DEPARTURE

During the sixteenth century the average emigration to all destinations was around 3,500 a year, with 2,000 of those sailing to the East. This he reckoned was about 2.5 per thousand of the population, which numbered 1.4 million. The rate per thousand then fluctuated between 3.5 per thousand in the early seventeenth century and 1.5 per thousand in the eighteenth century, when Portugal's population reached 2,600,000. Even given all the uncertainties about the numbers, and the fact that some areas of the country were more affected by emigration than others, these figures do not suggest that Portugal was suffering an insupportable loss of population. Moreover, since the large majority of these emigrants were men, the demographic effect on Portugal was much less than it would have been had large numbers of women emigrated. Nor was the loss of manpower as serious for the economy as the numbers might suggest, since it is probable that in the fifteenth and sixteenth centuries the loss through emigration was partly compensated by the importation of African slaves, whose numbers may have amounted to as much as half the number of those who emigrated.

Table 1: Emigration from Portugal

Years	Numbers of emigrants	Average numbers per annum
1400–1500	50,000	500
1500–1580	280,000	3,500
1580–1640	300,000–360,000	5,000–6,000
1640–1700	150,000	2,500
1700–1760	500,000–600,000	8,333–10,000
1760–1850	1,500,000	16,666

Source: Vitorino Magalhães Godinho, 'L'Emigration portugaise (XVᵉ-XXᵉ Siècles), une constante structurale et les réponses aux changements du monde', *Revista de História Económica e Social*, 1, Jan–June (1978), 8–10.

37

3

POINTS OF DEPARTURE

THE ATLANTIC ISLANDS

There are five groups of islands in the Atlantic which, since the fifteenth century, have played a very important part in the history of Portugal, although they are given very little attention by historians who are usually preoccupied with developments on the Iberian peninsula. Yet the long history of the Portuguese diaspora is as much a story of the people who left the islands as of those who left mainland Portugal.

The Canary Islands

The Canary Islands are the group nearest to Europe and have been known to Europeans since Roman times. From the late thirteenth century Portuguese seamen regularly visited the islands to raid for slaves or to hunt seals in the neighbouring Moroccan waters. Attempts were made by Portuguese, Castilians, French and Genoese to settle, but these were largely unsuccessful since the islands had a native population which fiercely resisted conquest. During the fifteenth century sovereignty over the islands was contested between Portugal and Castile until the dispute was finally resolved in favour of Castile in 1479. By that time a considerable number of Portuguese had settled on the islands and remained there as Castilian subjects, Castilian sovereignty not preventing further Portuguese migrants coming to join their compatriots. The Canary Islands provided many of the early settlers in Cuba and it is likely that it was from the Canaries that a number of Portuguese joined Spanish expeditions to the New World. For example, there was a large contingent of Portuguese in the expedition that Hernando de Soto led into the North American interior in 1539, including the chronicler of the expedition.

Madeira: settlement and onward migration

The settlement of Madeira and Porto Santo began after 1419 as the Portuguese were anxious to pre-empt any move to occupy the islands by the Castilians. To organise the settlement of these islands, and later the Azores and Cape Verde Islands, the Portuguese Crown appointed hereditary 'donatary captains' who assumed the responsibility for settling, defending and developing the islands in return for being able to exercise jurisdiction, allocate land, found towns, collect taxes and enjoy seigneurial rights over fisheries, mills, bread ovens and wine presses. Unlike the military nobility who served in the Moroccan fortresses, the men who took up the island captaincies intended to settle and found families, though during the fifteenth century there was some reluctance on the part of the upper echelons of Portuguese society to take up these opportunities, and at least two of the early island captains (Bartolomeu Perestrello and Antonio di Noli) were Genoese and one, Josse Huerter, came from the Netherlands.

Settlers were offered land according to the terms of the *Lei das Sesmarias*, and Madeira, in particular, proved attractive to settlers. The island was well watered and fertile but was covered by trees. The earliest settlers burned away tracts of forest—the Venetian traveller Cadamosto recalling that so fierce were the flames that the settlers had to stand in the sea for two days until the fires had burnt out and they could come ashore. Malvoisie grapes were introduced and flourished, and Cadamosto claimed that ripe grapes could be picked in Holy Week. Sugar and wheat were also grown and the island produced sawn timber (while the natural forests lasted) and wood for bows and crossbow bolts.[1] By 1460 there were two established towns, Funchal, the most important, becoming in 1514 the seat of a diocese which had supervision over church affairs in Africa and Asia until 1551. The neighbouring island of Porto Santo was also settled, though the drier climate of the island and the fact that it was soon overrun by wild rabbits discouraged intensive agriculture.

Agriculture, particularly sugar production, increased the demand for labour and as early as the 1440s voyages were being organised by the captains to obtain slaves in the Canary Islands and on the African coast. Slaves were brought to Madeira to produce the wine and sugar that were sold in Portugal, their arrival adding new elements to the Portuguese diaspora that was now beginning. In this way the triangular Atlantic trade was first articulated, though not in the classic form of later years. To attract settlers, the Crown granted commercial privileges which took the form of a remission of duties for goods imported into Portugal; and as the economies of the Atlantic islands developed, intricate commercial networks grew up linking the island groups to each other as well as to Portugal and the African mainland. As so much of the wealth of the islands was derived from trade, it is not surprising that the leading island families became a mercantile aristocracy which took an active part in commerce.

The social and economic structures that determined how Madeira would develop had already been put into place during the first century of settlement, structures that were to be copied on the other islands settled by the Portuguese. Land was concentrated in the hands of relatively few owners, who established entails and rented out the land to tenant farmers. The landowners also controlled the irrigation system, the *levadas*, on which the farmers depended to raise their crops. The concentration on growing sugar, and later on producing wine for export, resulted in high prices for food which benefited the large landowners and merchants but frequently led to famine for the other islanders. Moreover, the steep mountain valleys of Madeira, very picturesque as they seemed to later visitors, limited the amount of land available for farming, so much so that cattle had no pasture and had to be stall-fed and there was no room for surplus population. From at least the seventeenth century there was a constant food deficit and the island was unable to feed its growing population. John Barrow, the man who was to mastermind Britain's exploration of the Arctic, visited Madeira in 1792. He described how

the proprietor of the land and the collector of taxes for the Crown both attend at the press; the latter takes out of the tub his tenth of the whole must, after which the remainder is equally divided between the land-owner and the tenant. Each takes with him a sufficient number of porters to carry away their respective shares, sometimes in barrels, and sometimes in goat-skin *borrachas*, to the cellars in Funchal. The English merchants usually supply the farmers beforehand with money, to enable them to make a more extensive tillage.[2]

In the seventeenth century the British established a factory under privileges granted to them in the treaty signed between Portugal and the Commonwealth government in 1654. Over the course of the next 200 years British merchants, who provided the islanders with the main market for their wine, came to have a firm grip on the economy of the island, typically buying up the grape harvest at prices fixed by themselves. East India Company ships regularly called at Funchal and a sizeable British community established itself there. To Barrow, 'the penurious and solitary life of the Portugueze forms a striking contrast with the splendid and convivial manner in which the houses of the English merchants are constantly kept open for the accommodation of strangers who may call at the island'.[3] In 1807, during a critical phase of the Napoleonic Wars, the British occupied Madeira and for three months the island was even annexed as a British colony before being handed back to Portugal.

With the decline of Madeira's sugar industry in the seventeenth century, emigration to Brazil began and the regular visits of foreign ships provided an easy opportunity for those wanting to leave an island that was now suffering from serious over-population. Madeira's population had grown steadily from around 25,000 in 1580 to an estimated 67,000 in 1800 and, in spite of substantial emigration, to 148,300 by 1900.[4] Emigration on a large scale began in the 1830s, the presence of the British community creating many opportunities for departure. Emigrants found it easy to obtain a passage, many departing without passports from the neighbouring Deserta Islands, away from the controls that the Portuguese administration tried to implement. From the British West Indies and later Hawaii came agents intent on recruiting labourers with knowledge of the sugar industry, and in the first decade after 1835 12,000 Madeirans departed for British Guiana alone, a total of 36,724 Madeirans settling in that colony between 1841 and 1889.[5]

Emigration from Madeira was increased by a rather bizarre development which led to a major exodus from the island. In 1838 an evangelical Protestant doctor called Robert Kalley had brought his wife to Madeira for health reasons. As a result of his work as preacher and doctor the charismatic Kalley built up a large community of converts. Persecuted by the authorities, Kalley eventually decided to move to Trinidad and was accompanied by many of his converts, who eventually numbered over 2,000, many eventually relocating to Illinois.[6]

As the nineteenth century progressed, agricultural conditions on the islands deteriorated. Famine conditions resulted from the failure of the

POINTS OF DEPARTURE: THE ATLANTIC ISLANDS

potato crop in 1847, and diseases affecting the vines in the following decade severely damaged the island's economy and drove still more Madeirans to emigrate. Thereafter the numbers grew steeply. Madeiran emigrants tended to follow a chain of migration and to form close-knit communities at their destinations. Unlike the Azoreans who headed for the United States and later Canada, the favoured destinations of Madeiran emigration were the British and French Caribbean islands, Hawaii, Angola and South Africa.[7]

The Azores

The settlement of the Azores began in the 1430s but proceeded more slowly than that of Madeira. The nine islands of the archipelago were more distant from Portugal and their climate was less favourable for the production of wine and sugar—though in later centuries oranges and tea were to be grown successfully. The Azores were distributed as captaincies, but settlers had to be recruited from as far afield as the Netherlands, the first captain of the islands of Pico and Faial being Josse Huerter, a Netherlander who apparently attracted between 1,000 and 2,000 Flemish immigrants. The Azorean settlers adapted to their new oceanic world by establishing a thriving fishing industry and were soon undertaking voyages of their own further into the Atlantic. In fact the Azores became a new base for maritime exploration, and expeditions were organised by Azoreans to lay claim to islands which they believed lay beyond their horizons to the west.

By the middle of the sixteenth century the islanders were growing wheat and rearing cattle. A number of towns had been established, and in 1546 Ponta Delgada on the island of São Miguel was made a city with a Senado da Câmara. The Azores were, however, beset by problems. The islands lay in an active volcanic zone which caused frequent earthquakes and eruptions. An earthquake in 1522 totally destroyed the town of Vila Franca do Campo on São Miguel, when allegedly 5,000 people were buried in its rubble. There were also seismic events in the islands' politics. From the 1570s British pirates frequented Azorean waters attempting to waylay the Spanish silver *flota*, while the Portuguese pretender, Dom António, tried to use the islands as a base against Philip of Spain in the 1580s. Sea battles took place off the Azores and the islands were invaded and bloodily subdued by Spanish forces. 'In 1579,' wrote Gaspar Fructuoso, the sixteenth-century

43

Azorean historian, 'a year of penury, like so many years before it, the islanders were so mired in poverty that they could no longer continue as they were.... Some were persuaded to emigrate to Brazil to escape their misery....' The first migration in Azorean history had begun.[8]

After Portugal's declaration of its independence from Spain in 1640 the islands no longer played a key role in Atlantic commerce. However, the production of wheat was of importance to Portugal which always suffered a deficit in wheat production. The islands also produced quantities of woad which was sold as a dye to the English. Meanwhile volcanic eruptions continued to cause loss and hardship—there were serious eruptions in 1614, 1630, 1649, 1652, 1659, 1672 and 1718—and to undermine the ability of the islands to support their population.[9]

The population of the Azores initially grew relatively slowly, but by the middle of the seventeenth century it had outstripped that of Madeira. The most populous islands were São Miguel, Faial and Pico with 30,000, 9,000 and 10,000 inhabitants respectively. In the first half of the eighteenth century the Azores as a whole had a population density of 48 per square kilometre compared with 17–20 per square kilometre for mainland Portugal; and by 1796 the population of the archipelago stood at 156,256—a density of 66.6 per square kilometre.[10] The pressure of population was becoming severe and increasingly during the eighteenth century voices were raised suggesting that emigration would help restore some equilibrium between population and the land. In fact significant numbers of islanders had already begun to emigrate to Brazil, attracted by the discoveries of gold and diamonds and the opening of virgin land in the south, the settlement of Santa Caterina receiving an influx of 5,915 Azoreans and Rio Grande do Sul 1,400.[11] In spite of this, at the end of the century the captain-general, Denis Gregório Mendonça, referring specifically to the island of Terceira, bemoaned the fact that few men and virtually no women were emigrating, and asked: 'What disorders will result from this excess of population, the largest part of which is poor and miserable? The women prostitute themselves, men become robbers and everyone becomes a burden and inconvenience to the public.'[12]

By the middle of the nineteenth century the population had risen to nearly 250,000 and emigration was being recommended as a matter of urgency. Most of this growing population were rural farmers, but as land had been concentrated in the hands of a few large landowners who established entails to safeguard their family inheritance, the bulk of the population either rented small parcels of land or worked as wage labourers. Tenancies were usually for only a small number of years and, as the population grew, competition for land pushed up rents and increased economic instability. Wage labourers also suffered since work was only available on an irregular basis for much of the year. As a large part of the grain that was produced was exported by the commercial and landowning class, in defiance of royal decrees trying to limit the practice, the price of food was always very high and the population experienced famine conditions even in years of plenty.[13] By the early nineteenth century much of the population lived in extreme misery. As one observer wrote in 1806, outside the towns, substantial houses 'give way to four low walls, covered by a miserable thatch of straw; and in this mean and wretched refuge, built frequently on someone else's land, lives a family of real proletarians, without any property and without any employment'.[14] In 1800, out of 5,651 people on the island of Terceira whose occupations are recorded, half were day labourers; while in Faial out of 5,228 half were tenant farmers and a quarter were day labourers.[15] The parallels with the history of Ireland are striking.

Attempts to bring more land under cultivation and to enclose the grazing pastures and woodland on the higher hillsides, measures which might have led to improved agricultural output, were firmly resisted both by the landowners and also by the poor who depended on access to these areas. As Luís Mendonça and José Avila wrote, 'in the opinion of one of the civil governors of Angra, the failure to make use of the waste lands figures as one of the principal causes of the phenomenon of migration'.[16]

The social structure of the Azores meant that, for the majority of the population, the whole family, including children, had to work on small family farms or in casual employment. There were few spare resources available for education, or capital for setting up businesses. There were no industries on the islands beyond domestic artisan crafts and some construction, and fishing was the only supplement to agriculture. Although the growing of woad in the seventeenth century and of oranges for the European market in the nineteenth gave the islands an opportunity to develop exports and accumulate capital, the Azores did not benefit as Madeira did from a large expatriate community. Moreover the Portuguese elites preferred to spend their wealth embellishing churches rather than investing in infrastructure or industry.

However, some foreign ships did call and from the 1760s onwards the islands were increasingly visited by British and American whalers. Until whaling was finally banned in 1987, Azoreans hunted the whales using small open boats, landing the carcasses on the beaches for the messy business of cutting and boiling.[17] By the mid nineteenth century whaling had become a big business for shipowners, particularly those from the eastern seaboard of the United States. Azoreans were recruited as crew on the whalers, some eventually rising in the ranks to provide the United States with skippers for its whaling fleet. In this way there began a small exodus of adventurous Azorean men to the United States, establishing communities that soon set in motion a chain migration across the Atlantic.

However, in the Azores, as elsewhere, there was never a simple equation whereby poverty equalled a decision to emigrate. When large-scale emigration began it was not always the poorest who sought to leave the islands first. Emigration, which may sometimes appear to have been a mass movement, was in fact always made up of the decisions of individuals, and in making these decisions the factors that appear to have been decisive were whether the individual knew someone who had already emigrated, whether he or she had the means to pay for a passage and maintain himself or herself in another country, and whether the opportunity to emigrate presented itself.

Azorean emigrants took with them a distinctive culture which set them somewhat apart from other Portuguese. The peasants and day labourers of the Azores had led a very isolated existence. Not only were the islands located 900 miles from Portugal, but the communities were dispersed across nine islands, some of them, like Corvo, very small. Even on the larger islands communities might be very cut off from one another other. Below the towering cliffs of São Jorge small villages had been built on the *fajãs*, patches of land formed on the edge of the sea by landslips or the estuaries of small streams. These villages might only be accessible by precipitous mountain paths or by sea. As Jerry Williams wrote,

virtually all of the inhabitants were born, reared and eventually died on the island of their birth. Frequently, the whole life cycle took place in a single village. Living in the same village generation after generation eventually resulted in an extended family system whereby virtually everyone in a particular village was related, either by blood or through an intricate and reciprocal system of god-parentage.[18]

When individual Azoreans began to emigrate, members of the extended family soon followed and the close-knit village community was, in part, recreated wherever the migrants ended up. It has been suggested that this factor, as well as the continuing poverty of life in the islands, probably accounts for the relatively small number of Azorean emigrants who ever returned to the islands.

Emigrants also took with them the festivals associated with the Holy Spirit. This cult had been introduced into Portugal from Germany by Saint Isabel in the fourteenth century, and although the somewhat riotous celebrations which grew up had gradually been banned in Portugal, they continued to flourish in the Azores where they were believed to offer protection against the earthquakes and epidemics which periodically devastated the islands. Although attempts were made to suppress this cult, it became the focus for an insular religious culture which coalesced around the so-called *impérios*, elaborate little chapels which each community erected and where the 'emperors' and 'empresses' were crowned.[19]

By the early twentieth century conditions in the Azores had changed little from a century earlier. The economy was still largely based on agriculture and the only industries, mostly located on the island of São Miguel, were concerned with processing the sugar, tobacco and tea grown on the islands. Only 12 per cent of the population found employment in these industries.[20] As late as 1978 it was estimated that 70 per cent of the land in the Azores was still being farmed on a small scale by tenant farmers.[21] The rise of dairy farming in the twentieth century, while providing the islands with an export commodity, put further pressure on the land available for peasant farmers; but ironically it provided Azorean emigrants with the basic skills which they were successfully able to exploit in the dairy farms of California.

Alfred Lewis's novel *Home is an Island* describes rural life in the Azores before the First World War. It is a tale steeped in nostalgia in which the islands are a kind of forgotten Eden. The parents of the young José are part of a close-knit and supportive village community, but they can envisage only two possible futures for their son: to become a priest or to emigrate to America. The emigrants may have left the islands but had not entirely abandoned them. The boy, as he grows, is aware that

every house had its own past; from every home had departed, one day, a young man. A few went to America, some to Africa and Brazil. Not all of them came back. And so the spirits of those who had died, pursued by nostalgia, even in death, returned. They came back as strange never-before-seen birds; or as a sign, any noise, issuing from the forests of the island; perhaps the falling of a stone from an apparently sound wall; or the rasping of a window pane by an insect.[22]

The Cape Verde Islands and Guinea

The Cape Verde Islands, discovered in the 1450s, were situated on the latitude of the Sahara; although possessing rich volcanic soils, they suffered from irregular rainfall. Moreover they were far from Portugal. Granted like Madeira and the Azores to 'donatary captains', the islands struggled to attract immigrants. In 1466 the Crown granted the settlers special commercial privileges to enable them to develop trade with Guinea, but there were still relatively few settlers when the islands were attacked by a Castilian fleet in 1474 and the people, including the captains, were deported. By the end of the fifteenth century only two of the islands, Santiago and Fogo, had a sizeable population. To resolve the difficulties in populating the islands, the captains began to import slaves in large numbers to provide a workforce and, as the demand across the Atlantic grew, to be sold on to Spanish America.

Although the Portuguese population remained small, the islands came to assume an importance out of all proportion to the size of their settlements or the productivity of their agriculture. Lying on the main sea routes taken by sailing ships, they provided convenient ports of call for ships bound for the Estado da Índia or Brazil. Frequently visited by fleets, a racially mixed population was swollen by the members of ships' crews left behind as well as by the slaves imported for onward sale.

Most of the settlement was concentrated in and around the port-city of Ribeira Grande on the island of Santiago, which in the sixteenth century enjoyed considerable wealth as a centre for trading with West Africa as well as for servicing India- and Brazil-bound fleets. In 1513 the *corregedor*, Pedro Guimarães, described the population of the Ribeira Grande as follows:

There are fifty-eight settlers who are *vizinhos*, white men of honourable status. There are sixteen black *vizinhos* and there are fifty-six *estantes estrangeiros* who are natives of your kingdoms. There are four unmarried women and ten black women as well as other foreigners who are now here with their ships and will leave. There are twelve clerics and three friars among whom are two preachers.[23]

This description gives a good idea of the divisions of status within the Portuguese community. Clear distinctions were made between *vizinhos*, men of substance who could hold public office, and the so-called *estantes estrangeiros* who were new arrivals from Portugal, and between the white and the free black population. During the sixteenth century the population grew until Santiago had between 500 and 600 *vizinhos*. Many of the *vizinhos* had acquired entailed estates (*morgadios*), and later in the century there emerged a clear distinction between *vizinhos* and *moradores*, the former being men of property who monopolised local offices while the latter were immigrants who acquired their status by four years of residence. In 1546 black *vizinhos* were included among those who might hold public office, and among the privileges of their status were membership of the Misericórdias and religious brotherhoods, the right to elect town councillors, the right to serve in the militia and to aspire to the holding of *morgadios* or *capelas*. The ordinary *moradores* were often excluded from ownership of *morgadios* and made their living through trade with Guinea, importing among other things grain for sale to the visiting fleets.[24]

The *vizinhos* and *moradores* had originally been European Portuguese, but there was a steady erosion of the racial exclusiveness of these categories which gathered momentum in the seventeenth century. Legitimate children inherited their father's status even when their mothers were black, while illegitimate children could be declared legitimate by a royal letter. This process of legitimisation, which opened the door to inheriting property and holding public office, bound the Cape Verdeans strongly to Portugal. However remote metropolitan Portugal might seem from the everyday life of the islands, the need to obtain recognition of one's social, and hence economic, status from a distant Portuguese king bound this diasporic population back to the homeland by strong if invisible ties.[25]

Below the *vizinhos* and *moradores* was the mass of the population, white, mulatto and black, some slave and some free, who were excluded from the ownership of the relatively small areas of good land and had to live either as rent-paying peasants or by eking out a living as artisans or farmers in the drier and more remote areas. Thus the social divisions of the islands were not just those of master and slave but of the few wealthy landowners and merchants and the landless poor.[26]

As well as slaves there were also free black immigrants. Lisa Andrade describes how 'in the peopling of the islands there was not only the slaves but also the free blacks ... who spontaneously accompanied the merchants, missionaries and ships' captains; many among them spoke the Portuguese language and some went to Santiago to be made Christian'.[27] To these she might have added refugees from the wars of the mainland, particularly important following the 'Mane' invasions of the second half of the sixteenth century.

Charles Boxer wrote of the Cape Verdean population: 'Over succeeding centuries the racial amalgam in the islands was complete, the Negro element predominating in the physical make-up and the Portuguese in the cultural façade.'[28] The Cape Verdean population of the sixteenth century had strong economic and social ties that bound them closer to Africa than to Portugal. The islands became centres of the African diaspora as slaves were brought to the island for onward sale to the New World after undergoing a brief and superficial *ladino* 'make-over'. As for the free inhabitants, although few had ever seen Portugal or had any close relations with metropolitan Portuguese, they retained a strong sense of being Portuguese and of enjoying the rights and privileges of subjects of the Portuguese Crown. And as free blacks in the dangerous world of the eighteenth-century Atlantic, they might use their Portuguese citizenship to claim exemption from capture and enslavement. The Jesuit António Vieira, writing in the seventeenth century, described 'clergy and canons as black as jet, but so well-bred, so authoritative, so learned, such great musicians, so discreet and so accomplished that they may be envied by those in our own cathedrals at home'.[29] This Portuguese identity did not depend on race as such but was fixed by a wide range of cultural markers which included names, devotion to the Catholic church, house types and urban space, and European technologies. Their African heritage was most clearly seen in skin colour and phenotype, in agriculture, food and cooking, domestic life generally (for example the carrying of babies tied to the back of the mother) and a wide range of beliefs and practices which defined their understanding of the real and spiritual world. In between the European and African grew up a musical tradition, typically represented in the morna, and a creole language that drew on both the European and the African heritage.

However, most of the island communities were desperately poor. A sad portrait of the convict settlement in the Cape Verde Islands is given in the account of George Fenner's visit in 1566. Having found 'five or six small houses' on Boa Vista, the English fell in with two Portuguese

who 'were but poore & simple, and gave each of them a paire of shoes'.
They then sailed to a small island, possibly Sal, where they found

in all the Iland... not above 30 persons, which were banished men for a time,
some for more yeeres, some for lesse, and amongst them there was one simple
man which was their captaine. They live upon goats flesh, cocks, hennes, and
fresh water: other victuals they none, saving fish, which they esteeme not, neither have they any boats to take them.

The rent to the landowner was paid in skins and 'hath bene sent
foorth of the sayd Iland into Portugall 40000 skins in one yeere'. The
islanders also had 'great store of the oyle of Tortoises'.[30]

The careless exploitation of the islands and the attempts to grow
exportable crops, but chiefly the grazing of animals, damaged the fragile ecology. Although the islands were covered with vegetation when
first discovered, by the eighteenth century many of them had become
barren and semi-desert. Today Boa Vista looks like an island fragment
of the Sahara, but driving over the island reveals that at one time it was
divided into estates by long stone walls, and that there were farms and
villages which now lie abandoned in the interior. In some islands desert conditions were so severe that they would not support any inhabitants—in spite of possessing in Porto Grande a magnificent protected
anchorage, the island of São Vicente was almost totally unpopulated
the few wretched individuals on the island were described in 1836 as
living in a state of 'nudez absoluta'.[31] However, although the environment of the islands deteriorated and the severe climatic conditions
made agriculture increasingly difficult, the population continued to
grow, showing a remarkable fertility in spite of the frequent devastat-
ing famines and consequent high rates of mortality. Unable to survive
through agriculture, the islanders exploited whatever meagre resources
they could. Orchil, a form of lichen, was collected, but its sale was controlled by monopolists appointed by the Crown;[32] purgueira seeds were
exported for the Portuguese soap industry; and the manufacture of cotton cloth, salt and rum continued for the African market.

Almost from the beginning of settlement in the fifteenth century, the
Cape Verdeans had looked beyond their islands to make a living, and
emigration, temporary, seasonal or semi-permanent, became rooted in
their culture. Islanders would cross to Guinea to trade or to plant seasonal crops in the so-called pontas, wetland farms leased from local
African communities. There were also opportunities presented by visiting ships. There were always ships at anchor off the main island of

Santiago enabling islanders to make a living selling to the visiting sailors or shipping aboard foreign vessels as crew. The main ports of the island were surprisingly cosmopolitan and their population a mixture of peoples from all over the world. They were places where slavers, pirates and the crews of East Indiamen rubbed shoulders with slaves from Africa, convicts and prostitutes. The administrators, priests and officials from Portugal were few in number and largely strangers in their own land.

Barrow, who visited Santiago in 1792, commented that

the only Europeans we saw were the Governor, his secretary, the officer commanding of the troops, a raw-boned Scottish serjeant six feet high, and his wife... The clergy were people of colour, and some of them perfectly black. The officers of justice, of the customs, and other departments in the civil and military services, the troops, the peasantry, and the traders, were all blacks, or at least so very dark that they could scarcely be supposed to have any mixture of European blood in their veins. Yet most of them aspire to the honour of Portugueze extraction, and are proud of tracing their origin to a race of heroes who, disdaining the restraints of laws at home, contrived to get themselves transported abroad, where their free and ungovernable spirits could exert themselves without control. The Cap de Verd islands were to Portugal what Botany Bay is to England, an asylum for convicted criminals.[33]

Each of the other islands, he says, 'has its black governor, who is solely dependent on the governor General. The power and situation of the latter are little to be envied. Disease and want surround his habitation, and misery is ever before his eyes'[34] The islands had been suffering three years of drought.

In expressing my surprize to the secretary, that the mother country, so far from employing precautions, had taken no steps to procure succours, against a calamity so dreadful and of such long continuance, he observed that the Court of Lisbon considered these poor islands, and the few black subjects scattered over them, of too little importance to demand any part of its care or attention; that they produced very little revenue to the Crown, which arose chiefly from a monopoly of the slave trade on the coast, and from the sale of an exclusive privilege of supplying the Brazils with salt.[35]

'In short', Barrow says, 'the whole place is so miserable that I shall forbear any further description.'[36]

In the mid eighteenth century the rise of the American whaling industry brought whalers to the island of Brava as their principal port of call. Cape Verdeans sold their services to the Americans as crews for the whaling ships, which were often absent from the United States for years on end and found difficulty recruiting American crews. By the nineteenth century expert Cape Verdean boatmen and harpooners were actively sought and, like the Azoreans, many became officers on board the whalers. When the ships eventually docked in New Bedford or Nantucket the Cape Verdeans came ashore. Some stayed and small communities of 'Bravas' were formed. Once Cape Verdean communities became established, the end of the migration chain had become firmly anchored. More and more islanders crossed the Atlantic to join their countrymen, some braving the ocean in open boats, others as crew or stowaways, and the numbers rose as drought and famine affected the islands ever more frequently.

In the 1850s ships powered by steam began to replace sail, and in the 1860s the first submarine telegraph cables were laid. Porto Grande on the island of São Vicente now came into its own as a coaling depot. British coaling firms set up shop and the population of barren São Vicente grew rapidly. To join the coaling companies came the Western Telegraph Company and its employees. A sizeable foreign community grew up in what was cheerfully known as the 'Cinder Heap', with its golf course and cricket club, and by the last quarter of the nineteenth century Porto Grande had become one of the busiest ports of the Atlantic. People from all the islands came to São Vicente to seek work, attracted also by the opportunities to find a passage to America or Brazil. The opportunities for Cape Verdeans to emigrate were now plentiful and their diaspora had begun.

No figures exist to tell the story of emigration in the nineteenth century, but figures from 1900 until 1920 (when the United States first put up barriers to Cape Verdean immigration) show that 18,629 islanders left officially for the United States with a further 1,968 going to destinations in South America. One can only speculate how many went unofficially to avoid paying for passports or to escape military service.[37]

Migration and social mobility in the history of the Atlantic islands

The Portuguese who started the settlement of Madeira and the Azores in the early fifteenth century were not intending to abandon Portugal but to create an extension of their homeland in the virgin land of the islands. They belong with earlier generations who had colonised the empty lands and frontier districts of Portugal itself during the era of the *reconquista*. The greatest attraction for settlers of all classes was the availability of land. As Alberto Vieira put it, 'the greed for land and titles on the part of second sons and of the lesser aristocracy of the kingdom contributed to feed the diaspora'.[38] Land was granted by the captains according to the social status of the applicant, with the result that the largest part of the land was allocated to high-status families, most of whom resided in the islands, intermarried and came to form a close-knit island aristocracy, their social position secured by their economic privileges and by their entailed estates. Alongside these elite families there grew up a class of smallholders who paid tithes to the Order of Christ and dues on mills and wine presses to the captains. In short, this was a reinvention of the rural society of Portugal.

These early migrations and settlements established a pattern that was to characterise the Portuguese diaspora throughout its history. Among those who left Portugal, especially those who went to Cape Verde or the Guinea islands, there were few women—in Vieira's expressive phrase, 'the discoveries appear to have to been conjugated in the masculine'.[39] For the survival of their communities, female slaves had to be imported to substitute for the Portuguese wives who were not there. To supplement the numbers of those willing to emigrate to the islands, the Crown added *degredados* whose sentences were commuted to exile, a policy that was to continue in one form or another until the middle of the twentieth century. There were also a large number of settlers who were not subjects of the Crown of Portugal at all. Although replicating the rural society of Portugal in many important respects, the settlement of the islands inevitably involved a higher degree of social mobility than was to be found in Portugal, a tendency that was to characterise Portuguese overseas settlement over the centuries. Another trait visible in the early Portuguese migration within the Atlantic basin was the readiness to settle in lands other than those of the Portuguese Crown, in the Castilian owned Canary Islands or in the Americas, or within African kingdoms on the African mainland.

In the fifteenth century a high degree of mobility was also evident among the population. There was considerable movement of population between the islands, beginning with the leading families themselves. Maciot de Bettencourt, for example, surrendered his claims in the Canaries to the Infante Dom Henrique in return for land in Madeira, while Rui Gonçalves da Camara, second son of the captain of Funchal, obtained the captaincy of São Miguel in the Azores. Some of those who settled in Madeira soon moved on and Vieira has described the island as being 'a pole of convergence and redistribution of the migratory movement'.[40] Information about the population of São Miguel in the Azores in the sixteenth century shows that 59 per cent of families had their origin in Portugal and 24 per cent in Madeira.[41] Skilled Madeiran sugar growers also moved to the Canary Islands and to the Cape Verde and Guinea islands where their sugar-making skills were much in demand, the Guinea islands soon outstripping Madeira in the production of sugar.

Alongside sugar production there was commercial movement between the islands and the beginnings of a large-scale slave trade. Already the Portuguese diaspora was forming a complex pattern as the movement of settlers from Portugal and the islands met and merged with the forced diaspora of slaves from Morocco, the Canary Islands and western Africa, creating populations that in their cultural orientation were a blend of both Portuguese and African. Francis Rogers, an American of Azorean origin, describes this mixed heritage of the Atlantic islanders.

In its original efforts to people the Adjacent Islands [Madeira and the Azores] the Portuguese Crown undeniably had recourse not only to foreigners but also to some very unsavoury elements among white Portuguese men, to jailbirds to whom it gave the opportunity of exile in the islands ... Blacks, Moors (both Moriscos and captives) baptized Jews (New Christians), Spanish priests, prelates, and others, and mercantile Italians, French, English, and Germans. Slaves were definitely present, Blacks and, to a lesser extent captive Moors; and hanky-panky involving white men and female slaves resulted in the presence of some home grown mestiços.[42]

This initial phase of the Portuguese diaspora created new bases for further maritime expansion and new centres of population which in time would experience the pressures of over-population and declining agricultural yields and would generate fresh migrations. As the Portuguese diaspora unfolded in the succeeding centuries, it became as much a diaspora of the islanders as of the metropolitan Portuguese.

By the end of the eighteenth century all three groups of islands were experiencing the effects of the imbalance between the needs of a growing peasant population and the concentration of land in the hands of a few landowners. All three island groups also suffered the effects of periodic natural disasters: the diseases which attacked the Madeiran vines, the earthquakes in the Azores and the droughts that afflicted the Cape Verde Islands. The Portuguese Crown had arrived at a solution to these recurring problems—a solution that did not require it to confront the problems of land reform or economic development of the islands. Emigration killed many birds with a single sling shot: poor families were provided with relief, empty lands in Brazil and later in Africa would be colonised, social tensions that periodically led to civil disturbances were eased, and the islanders left behind would benefit from money remitted to their families. So during the reign of João V emigration from the islands to Brazil was encouraged, and in the reign of Salazar two hundred years later emigration to Africa was seen as the state's best answer to famine and over-population.

The Guinea islands

The last group of islands settled in the fifteenth century were the four Guinea islands—Fernando Po/Bioko, Príncipe, São Tomé and Anobom—discovered by the Portuguese from the 1470s onwards. These volcanic islands lay near the equator and were covered with thick rainforest. Unlike the Cape Verde Islands they did not suffer from lack of rain, but they were situated even farther from Portugal.

Settling in these islands meant almost certainly a permanent separation from Europe and a commitment to living in tropical Africa. Although the islands were reached in the 1470s, few settlers answered the call of the captains to whom the Crown granted the islands of São Tomé, Príncipe and Anobom. The fourth island, Fernando Po, was not settled at all, probably because it was already peopled by Africans and the Portuguese had no desire to undertake the kind of conquest that in the Canaries had proved so difficult. Among the early settlers to Guinea were convicts and, allegedly, Jewish children taken from their parents and sent to help populate the islands. Whatever the truth of this story, the belief that there was a strong Jewish influence in the islands was to persist, so that the islands were bound not only back to Portugal but into the wider world of the Sephardic diaspora.

Once the sugar-growing potential of the islands had been established, the lowland areas in the north of the town of São Tomé were distributed as *morgadios* to sugar planters. As well as experienced sugar growers from Madeira, the early settlers numbered Genoese, French and Castilians and men 'of any other nation who want to come to live here and all are accepted with a good will'.[43] Sugar prospered and São Tomé became even more commercially successful than

Madeira or Ribeira Grande. Seventy ships a year were said to visit the islands by the 1550s to take off the sugar and to bring a wide range of imported goods for the settlers.

The captaincy of São Tomé was abolished in 1522 and the island was placed under a governor and made an episcopal see. The main town was given a Senado da Câmara in 1534, which placed it on the same institutional footing as Lisbon, after Funchal only the second such city outside Portugal. However, European settlers found difficulty in establishing themselves in the islands because of the climate and the disease environment. Large numbers of slaves were imported to work the plantations and to provide wives and concubines for the settlers. Indeed a royal decree specifically allowed the importation of African women for the purpose of 'populating the island'.[44] As a result the Africanisation of the São Tomé population took place even more rapidly than that of Cape Verde. The Portuguese pilot who wrote an account of São Tomé in the middle of the sixteenth century records that 'when the wife of a merchant dies, he takes a negress, and this is an accepted practice, as the negro population is both intelligent and rich, bringing up their daughters in our way of life, both as regards customs and dress'.[45] In the middle of the sixteenth century there were sixty or so sugar mills operating with possibly as many as 10,000 slaves, while the free population of São Tomé probably rose to 600–700 heads of households by the mid sixteenth century before going into decline as sugar production increasingly relocated to Brazil.[46]

Apart from the transient seamen, merchants and royal governors, the population soon became made up largely of free blacks and mulattos who enjoyed a relative immunity from tropical diseases. By the end of the sixteenth century São Tomé, equipped with the institutions by which metropolitan Portugal governed its territories, presented what Boxer described as 'a rather peculiar society'. The brothers of the Misericórdia, the town councillors, the cathedral canons, the owners of the sugar plantations and the captains of the militia were all prestigious Portuguese of the local society. But they were all black and the women, as in other creole societies brought into being by the transient maritime Europeans, were a powerful as well as permanently resident influence in this society. There was therefore a marked process of creolisation of their Portuguese identity, because of the imperatives of the climate as well as the presence of so many Africans. The anonymous pilot described a society where the population built wooden houses either on stilts or with an upper floor as protection against insects, adopted African food crops and relied on African remedies for the fevers and venereal diseases which so seriously affected the newcomers. He also describes the social life which brought the settlers to dine in each other's houses, especially during the periods of great heat.

The islands enjoyed great prosperity until the 1590s when a combination of circumstances led to the decline in sugar production. The plantations began to suffer increasing depredations from bands of maroons (runaway slaves) and the islands were attacked by pirates and by the Dutch. In 1641 the Dutch actually took possession of São Tomé and held it until 1648. By the mid seventeenth century most of the sugar planters had given up the struggle and relocated to Brazil, while São Tomé survived as a tiny community of black Portuguese who made a living from local trade in the Gulf of Guinea and from the visits of the occasional European ship. Príncipe and Anobom, also peopled by black Portuguese, remained under the overall control of their absentee 'donatary captains'.

Largely cut off from Portugal, the population of the islands developed a rich syncretic creole culture. At least three different creole dialects were spoken in the islands: the São Tomense speech, the speech of the so-called Angolares who were the descendants of the maroons of an earlier age, and the dialect spoken by the tiny community in Anobom. The creole culture found expression in traditional dramatic presentations: the *Tchiloli*, also called 'The Tragedy of the Marquis of Mantua', and the dance drama called *dança Congo*, Africanised versions of European renaissance theatre of the sixteenth century. These dramas, although of European origin, became an indigenised expression of the creole identities of the population.

Few if any of the islanders had ever been to Portugal and they continually adopted a highly independent stance vis-à-vis the governors and bishops sent by Lisbon—so much so that the Portuguese governors relocated to Príncipe in the eighteenth century to escape their influence. They were nevertheless bound to the metropolis by the invisible threads of rank and status. From Portugal came recognition of their status as town councillors and cathedral canons, confirmation of their land titles and even grants of the habits of knights of the Military Orders. It was the sanction of Lisbon that maintained the social structure of the islands and the status of the free São Tomean families. Moreover, it was as free subjects of the Portuguese Crown that the São

Tomeans were able to maintain their security and independence in an Atlantic world where a black skin was often seen as synonymous with slave status. The free black population became known as the *forros* (freemen) and formed the elite which, after suffering an eclipse during the late colonial period when the island was partitioned among cocoa-producing companies, regained power when São Tomé became independent from Portugal in 1975.

The Guinea islands differed from the other groups in that they never developed migration to the United States. However, there were close ties with Brazil and it was from South America that the cocoa bean was introduced early in the nineteenth century. Networks were also established with Africa. Just as the Cape Verde Islands had become the point of departure for *lançados* trading and settling along the rivers from Senegal to Sierra Leone, so Portuguese based in São Tomé and Príncipe traded with the African states of the Gulf of Guinea, many of them settling in the Kongo kingdom, Benin or the Itsekiri Kingdom. The Guinea islands thus became a point of departure for a further wave of 'Portuguese' emigrants to Africa. However, here the parallels with the other Atlantic islands cease. In the nineteenth century large numbers of emigrants left Madeira, the Azores and the Cape Verde Islands for the New World. By contrast São Tomé became a destination for immigrants. Thousands of labourers were forcibly contracted in Africa for work on the cocoa plantations and Cape Verdeans driven by famine to leave their islands were also contracted to work in São Tomé. When considering the economics of labour and the forces that control the flow of migrants, the Guinea islands have to be placed in the same category as the islands of the Caribbean.

4

THE DIASPORA OF THE SEPHARDIC JEWS

The Portuguese New Christians and the Sephardic diaspora

Religious persecution has been one of the principal factors driving Portuguese to emigrate, as it was for their English counterparts in the seventeenth century. If there was no single iconic departure like that of the Pilgrim Fathers, there was a constant flow of Jewish and New Christian emigrants who left Portugal from the end of the fifteenth century, either to escape active religious persecution or to find places to settle where they could practise their religion without fear of molestation.

The origin of the dispersal of the Sephardic Jews has been frequently described, and the constant movement and settlement of those involved produced a bewildering complexity that marks it as one of the first examples of a truly global diaspora. During the Middle Ages there had been large Jewish populations in all the Iberian kingdoms and, in spite of sometimes violent outbreaks of anti-Semitism, this population had survived and prospered, particularly in the worlds of finance and commerce but also in medicine and urban artisan trades. Alongside the Jewish community, and placed, so to speak, between it and the Christian population, were the *conversos*—Jewish families that, for one reason or another, had converted to Christianity. Following the anti-Semitic riots of 1391 the emigration of Jews from the peninsula had begun on a small scale, but much larger numbers of Jews had con-

61

verted and in the following century this *converso* community became a group with a distinct identity within Castilian and Portuguese society. In time, being a *converso* became an inherited status and no longer simply implied a recent religious conversion. As practising Catholics the *conversos* became eligible to hold municipal and even ecclesiastical office, could own land and were able to contract marriages with noble families. It was the wealth, success and rising social status of *converso* families, as well as the suspicions that they remained crypto-Jews, that fuelled increasing hostility from 'old Christians' in the middle years of the century.[1]

During the fifteenth century Castile experienced very disturbed social conditions culminating in the civil war which followed the death of Enrique IV in 1474. The victor in this civil war, the Infanta Isabella, who had married Ferdinand of Aragon in 1469, was under strong pressure to adopt policies to unite her kingdom and to forge closer links with her husband's realm. This prompted her to respond to demands from within the church to establish an Inquisition to inquire into the religious orthodoxy of the converted Jews. The Inquisition was established in 1480 and at first concerned itself not with practising Jews and Muslims but only with the *converso* population. In 1492, however, the decision was taken to expel all orthodox Jews from the two kingdoms. It is probable that around 70,000 people were affected by this order and in the next few years there was a mass departure. Some Jews followed earlier emigrants to the more tolerant climate of Italy, while others went to North Africa or the Ottoman territories, settling in already established Jewish communities in Adrianople, Salonika and Istanbul itself. About 30,000 crossed the frontier into Portugal. The arrival of such large numbers of religious refugees presented a challenge to Portugal's traditional policy of toleration. The king, Dom João II, granted 600 families the right to settle permanently but decided that the rest of the refugees would have to leave the kingdom. However, the future of the Portuguese Jewish and *converso* population was still undecided when the king died in October 1495, to be succeeded by his cousin, Dom Manuel. As the famous Jewish mathematician Abraham Zacuto put it, 'We [in Portugal] had the enemies on one side and the sea on the other.'[2]

Dom Manuel wanted to secure a marriage with the daughter of Isabella of Castile and agreed to expedite the expulsion of Castilian Jews from Portugal. After due consideration his orders took a form which was to have a profound influence on the history of the Sephardic Jews. All Jews resident in Portugal were ordered either to leave the country or to convert to Christianity. To those who converted Dom Manuel promised that there would be no inquiry into their faith for the next twenty years—that is, that there would be no Portuguese Inquisition. In the years 1496 and 1497, therefore, there was a renewed exodus of orthodox Jews from the Iberian peninsula while large numbers apparently accepted Manuel's amnesty and formally converted to Christianity. Those who neither left nor converted were subject to forced conversion and their children were taken away from them. It was then that, allegedly, 2,000 Jewish children were dispatched to help form a Portuguese community in São Tomé. The Iberian Jewish community now split to follow two paths: one part had left the Iberian peninsula and had begun to settle in other lands, while a second group, approximately equal numerically to the first, remained in Portugal where they became known as New Christians.[3]

The Jews who departed at first settled throughout the Mediterranean lands, some finding a safe haven in the fortified towns that the Portuguese controlled in Morocco, while others went to the rudimentary settlements in West Africa and even to the Estado da Índia. It was felt that there was no need to expel such valuable citizens from these extra-territorial fragments of the Portuguese monarchy. Although there was a violent outbreak of anti-Semitism in Lisbon in 1506, the New Christians who remained prospered during the reign of Dom Manuel (1495–1521). Members of New Christian families not only maintained their prominence in commerce but received royal appointments, some even becoming members of the royal council. Others were appointed to the Military Orders of knights or to positions in the church, while still others married into the old aristocracy of Portugal. Dom Manuel's solution to the crisis of the 1490s had led to a great expansion of New Christian influence throughout the kingdom.

Portuguese in Spanish America

Many Jewish families which had left the Iberian peninsula retained links with the New Christians, and through them the Jewish business community was able to trade and invest in the commercial networks that opened up in the Atlantic and Indian Oceans. New Christian and Jewish money was soon helping to finance the growth of both Spanish and

Portuguese Atlantic trade, and for the first half of the sixteenth century there was no Inquisition outside the Iberian peninsula to restrict their activity. After the union of the Spanish and Portuguese Crowns in 1580, all trade restrictions between Portugal and Castile were lifted and the Portuguese had free access to Spanish markets. The result was renewed impetus to the diaspora as Portuguese New Christians moved in numbers not only to the Spanish-controlled Netherlands, where they had already been long established and where the royal factory at Antwerp formed a focus for their activities, but also to Spain itself where the port of Seville, through which all trade with America was channelled, was conveniently close to the Portuguese frontier. From Seville many travelled to the Spanish territories in America.[4]

Portuguese were not allowed by law to settle in the Spanish Indies, but circumventing this embargo was only too easy. Large numbers of Portuguese sailors shipped aboard Spanish vessels, while the existence of a sizeable Portuguese community in Seville meant that the passage of an illegal emigrant at San Lucar was easy to arrange. Moreover the growth of the slave trade between Portuguese ports in Africa and the Spanish Indies allowed increasing numbers of Portuguese to take ship from the Atlantic islands to the New World. It was also easy for Portuguese who settled in Brazil after 1530 to move on to the burgeoning Spanish settlements on the Río de la Plata.

By the 1630s Portuguese were estimated to form around 6 per cent of the population of Mexico City and Cartagena de las Indias. Another estimate suggests that at the time of the break-up of the union of the Crowns in 1640 there may have been around 10–12,000 Portuguese in Mexico alone and 6,000 Portuguese New Christians in Spanish America as a whole.[5]

In contrast to the pattern of emigration in later centuries, the Portuguese who settled in Spanish America did not share a common background within Portugal itself, for the records of the Inquisition show that those Portuguese whom it examined came from 91 different places. However, these Portuguese trading communities enjoyed a distinctive communal life, which helped them to retain a strong Portuguese identity. This in turn provided additional strength to the commercial networks and the system of trust and credit on which so much commercial activity depended. In the larger cities like Mexico City or Potosí the Portuguese congregated in their own areas, and many maintained large houses where separate families lived together. Security may have been a paramount consideration but there were social pressures as well. As Daviken Studnicki-Gizbert expressed it, 'Compadrazgo (godparentage) obligations forged at the birth of new members of the community created bonds of fictive kinship; hospices were built to lodge sojourners; chapels and confraternities devoted to the Portuguese Saint Anthony provided a symbol of collective affiliation as well as a space where Portuguese migrants could gather and organize various forms of mutual aid.'[6] The larger Portuguese communities might also establish a branch of the Santa Casa da Misericórdia.

If Jewish rites were practised within the Portuguese community, it was in secret. Sometimes these were mingled in an eclectic way with Christianity, as for example in the veneration of images dedicated to Saint Moses.[7] The social and business worlds of the Portuguese New Christians in Spanish America were closely intertwined. Families tried to marry their sons and daughters to existing or prospective business partners, and the clandestine practice of Jewish rites became, through fear of the Inquisition, a bond which reinforced the trust on which the conduct of business depended.

After Portugal broke away from Spain in 1640, Portuguese were no longer welcome in Seville or in Spanish America and the once thriving Portuguese community began to receive the unwanted attentions of the Inquisition. Many left for other Atlantic destinations while those who survived assumed Spanish nationality and a Spanish identity, which effectively dissolved the ties of Portuguese separateness. Within a generation the Portuguese had become absorbed into the local Spanish creole population.

New Christians and Jews in West Africa

Many New Christians took the opportunities presented by Portugal's overseas expansion to establish themselves in the Atlantic islands or as lançados on the coast of western Africa. There many reverted to Judaism or were able to practise mixed marrano religious rites. African rulers were not concerned with the religion of the 'strangers' who settled in their kingdoms, and for this reason many New Christians who 'had been born in Portugal … came here to declare themselves [Jews] because the kings of the land protected them and they could not be punished'. They settled so that they 'could practise in freedom their own religion and law'.[8] In the first half of the seventeenth century there was a thriving Jewish population at various points along the rivers of upper Guinea, but it appears that these gradually became merged with the wider Luso–African community and separate Jewish communities had largely disappeared by the end of the century. One reason given for this disappearance was the custom whereby Portuguese who settled in western Africa married local women. As a Jew has to be born to a Jewish mother, it was inevitable that with these marriages no permanent Jewish presence would be able to take root. New Christian influence, however, remained strong in the Cape Verde Islands and in São Tomé, where the conflict between the local *moradores* and the episcopal authorities gave rise on the part of the latter to hysterical accusations of Judaising—one bishop actually claiming that he had seen midnight processions in which a Golden Calf was carried through the streets. Toby Green has argued that the New Christian community in Cape Verde was instrumental in the process of creolisation and in the creation of the trans-Atlantic networks that led to the expansion of the slave trade. His argument is that the New Christians were used to living with a dual identity—that of Jew and Christian—and possessed the cultural flexibility which enabled them to trade profitably in the upper Guinea region. Less convincing is his argument that the New Christians brought with them their experience of violence in the Iberian peninsula and that, having escaped persecution in the Iberian peninsula, their becoming pioneers of the slave trade involved 'some form of psychological transference for a group whose estimation of humanity cannot have been very high following recent events in Portugal'.[9] More likely the Portuguese New Christians became involved in the slave trade simply because they derived great profits from it.

The Portuguese Inquisition

During the first part of the sixteenth century the New Christians and Jews who left Portugal often joined the Iberian communities outside the peninsula that were dominated by Old Christians. However, life became more complicated when the Inquisition was established in Portugal in 1536 (with oversight of the Atlantic settlements) and in Goa in 1560. Meanwhile branches of the Spanish Inquisition were set up in Mexico and Lima, also in the 1560s. New Christians living in Portugal and its overseas settlements and in Spanish America were now subject to investigation and this precipitated further emigration. For the next two hundred years the Inquisition and the Crown played cat and mouse with the New Christian population of Portugal. The Inquisition initiated trials and investigations, which forced the New Christians to seek amnesties from the Crown in return for large payments. Periods of active persecution were thus followed by periods of tacit toleration, which in turn prompted further persecution and further amnesties.

During the period from 1580 to 1640, when the Spanish and Portuguese kingdoms were united, the Portuguese New Christians were by and large protected by the Spanish Crown and had unprecedented opportunities to expand their commercial activity in Spain and Spanish America. The Spanish Crown offered its protection in return for the financial backing of the New Christians, and investigations by the Inquisition were discouraged. The protection offered was particularly effective between 1621 and 1643, during the ascendancy of the Count Duke of Olivares. During that time large Portuguese populations were established in Spanish America, while in Europe the New Christian bankers largely superseded the Genoese as the main financiers of the Spanish monarchy and as contractors for the *asiento*—the supply of slaves to the Spanish possessions.

However, after the Portuguese declared their independence in 1640 and enthroned Dom João IV as king, the Inquisition became more active in its persecution of New Christians. The king tried to prevent this persecution, as his Spanish predecessors had done, and for the same reason: the financial resources of the New Christian mercantile community were needed to support the Crown's attempt to stimulate the Portuguese economy by creating overseas trading companies and domestic industries. The Inquisition, on the other hand, was encouraged in its persecution by elements among the nobility and common people who systematically tried to undermine any economic enterprise that was supported by New Christian capital, even when it had the backing of the Crown. The result was that the years from 1640 to 1730 saw some periods of very active persecution and, in consequence, increased flows of emigration.[10]

During the seventeenth century, while the fortunes of the New Christians in the Iberian peninsula fluctuated, outside Spain and Portugal they experienced great commercial success and were among the leaders in the development of European capitalism. It has been suggested that one reason for the success and prosperity of the Portuguese mercantile class (Old and New Christians alike) in the Atlantic world was the very fact that outside Portugal the influence of the nobility was very much less and in many areas non-existent.[11] Whatever the reason, the seventeenth century provided striking proof of the contention that the major contribution of the Portuguese to European civilisation was made by exiles and *estrangeirados*, not by Portuguese resident in Portugal itself.

The 'Portuguese nation' in the Dutch colonies

Persecution by the Portuguese Inquisition was never prolonged or effective enough to persuade all the New Christian families to emigrate, but it was sufficiently threatening to convince many of them to invest their wealth outside Portugal. This trend became more marked after the split between Portugal and Spain in 1640. As access to an undivided Atlantic economy was now impeded by war, many New Christians moved to France or the Netherlands where a large Portuguese Sephardic population was already established. The Dutch occupation of northern Brazil (effective between 1630 and 1654) and the increasing Dutch presence in Africa presented the Portuguese New Christians with fresh investment opportunities. New Christian money was invested in sugar and slaves as well as in the Dutch Charter Companies and in Dutch trading voyages to West Africa. During the Dutch occupation of Recife, the New Christian population in northern Brazil rose to between 850 and 1,000 and may have constituted as much as half the white population of the colony.[12] When the Dutch were eventually expelled from Brazil in 1654 many New Christians departed once again and moved to the Dutch and English colonies in North America.

Curaçao was another area of settlement. Declared a free port by the Dutch in 1675, the island developed as a commercial centre rather than a plantation colony. Many Sephardic Jews from Amsterdam settled on the island, and by 1726 they owned 200 vessels and dominated the regional trade. Numbers rose from 600 in 1702 to 1,500 in the mid eighteenth century when they constituted a quarter of the island's white population.[13] At the same time there were 400 Jews in Jamaica and around 1,000 in Suriname. The dominance of the Sephardic Jews in the Dutch West Indies was one reason for the rise of Papiamentu, a Portuguese-based creole language that was used by Sephardic traders and their African associates and which survives as a living language in the twenty-first century.

Sephardim in Europe

Following the establishment of the Inquisition in Portugal in 1536, substantial numbers of New Christians began to leave Portugal and to establish exile communities in many of the major ports of Europe. The people who made up these communities were often referred to simply as 'Portuguese' or the 'Portuguese nation', and modern scholarship has described them typically as 'Port Jews' (as opposed to the 'Court Jews' who operated directly under the protection of European monarchs). The leaders of these exile communities came from wealthy merchant families and maintained ties with other Sephardic communities in Europe and with kin back in Portugal. Not all traced their origin to Portugal, for some were descendants of Spanish Jews who had not crossed into Portugal following the expulsion in 1492 but instead had directly sought refuge in Italy or the eastern Mediterranean. These formed a separate group of orthodox Jews who had never undergone conversion and who did not integrate easily with the *converso* or New Christian exiles who arrived at a later date.[14] These orthodox Sephardim apart, the New Christian diaspora was aided by the fact that most of the exiles were at least nominally Catholic. This made it easier for them to be accepted in Catholic societies like the Italian states or in France where Henri II issued *lettres patentes* to 'Portuguese' merchants who wanted to settle in the south-west of France. However, there were dangers once these New Christians tried to revert to Judaism: many of them, once they were safe from the Inquisition, decided to throw off an assumed Christianity and return to the Jewish faith. This made them vulnerable to local laws against apostasy. Not surprisingly it was the wealthiest Sephardic families that found it easiest to find toleration, safe conducts and permissions to reside.

The experience of the Portuguese who settled in the Medici port-city of Livorno illustrates what happened to the first generation of the Sephardic diaspora. New Christians from Portugal had settled, with encouragement from the Grand Dukes, from as early as the 1540s. When the Sephardic community was granted special privileges in 1591, among them immunity from Inquisition inquiries, many openly reverted to Judaism. By 1634 the community was solidly Jewish and there were no longer any New Christians as such—'crypto-Judaism ceased to be a pressing social phenomenon'.[15] Livorno now became a major centre of the Sephardic diaspora. The community there grew steadily throughout the seventeenth century and by 1738 numbered 3,687. Throughout the rest of the eighteenth century Jews constituted around 10 per cent of the city's population.

In northern Europe the main city where Portuguese New Christians settled was Amsterdam, which since the late sixteenth century had become the centre of opposition to the Spanish monarchy and its monopolistic commercial pretensions. Portuguese New Christians were welcomed because, as Yosef Kaplan puts it, 'these Jews were an attractive economic factor during the Age of Mercantilism thanks to their experience in international trade, their ability to mobilise resources from a population dispersed around the world, and, no less, their connections with the Iberian Peninsula'.[16]

Although direct migration from the Iberian peninsula accounted for much of the growth of the Amsterdam Sephardic community, some of the migration to Amsterdam seems to have come from communities established in south-western France, suggesting that there was a staged migration, particularly important for those of limited means for whom south-western France was the initial refuge nearest to the Iberian peninsula. Others moved on from Antwerp and Venice as the economic fortunes of these cities declined. Indeed the Venetian 'ponentine' community contributed materially to the establishment of the community in Amsterdam, providing it with one of its first rabbis, Joseph Pardo, and the model for the *Dotar*, its dowry society.[17]

The Portuguese and Spanish New Christians who began to settle in Amsterdam in the 1590s arrived as nominal Catholics and, although the crypto-Judaism of many of their number was well known, the municipal authorities turned a deaf ear to the protests of the Calvinist clergy. In 1616 they issued a set of regulations which were to govern relations with the Jewish community for the next two hundred years. These regulations contained three prohibitions. The 'Portuguese' were not to convert Christians, were not to speak against the Christian religion, and were not to have sexual relations with Christian women.[18] At about the same time the Portuguese exile community founded the institution that became known as the *Dotar*, to provide dowries for poor girls. The existence and practice of the *Dotar* became central to the way that the Portuguese community defined itself. According to Miriam Bodian it gave 'institutional expression to "the Nation"' and showed clearly how the Amsterdam Sephardic community aspired to a leadership role in the whole Sephardic diaspora.[19] The criterion for receiving a dowry was to be an established Portuguese New Christian or someone of Jewish lineage, and it was to be open to Sephardic Jews wherever they lived. Dowries might even be given to *bona fide* New Christians who had not yet returned to Judaism.

As more and more of the New Christians 'came out' as practising Jews, a number of separate communities were organised which came together in 1622 to create the *Imposta*, a governing body whose statutes were based on those of the Venetian Jewish community. This move to consolidate the organisation of the 'Portuguese nation' was prompted by the arrival of increasing numbers of Ashkenazim.[20]

The numbers of Portuguese in Amsterdam stagnated while the war between the United Provinces and Spain continued but grew rapidly after 1648, numbering around 3,000 by 1680. As the largest and richest Sephardic community in northern Europe the 'Portuguese nation' in Amsterdam held an influential and even dominant position in the diaspora. As Miriam Bodian explained, 'Dutch society actually encouraged… the cultivation of a distinct Portuguese–Jewish identity [and] provided the conditions that allowed the community to develop its own "expansionist" role as a nerve centre for the entire Atlantic "Portuguese" diaspora'.[21] Other Sephardic communities in northern Europe often sought rabbis and teachers from the Amsterdam intellectual elite. In the Jewish communities in southern France, for example, the 'persons appointed as representatives of the [Amsterdam] *Dotar*… were undoubtedly informal authority figures in their settlements'.[22]

The members of the 'Portuguese nation' in Amsterdam 'retained an intensely proud sense of their Iberian identity, reflected in their language use and in their patterns of cultural consumption'.[23] Throughout the seventeenth century they conducted their correspondence in Portuguese and retained a strong interest in Iberian theatre and literary culture. To safeguard their Iberian heritage they became increasingly exclusive. When the first Ashkenazi refugees began to arrive from Germany in the 1630s, 'they were not permitted to become members of the Spanish–Portuguese "Nation"'.[24] Indeed the Ashkenazim were considered to be of a different class and were often referred to as '*criados da Nação*'—servants of the Portuguese nation. The Portuguese community adopted regulations to exclude not only Ashkenazim but even members of their own community who married Ashkenazim. For their part Ashkenazi immigrants sought to benefit from the privileges already accorded the Sephardim and settled in their shadow—often as servants in the Sephardic households, as happened also in Denmark, Hamburg and London.

The rivalry between the two branches of Judaism took on an impressive architectural form. In 1670 the Ashkenazi community began work on the Great Schul on the Houtgracht in Amsterdam. Not to be outdone the Sephardic community built their own grand synagogue, the Esnoga, across the street. Opened in 1675 this magnificent building, as prominent as any of the city's churches, remains today as testimony to the wealth and taste of the people who built it—marking in an impressive manner what can now be seen as the high-water mark of the prosperity of Amsterdam's Sephardic Jews.[25]

As the 'Portuguese nation' grew in numbers and wealth during the seventeenth century, it also adopted regulations to exclude Jews with black ancestry and descendants of converts who could not claim descent from Abraham and membership of the tribe of Judah. As Yosef Kaplan wrote, 'the apologists among them did not hesitate to make generous use of the Iberian terminology of the days of the Statutes of Purity of Blood ... yesterday's segregated and downtrodden, who had been deprived of their honour by the Old Christians in Spain and Portugal, now hailed their own ancestry as a symbol of their Jewish identity'. And again, in

the purity of the *Nação*, the separatist strategy of the Western Sephardic diaspora shows itself in its fullest, most extreme form. Any reader of these regulations, who observes the manner in which it inquired into the pure "Portuguese or Spanish extraction" of candidates for membership in the congregations, cannot but recall the intense attention given by Iberian institutions and organisations at the time of the expansion of the Statutes of *limpieza de sangre* to verifying the pure origins ... of anyone who wished to join them.[26]

It is interesting to contrast this with the 'flexibility' with regard to race and intermarriage which Toby Green found in the New Christians of western Africa.

The sense of exclusiveness among members of the *nação* led to problems in accommodating the poor. The common solution was to arrange for the poor members of their community to be sent to London or to the Americas, thereby assisting and promoting the Sephardic diaspora.[27]

The Sephardic community in Amsterdam retained, in one form or another, its sense of being Portuguese throughout the eighteenth century, but the consciousness of an exclusive Iberian identity inevitably waned. One factor was the gradual drying up of the flow of New Christian exiles from Portugal. After a final burst of activity by the Inquisition early in the eighteenth century, the persecution of New Christians in Portugal largely ceased and was stopped altogether after Pombal's restructuring of the Inquisition in the 1760s and his granting of full civil rights to New Christians. No longer fed demographically by new exiles and spiritually by the consciousness of persecution, the forces which had been bringing change to the Sephardic community began to make inroads on its exclusiveness. In particular the declining wealth of the community, resulting from the more general decline in the Dutch economy, led to growing social divisions between rich and poor and a tendency for the wealthier members of the community to integrate with Dutch society. The use of the Portuguese language also declined until by the nineteenth century it was retained largely for liturgical and ceremonial purposes. The Napoleonic reforms, which brought about the total emancipation of the Jews but also the abolition of their autonomous institutions, further undermined the survival of a distinctive Portuguese '*nação*'. However, it was still possible in the nineteenth century for a Sephardic synagogue congregation to refuse burial rites to someone who had married an Ashkenazim.[28]

The story of the Amsterdam Portuguese Jews is especially interesting because it is so well documented and, as a consequence, so well studied. In many ways it shows the same trajectory of rise, consolidation and decline that was later followed by so many other Portuguese diasporic communities.

The Sephardic diaspora in Britain and Germany

Amsterdam was frequently a base from which Portuguese Jews moved on to other centres. Among the most important secondary destinations for the diaspora were Hamburg, Bordeaux (where the Sephardic population reached 1,500 by 1750) and London.

The rise of the Sephardic community in Hamburg reflected the changing pattern of commerce in the Atlantic world. Portuguese New Christians began to arrive in Hamburg around 1590 and, as they were ostensibly Catholics, were granted special privileges to settle in the city. By 1663 they numbered around 600. Through contacts in Brazil, the Hamburg 'Portuguese' began the refining of sugar which soon became the most important industry in the city, while links with the communities in Curaçao provided opportunities for manufactured goods from Hamburg to enter the closed markets of Spanish America.[29]

Jews had been granted formal permission to settle in England during the Protectorate, but the Sephardic Jewish community did not come directly from the Iberian peninsula and was first and foremost an offshoot of that of Amsterdam. It grew rapidly only after 1700, as the focus of finance and international trade shifted from the United Provinces to London. The movement of so many Sephardic families to London was a movement planned 'in deliberate consultation with Amsterdam and other Portuguese merchants seeking to maximise their advantages or to maintain their positions in international trade'.[30] This was not, therefore, an example of migration under pressure, though later in the 1720s and 1730s some refugees did arrive directly from the Iberian peninsula. Around 1720 the Sephardic population of London has been estimated to have been around 1,000, with a further 1,500 arriving during the next fifteen years.[31] The lack of formal controls on the movement of foreigners encouraged this immigration, and figures for the second half of the eighteenth century show that most Sephardic immigrants had their origins in the Mediterranean or the Low Countries rather than in the Iberian peninsula. Like its counterpart in Amsterdam, the Sephardic community in London at first assumed responsibility for all poor Jews who arrived. However, the growing numbers of both Ashkenazim and the Sephardic poor led to strict limitations being put on the amount of charity offered and to the adoption of policies either to send poor immigrants back where they came from or to forward them to the New World. When the royal charter was granted for the settlement of Georgia in 1732, the leaders of the Sephardic community took the opportunity to send many of the poorer members of their community to the new colony.[32]

In London the wealthy Sephardic families operating in the City of London found a society that was largely tolerant of religious heterodoxy, especially among the rich, although the City remained very reluctant to allow Jews to obtain official positions within its institutions. Many immigrants never formally became members of any synagogue and rapidly assimilated to the lifestyle of those around them, buying country properties, socialising with other wealthy merchant families and aping the manners of the landed aristocracy. As a result the Sephardic community in London never developed an identity as pronounced as that of the Portuguese *nação* of Amsterdam.

Characteristics of the Portuguese Sephardic diaspora

The Sephardic diaspora began as a forced migration exactly contemporaneous with the forced migrations of Africans resulting from the slave trade. However, in contrast to the experience of African slaves, it is clear that 'on the whole Jews not only adapted to the conditions of exile but often flourished within it materially and spiritually'.[33]

The Sephardic diaspora resulted in the establishment of a large number of Jewish communities throughout northern Europe and the Atlantic basin, which formed a network with ties to the Iberian peninsula. Some of these communities remained small, unstable and insecure but others put down roots, developing their own cultural life and themselves generating further emigration. As a result of settling and putting down roots in different countries, the Jews and New Christians of the Portuguese 'nation', in spite of their strong sense of identity, their elaborate commercial and family networks and their notable cultural conservatism, inevitably took on something of the nationality and cultural traits of the countries where they settled. However, this did not necessarily happen quickly and there is a notable contrast in this respect between the Sephardic communities of Amsterdam and London.

The culturally conservative Amsterdam community retained Portuguese family names and the use of the Portuguese language throughout the seventeenth century, adhering to an inherited Iberian culture through successive generations. In this way the community retained its sense of its own uniqueness. In the words of Miriam Bodian, 'in the fragmented, tolerant, particularistic world of seventeenth-century Amsterdam, Portuguese Jews felt no pressure to prove that they "belonged" to the majority society'.[34] As Daniel Swetschinski observes, 'ironically, there exists an unmistakeable parallel between this continued use of Portuguese in the diaspora and the erstwhile, imagined or real, preservation of Jewish customs in Portugal and Spain'.[35]

Although most Sephardic Jews had family histories of persecution in the Iberian peninsula, escape to Amsterdam, Hamburg or London did not mean that the exiles cut off all relations with their country of origin. Many maintained contacts in Portugal and some at the highest possible levels. Miriam Bodian gives the example of the brothers Jacob and Moses Curiel, members of whose family had been imprisoned and executed by the Inquisition, but who continued to serve the Portuguese Crown. Jacob became 'its agent in Hamburg from 1641 to 1644 and in return for his services, Dom João IV of Portugal made him a knight of his royal household, a rank later granted to his eldest son Moses ... agent of the crown of Portugal in the Netherlands from 1645 to 1697'.[36] Duarte Nunes da Costa, another exiled New Christian, was involved in negotiations for the release of the king's brother, held in Milan after the 1640 Portuguese revolt against Spain.[37]

The Sephardic diaspora was dominated by wealthy families. Although many of the community were poor, the high proportion of wealthy people among the migrants sets this phase of Portuguese emigration apart from most later phases which were characterised by the emigration of the poor. One striking statistic illustrates the level of education and social status of the 'Portuguese nation'. Among male Jewish migrants arriving in Amsterdam in the seventeenth century only 1 per cent were illiterate at a time when general male illiteracy in Dutch society ranged from 30 to 43 per cent.[38] In some respects the departure from Portugal of educated New Christians has to be seen in the context of a wider tendency for educated Portuguese—the so-called *estrangeirados*—to make their careers abroad. From the Portuguese community of the Sephardic diaspora were to come some of Europe's leading cultural and political figures—among them Rodrigo Lopes (physician to Queen Elizabeth and, possibly, the model for Shylock), Baruch Spinoza (who, however, fell out with the Sephardic community of Amsterdam), David Ricardo, Camille Pissarro and Benjamin Disraeli (whose grandmother was of the 'Portuguese nation').

Merchants of the Sephardic Jewish community formed voluntary groupings in which the networks of commerce, often bound together by marriages, were all-important and in which religious and communal ties and discipline were correspondingly weak. During the period of active persecution in the Iberian peninsula the communities of religious exiles might include not only confessed Jews but New Christians who had not abandoned their Christianity—though there was a marked tendency for them to do so once they had left Portugal behind. There were also *marranos* whose religious practice drew on both Christianity and Judaism. In these circumstances the religious foundations of the Sephardic communities were bound to be weakened. New Christians who had not yet returned to Judaism were accepted as part of the '*nação*'. New Christian martyrs were celebrated even if they had not formally reconverted; and New Christians, still practising their Christian religion, were able to apply to the *Dotar* for dowries for their daughters. In Amsterdam the 'Portuguese' came to see themselves as 'a colony of foreign merchants' as well as an 'association of religious exiles'.[39] As Miriam Bodian points out, 'there is, overall, a peculiar, polarized quality to the set of attitudes the "Portuguese" held about Iberian society. The great majority of them were able, it seems, to divorce the experience of *converso* persecution from the world of Iberian values and culture, demonizing the former and holding fast to the latter.'[40] This made the purity of Sephardic descent and membership of the *nação* more important than religious orthodoxy. This explains also how New Christians could be accepted but Ashkenazi Jews rejected.

Throughout the sixteenth and seventeenth centuries the use of the Portuguese language was one way in which members of the *nação* distinguished themselves, and this was true not only of Amsterdam. In the sixteenth-century Ferrara household of the rich Sephardic Lady Beatrix de Luna, 'the language spoken by both the young valets and the orphan girls who waited on the "lady" was Portuguese'.[41]

The 'Portuguese nation', constituted by the Sephardic diaspora, was essentially a society of rich merchant families who retained close ties with each other and established networks of family and commercial interest, literally throughout the world. It is the international, the globalised, nature of the Sephardic community which is particularly striking.

When we look again at the early modern Sephardic port Jews, we cannot help but be struck by the constancy of movement in their lives. As exiles and refugees, many moved restlessly from one home to another: variously back and forth in Christian lands, Muslim lands; in the Mediterranean ranging from Iberia, to Italy, to North Africa, to the Levant; to the west European Atlantic seaboard; to colonial possessions in the New World or the Far East. With families far-flung across countries and continents, the Sephardic world was one of both people and goods on the move.[42]

The De Luna family is an early example of this movement. From Portugal they moved to Flanders, 'then escaped undercover to Venice and later to Ferrara, and finally emigrated "out of Christianity" to Constantinople to return publicly to their Jewish faith'.[43] Throughout all this movement their sense of identity remained vital for the success of their financial and commercial dealings. A member of the Amsterdam 'Portuguese nation' sailing for Curaçao or Jamaica or moving to settle in Copenhagen or Livorno would find that his

'Portuguese' identity enabled him to establish the necessary business contacts and obtain the assistance of other 'Portuguese' in the region where he settled. This mobility and sense of being a community at home in all parts of the globe enabled the Sephardic Jews and New Christians to assume a wider cultural and even political role as 'interpreters'. In the ports where they settled, such as Amsterdam, Odessa or Salonika, they acted as intermediaries or brokers between Dutch and Iberians or Ottomans and Europeans.[44] Such a role was not always seen in a positive light, for Portuguese New Christians also maintained close relations with the Barbary corsairs and acted as their agents in the purchase of goods in Europe.[45]

Eventually this movement of the Portuguese Sephardic community outside the Iberian world would mark a parting of the ways. At first the Jews or New Christians who left Portugal had settled in the same areas as their Old Christian associates. In Spanish America or West Africa, New and Old Christians had lived and traded side by side. After the middle of the sixteenth century, and still more after Portugal's separation from Spain in 1640 and the expulsion of the Dutch from Brazil in 1654, their paths would separate and, although the Sephardic community retained a sense of its 'Portuguese' identity, direct contacts with Portugal or with other communities of the Portuguese diaspora became ever weaker. When in the nineteenth century a new wave of migration brought poor Portuguese to the coasts of the United States, they would have nothing in common, and probably no contact, with the community of Sephardic Jews long established there.

5

PORTUGUESE MIGRATION AND SETTLEMENT
IN ASIA

The spread of the formal empire and the carreira da Índia

Between 1497 and 1499 Vasco da Gama, a knight of the Military
Order of Santiago, made the first successful return voyage by sea from
Europe to India. After three follow-up voyages the Portuguese Crown
decided to create a new kingdom for the Crown of Portugal in the
East. Dom Manuel declared himself to be sovereign over the sea, a new
and audacious claim which had no precedent in any existing legal system. The new kingdom of the sea was to be called the Estado da Índia
(the State of India) and was to entitle, or at least enable, the king to
control the people and commodities which crossed his domain. The
principal objective was to enforce the Portuguese Crown's monopoly
over certain branches of international commerce—notably gold, ivory,
pepper, cinnamon and horses—and to control strategic materials that
might aid hostile Muslim powers. To make this ambitious policy successful all shipping in the Indian Ocean was to be licensed through the
issue of passes (called *cartazes*) and the levying of customs duties on
commercial cargoes. To enforce this, a fleet and an army were to be
stationed in Indian Ocean waters. The boundaries of the Estado da
Índia were never clearly defined but in practice the Portuguese were
only ever able to enforce their rule in any consistent way in the western Indian Ocean.

The Estado da Índia needed a seat of government and bases from which its fleets could operate. After a number of false starts a structure emerged based on four heavily fortified strongholds: Goa on the west coast of India; Ormuz controlling the access to the Gulf; Mozambique which acted as a way station for fleets coming from Europe; and to the east of India, the island port of Malacca which controlled the straits of Malacca, providing access to eastern Asia. As Portuguese pretensions met with strong opposition from many African and Asian rulers, aided by the Ottoman Turks, the Portuguese eventually extended their system until they had around fifty fortified settlements. The most important of these were Muscat and Bahrein which supported the base of Ormuz; Diu on the coast of Gujerat; Sofala and Mombasa on the East African coast, which supplemented the fortress of Mozambique; and Colombo in Sri Lanka. Along the coast of western India the Portuguese gradually took control of all the major ports except for Calicut: Damão, Bassein, Chaul and Bombay which constituted the so-called Província do Norte; Barcelor, Mangalor, Onor on the Kanara coast; and Cannanore, Quilon and Cochin which became the centre of their operations on the Malabar coast. In the distant archipelago of the Moluccas the Portuguese also maintained a fort at Ternate, from which they tried to control the trade in cloves. In many cases the Portuguese garrisons in these ports acquired extensive areas of the hinterland, especially Bardes and Salsette, the provinces surrounding Goa, the land inland of the ports of the Provincia do Norte, the Zambesi valley and the hinterland of Sofala in eastern Africa and the lowlands of Sri Lanka. Contrary to what is often asserted, the Estado da Índia was not exclusively a maritime empire but included very extensive mainland territories in Africa and India.

In addition to these fortified towns, which were under direct Portuguese control, there was a network of alliances with local rulers who allowed Portuguese to settle and trade in their dominions and who played an important role in maintaining the Portuguese commercial system. Prominent among these allies were the Sultan of Melinde and the rulers of Ethiopia in north-east Africa, while the Shah of Ormuz, the Sultan of Diu, the rulers of Cochin and Kotte (in Sri Lanka) and the Sultan of Ternate in the Moluccas became, in effect, Portuguese satellites.

The Estado da Índia was constantly at war with those Asian rulers who never accepted Portugal's claims to control the sea and the commerce between Asia and Europe. The most formidable enemies of the Portuguese were the Ottoman Turks, and when Portuguese naval power had finally disposed of the Ottoman threat in the 1550s, the Portuguese faced challenges from the rulers of Aceh in Sumatra, Kandy in the highlands of Sri Lanka and Calicut in south-western India. The cost of these wars and of maintaining the fleets and fortresses was prohibitive, so the Portuguese Crown gradually leased out its monopolies to its fortress captains or to the captains of the trading fleets, retaining only the pepper monopoly in its own hands (though even this was at times leased to syndicates of financiers in Europe).

Meanwhile new bases from which to carry on the very lucrative trade in silk between China and Japan had been established at Macao on the coast of China in 1556 and at Nagasaki in Japan in 1570, though these communities were largely outside the control of the authorities in Goa.

Each of the fortified port-towns of the Estado da Índia became the focus for a settlement of Portuguese. The population in these settlements was made up primarily of the soldiers and sailors who manned the fleets, the officials who administered the Crown's trade monopolies and the clerics who served the church. In addition there were some *degredados*, particularly in the early days of exploration, and some *orfãs do rei*—girls sent out to the east with dowries in the form of Crown appointments. As far as can be calculated, between 1497 and 1630 around 275,540 people left Portugal for the Estado da Índia, an average of 2,072 a year, twice the rate for departures from Castile for the New World.[1] However, the return fleets of the *carreira da Índia* were also fully manned, so that the net emigration to the East was only 1,024 per annum. Over the whole period from 1497 to 1700 the average net emigration was only 815 persons per annum, almost all of whom were men.[2] Europeans travelling to the Estado da Índia experienced very high rates of mortality both on board ship and at their destinations, and Charles Boxer considered that 'there were never as many as 10,000 able bodied Europeans and Eurasians available for military and naval service between Moçambique and Macao'. He went on to observe that although muster rolls showed 15,000 men 'entitled to draw service-pay... not more than 3,000 of these really existed'.[3] The number of European-born Portuguese in the East was never very large.

What sort of society did the Portuguese create in the various ports where they settled? The Portuguese in the Estado da Índia were essentially governed by the ethos and the needs of the military. Each fort had a captain and a permanent garrison (usually under strength). The captains of the major forts (Ormuz, Goa, Diu, Malacca, Mozambique) were often *fidalgos* or members of the nobility who held office usually for three years. The Estado da Índia as a whole had a fleet and an army which, during the half year when the monsoon was favourable, would take to the sea to pursue the Crown's military objectives. In between campaigns the soldiers were unemployed and left to their own devices, though some were supported as retainers by the captains ahead of the next campaigning season. After some years' service the soldiers could apply to become *casados* (married men)—that is, they ceased to be full-time soldiers and could embark on civilian occupations, though they were still liable to serve as soldiers in times of emergency. In Malacca, for example, the number of *casados* at the end of the sixteenth century stood at around 300.[4] The Portuguese residents in the settlements were sometimes referred to simply as *moradores* (inhabitants). They could also apply for leave to return to Portugal but it seems that very few did, largely because Portugal offered few if any opportunities for a good life comparable to those available in Asia.

The officers of the garrison and the officials of the royal factories lived in hope of reward from the Crown for their services, rewards that would take the form of promotion, transfer to more lucrative posts or grants of rents or land in the occupied territories. From the earliest days of the Estado da Índia, almost all Portuguese from the viceroy downwards were engaged in trade. Trade was legal for the *casados* provided they did not infringe the royal monopolies; the captains of the fortresses, in particular, took full advantage of their control of military force to carve out for themselves lucrative commercial opportunities.

Few Portuguese women ever made the journey to the East, so Portuguese men formed liaisons with African and Asian women, or with the mixed race women born of earlier unions. These wives, according to the Florentine merchant Francesco Carletti, were 'mostly those born there of Portuguese fathers and Chinese, Japanese, Javanese, Moluccan, and Bengali mothers... most of the women turn out to be very beautiful, and in particular well-formed as to person'.[5] The Portuguese usually recognised their illegitimate offspring, who thus became members of the Portuguese diasporic communities. By the mid sixteenth century, although the senior military and civil posts were still occupied by European Portuguese sent from Lisbon, the people who manned the forts and fleets were increasingly the Afro-Portuguese and Luso-Asiatics. The Portuguese communities in the East were on the way to becoming indigenised.

The larger Portuguese settlements, in particular Goa, Malacca and Macao, were formally incorporated into the Lusitanian world by the creation of a Senado da Câmara, established by royal charter, which governed their everyday lives. These cities, and many of the smaller settlements as well, had a Misericórdia which provided a large range of charitable and welfare activities and also acted as a bank for the Portuguese communities. Being a brother of the Misericórdia conferred a social prestige that was recognised throughout the Portuguese world. The church with its ecclesiastical organisation, its brotherhoods and religious houses provided further institutional cement for society. Portuguese settlements also had a militia in which all *casados* and *moradore*s were expected to serve.

The Portuguese in the East spread their wings

By the end of the sixteenth century the creative, outward looking, culturally alive Portugal of the Renaissance, which had produced the great navigators who had explored the world, the richly inventive Manueline architecture and a generation of poets, scholars and humanists, seemed to have died. The union with Spain had meant an end to the patronage which had been provided by the Portuguese Court in Lisbon and men of talent sought to make a career for themselves in the Spanish dominions. Although the Portuguese re-established their independence in 1640, and installed on the throne the musically gifted Duke of Braganza, it was only in the last decades of the seventeenth century that Portugal began to regain something of the cultural vibrancy of the Renaissance. The seventeenth century, the century of the 'little ice age' when the economy of Portugal stagnated and its population declined, was a century of warfare against the Dutch and the Spanish, and a period of introspection and barely repressed social tensions that found expression in the activities of the Inquisition. The mood is reflected in the paintings of Josefa of Óbidos (1630–84), an artist with a unique aesthetic vision unlike that of any other European artist of the period, but whose work was of a stilted, icon-like piety.

It was in the East that Portuguese, old Christians and New Christians alike, felt able to escape from the straitjacket of social hierarchy and religious orthodoxy. In the eyes of many sixteenth- and seventeenth-century travellers, the Portuguese settlements in Asia had already strayed far beyond the moral boundaries of European society and had acquired an exotic character wholly their own. Writers who attempted to describe Portuguese society in Asia were uncertain how to react to what they saw. Were they witnessing a European society hopelessly corrupted by Asian practices, or were they describing something new and different which had to be understood within its own terms of reference?

One of the most vivid descriptions of the Portuguese in Asia was given by the Dutchman Jan Huyghen van Linschoten, who served in the entourage of the archbishop of Goa in the 1580s and in 1596 published an account of Asia as he had seen it. Linschoten famously described how poor Portuguese emigrants, many of them, as we have seen, the sweepings of the jails, arrived in the East travelling alongside noblemen and their entourages. Once in the East all Portuguese acquired social status and assumed the manners of high social rank. The very poorest lived together in communal households sharing a suit of fine clothes in which to appear in public, but all had Indian servants and most found ways of rising up the social scale. Service to the Crown in the fleets and armies was one way, but many Portuguese preferred to become involved in trade, while others, according to Linschoten, made a living by becoming the lovers of Indian women and being rewarded for their services.[6]

This picture is confirmed by the Frenchman François Pyrard, who wrote in the 1620s. Pyrard borrowed a lot from Linschoten while adding to it his own observations: 'The Portuguese out there [India] engage in no mechanical arts, in whatever necessity they may be, but call themselves all gentlemen, and live like noblemen.'[7] All the Portuguese assumed the manners and style of nobility with the exaggerated codes of honour common in the sixteenth century, but 'these honours and titles, given by the soldiers to each other, are not used until they have passed the Cape of Good Hope, for then they abandon almost all their former manners and customs, and throw their spoons into the sea.'[8] 'The Indians', he says, 'were all amazed when we told them that these fellows were sons of porters, cobblers, drawers of water, and other vile craftsmen.'[9] A hundred years after Linschoten, when the Estado da Índia was already in steep decline, the Frenchman Jean Baptiste Tavernier recognised the same pretence:

The Portuguese who go to India have no sooner passed the Cape of Good Hope than they all become *fidalgos* or gentlemen, and add Dom to the simple name of Pedro or Jeronimo which they carried when they embarked: this is the reason why they are commonly called in derision *"fidalgos* of the Cape of Good Hope".[10]

The lifestyle of the Portuguese had moved a long way from that of the poorer classes of Europe from which most Portuguese seamen, soldiers and *degredados* were drawn. Linschoten describes the way of life of well-off Portuguese surrounded by slaves who not only supported their life of ease but earned a living for their masters by trading or prostitution. It was a world dominated by the people of mixed race, the children of Portuguese men and Indian women who in the next generation were physically indistinguishable from the Indians themselves but were recognised as members of the Portuguese community. Tavernier also noted that 'as they change in their status so also they change in their nature and it may be said that the Portuguese dwelling in India are the most vindictive and the most jealous of their women of all the people in the world.'[11] The women were closely guarded, leaving their houses only to go to church. In their houses they wore Indian clothes and ate Indian food and the houses themselves were described as having gardens for relaxation.

Linschoten, fascinated as well as shocked by the sexual license he witnessed, was describing a society which in his eyes had lost its martial vigour and whose wealth was ripe for the plucking. His judgment on the Portuguese became the stock in trade for many northern Europeans who subsequently tried to adjust to life in India. Famously the historian R. S. Whiteway, influenced no doubt by the pseudo-scientific ideas about race current at the time, could write as late as 1899 that among the causes of the decline of the Portuguese in the East was 'the deterioration of the Portuguese race caused by intermarriage with native races'.[12]

However, Pyrard, although also commenting on the sexual licence, found Portuguese society had many attractive qualities. He admired the hospital for the care of the sick and commented on the cultured society of the Portuguese for whom music was an essential pastime in their houses and during their parties held on the water or in the gardens of their country houses. Although they were addicted to gambling, he approved of the custom whereby those who were fortunate distributed largesse to the losers and even to onlookers. Linschoten and Pyrard were seeing characteristics which describe so many of the diasporic settlements of the Portuguese—their willingness to adopt local customs and practices, their relaxed sexual *mores* and their devotion to the saints and to the church—and also their love of gardens around their homes.

Another portrait of the Portuguese in the East comes from Francesco Carletti, who reached Japan in 1598 after crossing the Pacific from Mexico. He arrived just as the persecution of Christians was beginning, but found the trade between Japan and China carried on by the Portuguese still flourishing. Carletti witnessed a stand-off between Portuguese and Japanese on board the ship in which he was travelling. The ship's captain was 'Portuguese by nationality, though born in Nagasaki of a Japanese mother'.[13] The confrontation resulted from an insult given by a Portuguese to a Japanese sailor and Carletti witnessed both groups arming themselves and preparing for a fight which he realised would have led to the foundering of the ship. The exaggerated pride and a sensitivity to real or assumed slights on one's honour were traits that accompanied the high social status which Portuguese, often low-born, assumed in the East.

Carletti, ever attentive to the tastes of his patron, the Grand Duke of Tuscany, describes the sexual freedom enjoyed by the Portuguese—how visiting Portuguese merchants were able to obtain women very cheaply for the duration of their stay in Nagasaki—and he comments that 'many of the Portuguese find this Land of Cockaigne much to their liking—and, what is better, it costs them but little'.[14] The sexual licence of the Portuguese, he asserts, was in some measure the result of the monsoons:

the lubricity and idleness of those soldiers, most of whom are unmarried gentlemen with no belongings but cloak and sword, and those along with youth, which they use up in the pastime [sexual promiscuity], especially as during four months of the year they cannot sally forth in their ships because of the rains....[15]

There is in his account, as there is in that of Linschoten, a tacit juxtaposition of the extreme luxury and self-indulgence of the life-style of the Portuguese community in Goa and the perceived weakness of their commercial empire now under attack by the Dutch.

The missions, the padroado real *and the founding of Asian Christian communities*

The Portuguese presence in Asia was shaped not only by the Estado da Índia but also by the *padroado real*, the royal patronage over the church which had originally been conferred on the Order of Christ by successive papal bulls in the 1450s. With the accession of Dom Manuel to the throne in 1495, the mastership of the Order of Christ became vested in the Crown and the resources of the Order became in effect part of the royal patrimony.

The *padroado real* allowed the Portuguese Crown to collect tithes and other ecclesiastical revenues, appoint priests and bishops, summon church councils and issue decrees. It also laid on the Order of Christ the responsibility to establish parishes and episcopal sees, promote missionary activity and provide the funds needed by the Church generally. The king interpreted the *padroado real* as conferring jurisdiction over the church exclusively on the Portuguese Crown to the exclusion of interference from any other body, the papacy itself included. The rights and responsibilities of the *padroado real* were not confined to the territories of the Portuguese Crown but covered all Christian communities wherever they might be east of the Tordesillas line—the notional division of the world between Portugal and Castile agreed at the Treaty of Tordesillas in 1494. As a result, all Christians in Asia and Africa in ecclesiastic matters came under the jurisdiction of the king of Portugal—a vast extension of Portuguese power and influence, which was not bounded by any territorial sovereignty.

The early Portuguese voyages to the Indian Ocean were accompanied by priests, but they were there to administer the sacraments to the Portuguese themselves, not to act as missionaries. The Christian community therefore was limited to the Portuguese who arrived in the fleets and the women they married on the condition that they would embrace Christianity. The native Christian communities, the St Thomas Christians of Malabar and the Ethiopian Christians, refused to accept the authority of Rome.

There was little if any attempt at converting the heathen until the 1530s, when Goa became a See and the Franciscans, following their dramatic successes in Mexico, became active in Sri Lanka and South India. From the 1530s missionary activity grew rapidly and the Goan authorities began to take an authoritarian line with the Indians living under Portuguese jurisdiction in the Goan provinces. In 1541 Francis Xavier arrived in the East with the first Jesuit mission; over the next ten years he established Christian communities, served by Jesuit priests, in south India, Indonesia and Japan. Jesuit missions were also sent to Ethiopia in 1556 and East Africa in 1560. Meanwhile a policy of forced conversion was being pursued in Goa, where Hindu temples were destroyed and orphans and paupers were forcibly baptised. In 1560 the Inquisition was established, putting a final end to a period of relatively peaceful religious co-existence. Renewed efforts were now made to bring the St Thomas Christians into communion with the Roman Church and hence under the jurisdiction of the *padroado real*. Meanwhile, stimulated by the activity of the Jesuits, the Dominicans had stepped up their missionary effort, establishing themselves in Indonesia and, after the failure of the Jesuit mission there, in East Africa. Franciscans and Augustinians were also increasingly active.

By the end of the sixteenth century there may have been a million Christians in Asia—the highest concentrations being among the Goans, among the pearl fishers of South India, and in the eastern Indonesian Islands and Japan, where it has been estimated that there were 300,000 Christians. Early in the seventeenth century the Portuguese conquest of the lowlands of Sri Lanka resulted in still more conversions.

In one sense the *padroado real* made all Christians part of a world-wide community under Portugal's patronage, though many would have hesitated to think of themselves as Portuguese. However, conversion made it easy for many people in Asia and Africa to enter the Portuguese community, serving as soldiers or generally as clients of the Portuguese, marrying 'Portuguese' women and founding Christian Portuguese families. In the sixteenth and seventeenth centuries the Portuguese followed a deliberate policy of trying to convert the elite ruling families of Asia to Christianity. If they failed, not unsurprisingly, in the case of the Mughal emperors, they had some success among the *daimyos* of Japan and among those involved in the endlessly contested successions to Asian kingdoms, principalities and sultanates. Members of the ruling families would often undergo conversion to secure Portuguese aid, and if many of these converts eventually deserted the church, others assumed a distinctive Asian Portuguese identity, marrying Christian 'Portuguese' wives, taking Portuguese names and dressing in the Portuguese manner. Some of the members of elite families served the Portuguese in important positions as interpreters, ambassadors, commercial agents or military captains. Some even found their way to Europe, like the 'two Sinhalese princes who settled down in Portugal and lived the life of another "Don Juan" in the city of Lisbon'.[16] This made them part of a worldwide Portuguese community, helping to spread the new faith and with it the network of Portuguese influence.

Although the Catholic mission priests were expelled from Ethiopia and Japan in the 1630s, and in the latter Christianity was virtually wiped out, in other parts of Asia it was priests who, after official Portuguese rule went into terminal decline, consolidated the survival of Portuguese communities—notably in Sri Lanka under the Dutch and in the Indonesian islands of Flores, Solor and Timor where a Lusitanised Catholic community survived and, in a limited way, prospered.

The informal empire and the spread of Portuguese settlements beyond the control of Goa

Most of the missionary work in Asia had been undertaken in communities that were not under the control of the Estado da Índia, and it is clear that the missionary orders preferred to work without the direct interference of the civil authority. In this they were following the example of large numbers of lay Portuguese who had left the official settlements of the Estado da Índia to establish their independence or to seek their fortunes in other Asian states. The growth of these independent Portuguese communities, often referred to as the 'informal empire', was as marked as the expansion of the Estado da Índia itself.

The reasons behind this dispersal of the Portuguese in the East are many: life on board ships or in the Portuguese forts was hard and the pay was little or non-existent; the royal *regimentos* laid down rules that strictly controlled the daily lives of the soldiers and sailors who were subject to the whims of often tyrannical captains; and the administration of the royal monopolies placed barriers to commercial activity while the ecclesiastical authorities continually searched for religious heterodoxy. Portuguese residents in the towns of the Estado da Índia were not free to trade, or to marry, to make their fortunes or to worship as they pleased.

Many soon realised that they had skills that were highly marketable. In particular Portuguese soldiers, skilled in the use of firearms, were much in demand and large numbers of them deserted with their weapons to serve as soldiers in Indian or African armies, where they were well paid and treated as a privileged elite. Once settled outside the Estado da Índia, individual Portuguese were free to trade and to adopt aspects of Asian culture more to their taste. Many kept slave women and lived free from the prying eyes of the religious authorities. Others adopted the life of the freebooter, establishing their own pirate settlements in protected river estuaries, notably in the Bay of Bengal.

These were lawless communities, given to unpredictable and excessive violence, as the Venetian merchant Cesar Fedrici found when he visited Martaban (modern Mottama) in 1566: 'We found in the Citie of Martavan ninetie Portugales of Merchants and other base men, which had fallen at difference with the Retor or Governour of the citie, and all for this cause, that certain vagbondes of the Portugales had slaine five falchines [porters]of the king of Pegu.' The caravan accompanied by the *falchines* had camped overnight at Martavan and a quarrel had broken out with the Portuguese. 'The night following, when the Falchines were a sleepe with their companie the Portugales went and cut off five of their heads.' Events then spiralled out of control. War elephants were brought up which broke into the Portuguese warehouses where goods to the value of 16,000 ducats were taken in reparation. The Portuguese fled on board their ships but returned the following day bringing cannon with which they tried to bombard the city. Fedrici, not surprisingly, 'thought it a strange thing to see the Portugales use such insolencie in another mans Citie'.[17]

The pirate settlements in the Bay of Bengal are vividly described by the Augustinian friar Sebastião Manrique, who was sent to the mission at Hugli in 1628 and from there was appointed priest to the pirate community of Dianga near Chittagong. This settlement had originally been established in the sixteenth century by traders bringing goods to Arakan. It had been joined by Portuguese mercenaries fighting in the Arakan army and then by pirates who made a living raiding the coastal communities of the Bay of Bengal for slaves. The Portuguese pirates were lawless, ruthless and cruel, their captives arriving at Dianga with their arms immobilised by bamboo splinters thrust through the palms of their hands. Part of Manrique's task was to visit these slaves when they arrived at Dianga to try to convert them to Christianity, and he claimed that in this way he was able to make 2,000 converts a year.[18]

Some Portuguese renegades became the trusted servants and advisers of Asian rulers—like Francisco Serrão who sailed on the first Portuguese voyage among the Indonesian islands in 1512. Serrão was shipwrecked but reached safety on the island of Ambon. From there he travelled to Ternate where 'he became the Sultan's intimate counsellor and his right hand man in matters of war'.[19] He married a Javanese woman and died in 1521.

The Portuguese who left the Estado da Índia did not, however, intend to give up their Portuguese identity. Portuguese renegades, mercenaries and independent traders tended to congregate together to form their own quarters in Asian cities or to establish their own independent settlements. An example of the latter was the large Portuguese town that grew up near the supposed tomb of the apostle St Thomas, hence called São Tomé—today a suburb of Chennai/Madras. There were sizeable groups of Portuguese merchants in many parts of the Indonesian archipelago, including Patani and Macassar, while the most important of these independent Portuguese towns was the trading settlement founded on the coast of China near Canton, which became known as 'the City of the Name of God' or Macao. Macao was eventually brought partially within the orbit of the Estado da Índia, though the Chinese did not acknowledge Portuguese sovereignty there until the nineteenth century. In Japan the Portuguese port town of Nagasaki also remained free of the control of Goa. The largest informal Portuguese settlements, however, were in Bengal: the towns of Hugli and Dianga in the early seventeenth century having a population of over 700 Portuguese, making them larger than any other Portuguese town in Asia except Goa itself.

The decline of the Estado da Índia and the dispersal of the Portuguese

At the end of the sixteenth century the Dutch and English arrived in Asian waters and presented the Portuguese with a major challenge. Over the next sixty years the Estado da Índia was at war not only with its European rivals but also with increasingly aggressive foes in Asia. Slowly its formidable military structure gave way. Ormuz was lost in 1622, Malacca in 1641, Muscat in 1650, Colombo and the rest of Sri Lanka in 1656, Bombay was surrendered to the English in 1662 and the towns on the Malabar coast to the Dutch in 1663. When peace was finally made with the Dutch, the Estado da Índia was reduced to Goa, Diu, the Província do Norte and eastern Africa, though Mombasa and the settlements on the African coast north of Cape Delgado were subsequently lost to Oman in 1698.

The contraction of formal Portuguese power continued in the eighteenth century. Bassein and Chaul were abandoned to the Marathas in 1740 and in 1752 the East African settlements were removed from the control of the Goan viceroy and made a separate governorship. East of Malacca the Portuguese retained only Macao and the trading posts in Timor and Flores in eastern Indonesia.

When the fortresses and towns of the Estado da Índia fell to the Dutch or to local Asian or African forces, a process of dispersal and slow absorption began. Most European Portuguese would leave, retreating to strongholds still held by the Estado da Índia, though when the English took over Bombay and established themselves in Madras some wealthy upper-class Portuguese remained in those cities. The Abbé Carré describes the marriage of the daughter of a wealthy Madras Portuguese, Lucas de Oliveira:

I had been invited to a Portuguese wedding, which was celebrated with as much pomp and magnificence as if it was that of some prince or person of high degree. The English Governor was present, with the principal officers of the town and all the garrison companies under arms. After the church ceremony there was a procession round the precincts of Fort St George, which saluted it with all its guns, with many salvoes of muskets, and similar signs of rejoicing.[20]

Carré's account of the hazards of marriage with the daughters of Portuguese families established in India is both a reflection on the declining wealth of the Portuguese, which led them to become obsessive about their *fidalgo* status, and a more general cautionary tale about marrying in haste and repenting at leisure.[21]

The indigenous 'Portuguese' population was dispersed to other commercial centres, creating a series of small diasporas which served to spread the 'Portuguese' ever more widely around maritime Asia. A typical example occurred after the capture of Malacca in 1641 when the 'Portuguese' population of the city resettled in Macassar. Sometimes the Luso-Asian and indigenous Christian populations remained under the new rulers and negotiated a new and more subordinate role for themselves. When the Dutch began to establish themselves in India, Sri Lanka and Indonesia in place of the Portuguese, they frequently took Luso-Asian women as wives and incorporated parts of the Luso-Asian population into their settlements. In this way Batavia, in its early days, was largely a Portuguese-speaking and not a Dutch-speaking community. Large numbers of Asian Portuguese also remained settled in the territories of the East India Company in Bombay and Madras and took service with the Company as soldiers. Others entered French or even Dutch service. 'Portuguese' in English service were usually identified as just another section of the Indian population.

Once the Asian Portuguese were separated from the Estado da Índia, few if any European Portuguese ever joined their ranks. They became increasingly isolated, and grew away from the rest of the Portuguese world, cut off from continued contact with Portuguese culture, except through the church. However, they retained their separate 'Portuguese' identity, which was expressed in the observance of the Catholic Christian rituals, in the retention of Portuguese family names, in certain elements of Portuguese culture and in the use of creolised Portuguese speech. As Stefan Halikowski-Smith has expressed it,

the vast majority of "Portuguese" were ... dark skinned *mestiços* who had never been to Portugal, who appropriated certain items of Portuguese dress such as hats whilst neglecting others such as shoes, and were Christians out of status reasons rather than conviction. Indeed, their greatest claim to being "Portuguese" was often not via their blood, but the creolised dialects they spoke.[22]

He favours the use of the term the 'Portuguese tribe' to describe these people who became, in effect, another caste within Asian society.

The Portuguese language, now no longer the language spoken by the dominant elites in politics, law and trade, became fragmented into a number of regional creoles and dialects; by the nineteenth century most of these were spoken only by small groups in western India around Chaul or Cochin, in Malaysia in the region of Malacca, in Sri Lanka and in eastern Indonesia. The use of Portuguese creole dialects may, however, have had a greater importance than is at first apparent. It has been claimed that 'a Luso-Asian lingua franca ... served as the bridging tongue between not one, not two, but three European powers and the indigenous people'.[23] Apparently Frederick North, who was the British governor of Ceylon from 1798 to 1805, 'had to employ a Portuguese–Sinhala interpreter to accompany his ambassador to the court of the Kandyan king'.[24] The 'Portuguese tribe' acted out the role of cultural intermediaries long after the Estado da Índia lost its political power. The church continued to be supported by Jesuit, Franciscan or Dominican missionaries who recognised the jurisdiction of the *padroado real*, often in defiance of ecclesiastical authorities appointed by Rome or by the French; and within the church the Portuguese language survived as a kind of language of ritual, helping to keep alive a tenuous Portuguese identity.

During the eighteenth and nineteenth centuries the economic and social status of these Asian Portuguese communities inexorably declined. The Macassar Portuguese, numbering possibly as many as 6,000,[25] had relocated to Ayutthaya after being expelled by the Dutch from Macassar in 1660. In Ayutthaya they remained throughout the next century occupying a distinct quarter in the kingdom's capital but declining in wealth and economic status. In the East India Company territories also, the 'Portuguese' either took service in the Company's army in a position little different from the Indian sepoys or survived as low-paid clerks or petty traders. The so-called Mardijkers of Batavia were another fragment of the 'Portuguese tribe' which formed a substantial part of the city's population well into the eighteenth century. Eventually the use of the Mardijkers's Portuguese creole language died out, except for its retention for religious purposes in the Tugu area, though the use of Portuguese family names continued as a last vestige of their Portuguese origin.

In Sri Lanka a 'Portuguese' Catholic community survived under Dutch and British rule, being referred to incongruously as 'Portuguese burghers'. These were the descendants not of European Portuguese but of slaves, servants, clients and soldiers who had been brought to the island in Portuguese service. Apparently in the census conducted by the British in Colombo in 1800, 'the five thousand "Portuguese" were observed to possess a darker complexion than the locals themselves'.[26] Portuguese family names are still very common in Sri Lanka and the Burghers are still an identifiable group who live in the Batticaloa area. In Sri Lanka there was a live literary tradition, and prayers, ballads and poetry written in creole have survived from the nineteenth century. The creole ballads represent a tradition which the Portuguese took with them to their overseas territories. As Shihan de Silva Jayasuriya observes, 'the creole communities have been the bearers of these songs for several centuries and have kept them alive through an oral tradition for four centuries before they were recorded'.[27] Indo-Portuguese creole was still widely used until the end of the nineteenth century. In the twentieth century, however, the use of Indo-Portuguese dwindled to the point where it survives only as a liturgical language in some Catholic areas and as a language spoken at most by only a few hundred people in isolated rural communities. This is in marked contrast to the Portuguese creoles in the Atlantic, which are still widely spoken and have even achieved the status of national languages.

In the Lesser Sunda Islands of Timor, Flores and Solor in eastern Indonesia, a branch of the 'Portuguese tribe' survived and, in a limited way, flourished. During the sixteenth century the Dominicans had enjoyed some success in establishing Catholicism in Solor. When the Dutch captured Solor from the Portuguese in 1613, the 'Portuguese' Catholic population took refuge in Larantuka in Flores, where they were joined after 1660 by refugees from Macassar who brought with them items from the church treasury there. The Christian group became known as Larantuqueiros or Topazes.[28]

The term Topaze (also written Toepas or Tupassi) was widely used in India and Sri Lanka to refer to people of mixed race who spoke two or more languages.[29] The Abbé Carré, travelling in India in the 1670s, uses the term to refer to Christian Indian soldiers in Portuguese service.[30] In the Lesser Sunda Islands the Topazes originated from the contact of Portuguese traders with the local inhabitants and from the success of the Dominican missions in making converts. They formed a group who maintained an autonomous existence in Timor and Flores with an assumed Portuguese identity expressed through their dress (the term Topaz, it has sometimes been claimed, means people who wear hats), their use of Portuguese names and their nominal commitment to Catholicism. William Dampier, who visited the islands in 1699, wrote:

> These [the Topazes] have no Forts, but depend on their Alliance with the Natives: And indeed they are already so mixt, that it is hard to distinguish whether they are Portugueze or Indians. Their Language is Portugueze; and the religion they have, is Romish. They seem in Words to acknowledge the King of Portugal for their Sovereign; yet they will not accept any Officers sent by him. They speak indifferently the Malayan and their own native Languages, as well as Portugueze.[31]

Unlike other branches of the 'Portuguese tribe', however, the Topazes did not decline and lose all touch with Portugal. They remained prominent in the sandalwood trade with Macao, and this trade in fact sustained a tenuous Portuguese presence in the Far East as merchants from Macao continued to visit the islands to trade this valuable commodity, in the process helping to sustain the Portuguese identity of their Topaze trading partners. Although the leading Topaze families, like the Hornay and da Costas, fought hard to maintain their independence from the control of the Portuguese in Macao, they were also wary of being brought under Dutch rule and had to maintain a difficult balancing act to survive. For this reason it was convenient to have an official Portuguese presence in the main ports of Larantuka (in Flores), Lifau and Dili.

In the nineteenth century this presence, and the local influence of the Topazes, enabled Portugal belatedly to establish a claim to possession of East Timor and Flores. Although a formal partition agreement resulted in Flores being ceded to the Dutch in 1854, the Topazes continued to dominate Timor. Gervase Clarence Smith, writing of the late nineteenth century, described how

the Portuguese position in the area... depended almost entirely on a group of creoles much addicted to piracy, and on a number of petty chiefs who paid a small tribute and were often baptised catholics. Both creoles [Topazes] and chiefs who were tied to each other by marriage and other links, were involved in raids and wars, and the captives taken in such skirmishes were sold as slaves.[32]

East Timor remained a Portuguese possession with a small Portuguese population until 1975 when it was invaded and annexed by Indonesia. On achieving its independence in 1999 it decided to adopt Portuguese as its official language and to join the CPLP (the Comunidade dos Países de Língua Portuguesa).

António Pinto da França in search of the Portuguese in Indonesia

In the 1960s the Portuguese Consul General in Indonesia, António Pinto da França, enthusiastically travelled throughout the archipelago searching out artefacts, religious traditions and linguistic survivals of Portuguese provenance, uncovering the half forgotten relics of the Portuguese diaspora of the sixteenth and seventeenth centuries. His book *A Influência Portuguesa na Indonésia*, published originally in 1970, was a strange work of dedicated cultural archaeology.[33]

He found bells and inscriptions from Portuguese churches and a Portuguese cannon which had become a cult object to aid childless Javanese women. In Solo in central Java he heard of the cannon called Sutomi, according to local legend named after a princess called Sutomi but with an inscription clearly reading 'São Tomé'. In Ambon he saw Portuguese helmets used in local ceremonies and was shown the royal regalia of the Raja of Sika in Flores, which included gold objects presented by the Portuguese to his ancestors in the early seventeenth century. He visited the summer palace of the Sultans of Jogjakarta and recorded the tradition that it had originally been built by shipwrecked Portuguese. Nearby was a large stone slab, at one time used as a seat by Prince Senopati, bearing a Latin inscription. Elsewhere in Indonesia he thought he could detect Portuguese motifs in local song and dance and items of dress of Portuguese origin.

More intriguing were the linguistic relics. Pinto da França recorded the Portuguese family names in use in Ambon, Sulawesi and Flores and the numerous words of Portuguese origin found in the dialects spoken not only in Tugu and Flores but also in Ambon, Ceram and Sulawesi. He recorded that the Portuguese dialect was still spoken in the region of Tugu near Jakarta which had been a settlement of the so-called Mardijkers. He recorded the words of four songs with Portuguese dialect words—the dialect he thought was similar to the *papiah* dialect spoken near Malacca. In Flores, where Portuguese influence had been strong until the middle of the nineteenth century, he found that local Catholics maintained a Confraternity dedicated to 'Reinja Rosario' and still used Portuguese titles for its office holders. There he also heard prayers still recited in Portuguese. In Sika, also in Flores, where the king bore a Portuguese name, Dom Sentis Alexu da Silva, a Christmas play, the Sandiwara, was still produced using a curious Portuguese creole dialect, and he reproduced the text of this play as he was given it. He likewise noted down a Portuguese dialect song heard by Charles Boxer in a Jakarta restaurant in 1933.

The Portuguese Asians through Conrad's eyes

In the late nineteenth century, as the European powers scrambled for colonies in Africa, South East Asia and the Pacific, this carving up of the world was usually justified as the bringing of modern civilisation to backward peoples. To this claim there was always a racial gloss—being white was synonymous with being civilised. The Portuguese, however, were a problem. Were they really white? The country that had once produced *conquistadores* like Albuquerque was now seen as decadent, its European heritage diluted through intermarriage with Asians and Africans.

In his fiction Joseph Conrad put this simplistic view of the world to the test, but in so doing painted a most unflattering picture of the surviving relics of the Portuguese diaspora in the East. At the start of *An Outcast of the Islands* (published in 1896) Willems, the central character, described as 'the confidential clerk of Hudig & Co.',[34] a trading firm in Macassar, is married to a local woman, a member of the Da Souza family, who are descendants of Portuguese who had settled in the islands centuries before. Willems is a white European and 'fancied... he would be able as heretofore to tyrannise good-humouredly over his half-caste wife, to notice with tender contempt his pale yellow child, to patronise loftily his dark-skinned brother in law'.[35] We are told that he cannot imagine anything he might do which would lessen 'the submission of his wife, the smile of his child, the awe-struck respect of Leonard da Souza and of all the Da Souza family. That family's admiration was the great luxury of his life.'[36]

The Da Souzas represent the class of person for which European empire builders reserved special contempt—the person of mixed race who was neither truly European and civilised nor had the virtues of the 'noble savage'. In Willem's eyes they

were a numerous and an unclean crowd, living in ruined bamboo houses, surrounded by neglected compounds... they were a half-caste lazy lot, and he saw them as they were—ragged, lean, unwashed, undersized men of various ages, shuffling about aimlessly in slippers; motionless old women who looked like monstrous bags of pink calico stuffed with shapeless lumps of fat, and deposited askew upon decaying rattan chairs in shady corners of dusty verandahs.[37]

Willems had taken up the 'white man's burden'.

He heard their shrill quarrelings, the squalling of their children, the grunting of their pigs; he smelt the odours of the heaps of garbage in their courtyards: and he was greatly disgusted. But he fed and clothed that shabby multitude, those degenerate descendants of Portuguese conquerors.... They lived now by the grace of his will. This was power. Willems loved it.[38]

Coming back from a night out, Willems decides 'he had not talked enough about himself, he had not impressed his hearers enough'. So he makes his wife get up and listen to him: 'She was used to those night discourses now. She had rebelled once—at the beginning. Only once.'[39] So the non-European world, and with it Portugal and the Portuguese, had to listen to the lectures and bragging of the racially charged imperialists of the late nineteenth century.

In setting the scene for his novel in this way, Conrad is using Willems to present a view, widely held in northern Europe and America, about the relationship of the white man with the non-white. The non-white was seen as lazy, squalid, living off the charity of the white, lost in moral decadence. For the purposes of this story it is the mixed-race Portuguese who has to stand as the symbol of decadence. The relationship of Willems with the Da Souzas is structured to be the relationship of Europe with the non-European world. That this relationship is soon to be transformed, as the power of the white man leads inevitably to his moral corruption, is the very essence of Conrad's vision of empire.

Macao

With the decline and break-up of the Estado da Índia, there remained only two Portuguese communities in Asia able to sustain a viable economy and to remain centres of Portuguese culture: Goa and Macao. Each of these was to generate its own wave of emigrants in the nineteenth and twentieth centuries and to contribute to the multifaceted Portuguese diaspora.

In the sixteenth and seventeenth centuries Macao was a rich commercial city whose merchants traded with Japan and throughout the China Sea as far as the Moluccas and Timor. With the closure of Japan after 1639 the prosperity of Macao declined, though it retained a role in some East Asian trades. Macao remained under Portuguese control and until the middle of the nineteenth century was the only European port on the coast of China. Because Macao remained technically part of China, it became in effect a sort of semi-autonomous trading republic ruled over by its Senado da Câmara. Although there were always some European Portuguese based in Macao, most of the Macao 'Portuguese' were of mixed Chinese, Portuguese and Malay origin. They traded with the Topazes of the Lesser Sunda Islands and found other niche markets in the East, but increasingly the city became the resort of private traders trying to evade the East India Company's monopolies or the embargo on opium imports imposed by the imperial Chinese government.[40] As a commercial centre the city had constantly to reinvent itself, becoming in turn a hub for the trade in opium, gold, and contract labour and in the twentieth century a centre for gambling.

It was from Macao that Christian missions were despatched to Japan and China; and in China a small, partially Lusitanised, Christian community came into existence. Macao was also seen as offering a possible solution to the problem of peopling the hard-pressed Estado da Índia and there were plans to send orphan girls from Macao to provide wives in eastern Africa—an echo of the policy adopted towards orphans in Portugal itself.

In the nineteenth century Macao became a centre for the recruitment of Chinese labour, shipments of indentured workers being made to Peru and Cuba. Clarence Smith estimates that Cuba imported 125,000 Chinese and Peru 100,000 between 1847 and 1874.[41] These were not Lusitanised Macaonese and they have no real place in the history of the Portuguese diaspora; but they were recruited by Portuguese agents in Macao, some were shipped in Portuguese vessels and the trade was financed by Portuguese capital. Just as the origin of the transatlantic African slave trade had been linked to Portuguese overseas expansion, so this last phase of what was in effect a slave trade was generated in one of the Portuguese diaspora's most long-lived communities.

In the twentieth century there has been a considerable exodus of Macaonese who, of course, had Portuguese citizenship until the city was handed over to China in 1999. Many Macaonese took advantage of being Portuguese and moved to Lisbon from where there was free movement within the European Union, while others moved to the booming commercial centre of Hong Kong where, according to official Portuguese estimates, there were 20,000 Portuguese residents in 1997.[42]

The Goan diaspora

Goa became the capital of the Estado da Índia after 1530 and the centre of its military, political and ecclesiastical administration. As the city grew it attracted a very mixed population and became what the twenty-first century would call a multicultural community. Those Indians who adopted Christianity in time joined with the offspring of Portuguese and Indian women to form a population with a distinctly Goan ethnic identity which, while retaining Indian caste distinctions, was heavily influenced by Portuguese language, culture and ideas.

Individuals from this community were partially absorbed into the Portuguese ruling elite, having access to education, and occupying administrative and ecclesiastical positions within the Portuguese world. Goans, along with other Luso-Asians, were employed in various capacities throughout the Estado da Índia. Michael Pearson gives as an example the

very distinguished Xavier family... descended from a convert originally called Narsu Quenim, [who] apparently had no, or very little, European blood. Despite this they flourished in the eighteenth and nineteenth centuries. Family members held such official positions as interim secretary-general of Portuguese India, secretary to the governor general of Mozambique, president of the municipal council of Mozambique, and commander of the artillery in Lisbon's national guard. Others were a priest, a doctor, a headmaster, and the famous *littérateur* Filippe Nery Xavier.[43]

The Abbé Faria

Some Goans found their way to Europe along the pathways built by the centuries of imperial commerce. An intriguing example is the Abbé Faria, one of the best known and most vividly portrayed characters from the Portuguese diaspora.[44] The very ambiguity that surrounds him only emphasises the uncertainties that typify most diasporic identities. The Abbé Faria is a central character in the first part of Alexander Dumas' novel *The Count of Monte Cristo*. The hero of the story, Edmond Dantès, becomes Faria's fellow prisoner in the notorious prison, the Château d'If. In the course of the story the two make contact with each other, strike up a friendship and, when the Abbé eventually dies in his cell, Edmond escapes from the Château by substituting himself in the Abbé's shroud and getting carried out of the prison to be buried at sea. However, before his death the Abbé had imparted the secret of a hidden treasure that made Edmond's fortune and enabled the adventures of the rest of the novel to unfold.

Most commentators are agreed that Dumas based his Abbé on a real person, a priest called José Custódio de Faria who had spent fourteen years as a prisoner in the Château d'If. However, with the name and the coincidence of incarceration the similarities apparently end. In Dumas' story the Abbé is Italian, has been imprisoned for his activities as an Italian nationalist propagandist and had come across the information about the hidden treasure during his period as chaplain to an Italian cardinal. In his prison he had displayed immense ingenuity in making for himself writing materials and tools and had begun the laborious task of digging for himself an escape tunnel. Once he made contact with Edmond he became the young man's mentor, teaching him languages and advising him on the ethical conduct of his life and on the techniques of survival in prison. The Abbé suffered from some acute nervous disorder from which he eventually died—still a prisoner.

The real Faria was Goanese. He had travelled with his father to Rome and had taken holy orders. In France he had taken an active part in the Revolution and for that he had been imprisoned. However, he did not die in prison and on his release began a career as a scientist. He studied hypnotism and is acknowledged as one of the founders of modern psychoanalysis.

So, was there any link between the fictional and the real Abbé, apart from the name?

In Dumas' imagination Faria becomes a typical member of an enlightened intellectual elite, educated within the church, but able to become a master of contemporary science and to use his education, with its philosophical subtleties and casuistries, to chart a path through the turmoil of revolutionary Europe. Although coming from a priest-ridden background, he had nevertheless surmounted the superstitions of his age and had embraced the science of the Enlightenment.

A child of the Portuguese diaspora, the real Faria was also an *estrangeirado*, receiving his education and training in Italy. He had carried out experiments in hypnotism and research into the human psyche—strange, innovative and unorthodox areas of knowledge. This comes through clearly in Dumas' character: 'I am the poor mad prisoner of the Chateau d'If: for many years permitted to amuse the different visitants to the prison.' His understanding of mankind, he explains to Edmond, is based on the idea that humans have innate ideas: 'the natural repugnance to the commission of... a crime prevents its bare idea from occurring to you ... our natural instincts keep us from deviating from the strict line of duty.'[45] Dumas' character is a student, even a master, of human psychology and Edmond describes him as 'the wonderful being whose hand seemed gifted with the power of a magician's wand' and 'one gifted with supernatural powers'.[46] Later Edmond says of Faria, 'you who see so completely to the depth of things and to whom the greatest mystery seems but an easy riddle'.[47] The Abbé describes what it is to be a scientist and student of human psychology: 'to learn is not to know; there are the learners and the learned. Memory makes the one; philosophy the other.'[48]

The Goan diaspora in the nineteenth century

In East Africa, where Goans were usually known as Canarins by the Portuguese, they served as priests in the parish churches, traded for gold and ivory and became the holders of *prazos*, the semi-feudal grants of land and population which were made in the Zambesi valley region and in the Querimba Islands. As late as the 1880s some of the most influential figures in East Africa, like the warlord Manuel António de Sousa, were Goans.

With the contraction of the Estado da Índia in the eighteenth century and the decline of its economy, the Portuguese government was no longer able to provide career opportunities for educated Goans and it became increasingly common for them to seek employment in the territory of the East India Company—particular in nearby Bombay, which by the nineteenth century had a large Goan community, its members typically filling low-status clerical positions in government or business offices. Poorer Goans found employment as seamen or in domestic service.

The Portuguese established a medical school in 1842 in Goa, the Escola Médico-Cirúrgica de Goa, and Goan-trained doctors practised in other Portuguese colonies and in various parts of the British Empire. Zanzibar was one destination popular with Goans in the nineteenth century and many, including a number of doctors, found employment in the service of the Sultan. When the British took control of the areas that later became Uganda and Kenya, Goans from Zanzibar found expanded job opportunities working for the British administration or British companies, again filling clerical positions and sometimes more humble occupations like cooks.

Goans had Portuguese passports and had to be treated as Portuguese citizens by the British authorities, and this set them apart from other Indians. For the British, Goans had an advantage over other Indians in being Christian and having a partly European educational background. The Portuguese themselves appointed consular officials in East Africa from among the Goan community and this became an established practice until the end of the colonial regime. One Goan consul, a doctor named Rosendo Ayres Ribeiro, allegedly went on his rounds mounted on a zebra.[49]

It was not just the Goanese diaspora which gave the Portuguese some influence in British India, for this influence had another basis in the partial control that Portugal still retained over the Catholic church through the *padroado real*. The Portuguese continued to claim the right to make church appointments, even in branches of the church located in British India. Renamed the *Padroado Ultramarino Português* and, since 1911 (following the Portuguese Law on the Separation of Church and State), the *Padroado Português do Oriente*, the *padroado real* remained in much of Asia as the ghostly presence of the long defunct Estado da Índia. The sphere of its influence steadily contracted although its continued existence was confirmed by the Pope in 1928. It finally disappeared with the withdrawal of Portugal from Macao in 1999.

Not all Goans were Christian and, especially after the acquisition of the Novas Conquistas which greatly expanded Goan territory towards the end of the eighteenth century, rather more than half the population was Hindu. In the outlying port-towns of Damão and Diu, which still remained under Portuguese control, most of the population were non-Christians. Many Hindus, Parsees and Muslims from Portuguese-controlled territories traded, and even settled, throughout the Indian Ocean, and were especially prominent in the Portuguese-controlled ports in eastern Africa. Although this trading diaspora had its point of origin in the Portuguese ports of northern India, and although its members probably spoke and wrote Portuguese, they were only 'Portuguese' in the most marginal sense.[50]

Organised opposition to Portuguese rule in Goa began to emerge in the eighteenth century and continued with sporadic rebellions and conspiracies in the nineteenth century. These movements were too weak to destabilise Portuguese rule but did lead to political exiles joining the Portuguese diaspora in British India.

Although the Portuguese always considered Goa to be part of the pluricontinental kingdom of Portugal, it was only with the declaration of the Portuguese Republic in 1910 that Goans were explicitly given equal rights with metropolitan Portuguese and that the idea of equality of the Portuguese nation was given full expression. The Republic also offered the Asian and African territories of Portugal autonomy within what, in effect, was intended to be a federal structure.[51] However, any suggestion of Goan autonomy was ended with the demise of the Republic in 1926 and the passing of the Colonial Act in 1930 which, while affirming the unity of the Portuguese nation across the world, brought the administration of Goa directly under the control of Lisbon. As Salazar's Portugal tried to 'go it alone' in the world of the 1930s, seeking the elusive goal of autarchy and trying to stem the spreading flood tides of liberalism and communism, Goa became ever more detached from the developments taking place in British India. Goans increasingly looked outside the closed Portuguese world for education, for career opportunities and for political freedoms. According to Caroline Brettell, 'an estimate made in 1954 suggested that about 180,000 Goans were away from their homes'[52] and, as with Portuguese emigrants elsewhere in the world, the remittances sent back to their families were a substantial contribution to the economy of Portuguese India.

The determination of Salazar to view Goa as essentially a branch of the Portuguese nation led once again to increasing numbers of Goans, like the Cape Verdeans, being employed in the Portuguese colonial service in Africa. Caroline Brettell gives the example of Edgar Fernandes who arrived in Lisbon from Goa in 1958 and was employed in a technical capacity in Cape Verde and Timor.[53]

Goa and the Goan diaspora after 1961

After the independence of India in 1947 the political future of Goa became an urgent issue. Broadly speaking three different paths to the future were outlined. There were those, mostly Hindus who formed possibly 60 per cent of the population of Goa, who wanted unification with India and incorporation into the Indian Republic; then there were those who wanted independence for Goa apart from India; and thirdly those who wanted to remain as part of Portugal. The last group were mostly Goan Christians. The Goan diaspora was also divided along similar lines as to how it saw the way ahead.

In the event India invaded Goa in December 1961 and the territory, along with Damão and Diu, was fully incorporated into India. This resulted in yet another wave of the Goan diaspora. Some Goans, unwilling to be taken over by India, left for Portugal, escaping first to Karachi and then travelling by boat to Lisbon. Others went to the Portuguese African colonies, but there was a further dispersal after these colonies were granted independence in 1975. While some Goans joined the ranks of Frelimo or the MPLA, most left for Lisbon, Brazil or other destinations. Edgar Fernandes, as Caroline Brettell found out, had cousins in Canada, Britain and the United States.

The Goan diaspora, therefore, has four distinct elements and many subdivisions. First there are those who left while Goa was still under Portuguese rule; second there were those who left soon after the Indian take-over in 1961; third were the Goans who had already moved to Africa but after 1975 found they had to move again to Europe or the Americas; and finally there are Goans who have left more recently, taking advantage of the regulations drawn up in Lisbon in 1991 which allowed anyone who could establish that they, their parents or grandparents were born in Goa prior to 1961 to apply for Portuguese citizenship. This included Hindu as well as Christian Goans and greatly increased migration from India to Portugal and from Portugal to the rest of the European Union.[54]

Within the broad category of recent Goan emigrants there are various subdivisions, for example between Catholic and Hindu Goans or between those who had worked for the Portuguese dictatorship and those who arrived after its demise. To these divisions have to be added the divisions which have grown up between Goans who settled in Portugal and those who settled in Britain or the Americas. Moreover it was not only Catholic and Hindu Goans that left India and arrived in Portugal via the African colonies. There were significant numbers of Ismailis and Gujeratis who had made careers within the Portuguese empire, who spoke Portuguese and had been educated in the Portuguese colonies. Many of these also left the Portuguese African territories in the 1970s to settle in Portugal and from there spread to western Europe.

The Portuguese diaspora reaches Australia

It is probable that Australia was sighted by Portuguese navigators in the sixteenth century, but most improbable that there was any settlement there. During the gold rush of the early 1850s some Madeirans who had settled in British Guiana chartered a ship to go to Australia, but only a handful of Portuguese are recorded in any of the Australian states until the period of the Second World War. During the War Macao was not occupied but remained under close Japanese surveillance from Hong Kong. Portuguese Timor, however, was invaded by Japanese forces in 1942 and remained under their control until the end of the war. It was during the war that the first significant number of Portuguese and Luso-Asians departed for Australia to begin the formation of a Portuguese community there.

There was a renewed influx of Portuguese after the Indonesian invasion of East Timor in 1975 and by the 1980s the Portuguese community, mostly in the state of Victoria, numbered between 2,000 and 3,000. By 1997 the numbers of Portuguese in Australia had risen to 55,339, according to the often exaggerated statistics compiled by the Portuguese Ministry of Foreign Affairs.[55] Figures for 2010 compiled by the Centro de Investigação de Estudos de Sociologia (CIES) gave 18,520 people in Australia as having been born in Portugal.[56]

106

6

THE PORTUGUESE IN BRAZIL

In the mentality of humble people in the villages, someone going to Brazil signified, and still signifies, purely and simply the entry into the Land of Canaan.

(Guilhermino César)[1]

In the specific case of the Azores (as with the rest of Portugal generally) emigration was facilitated by the fascination which from early times was exercised by the colony of Brazil, at that time the "jewel of the Portuguese Crown", a fascination which continued far beyond the independence of Brazil.

(Luís Mendonça and José Ávila)[2]

The settlement of Brazil

The story of the settlement of Brazil is the story of converging streams of migration: New and Old Christian settlers originating from Portugal and the islands merged with the slaves (forced immigrants) brought from Africa to form the population of coastal Brazil, which in turn formed fresh streams of migrants who mixed with the native Americans and explored and eventually populated the interior—the *sertão*.

The first Portuguese ships to arrive in Brazil were probably those of Pedro Álvares Cabral who sailed along the Brazilian coast on his voyage to India in 1500, and the first Portuguese individual to remain in Brazil must have been the convict who is reported to have jumped ship to join the Indians. For nearly thirty years thereafter Portuguese ships regularly visited the Brazilian coast to collect the much sought after Brazil wood. Temporary camps were formed ashore, some of which eventually became semi-permanent, while a few Portuguese, similar to the *lançados* of upper Guinea, built lives for themselves on the coast, took Indian wives and raised families. However, until about 1530, the numbers involved were very small.

In 1532 a township with a permanent population was created at São Vicente in the south, and between 1533 and 1535 Brazil was divided into fifteen 'donatary captaincies'. The captains, few of whom were men of much substance, were supposed to organise the colonisation of their captaincies and had the right to allocate vacant land to settlers. The most successful captaincies were those of São Vicente in the extreme south, where a sugar industry was begun with capital invested by Netherlands sugar interests; and Pernambuco in the north, where sugar-growing was also started. In each case the success of the settlements was due to the active presence of the captain and his family and the good relations which were brought about by intermarriage with the local indigenous population.

It is of interest to note the prominent part played by women in these early settlements. When Martim Afonso de Sousa, the captain of São Vicente, departed for India in 1533, his wife, Ana Pimentel, who had remained behind in Portugal, sailed to take charge of the captaincy. She was officially named *governadora* in 1538 and governed the captaincy for ten years. When the captain of Pernambuco, Duarte Coelho, died in 1554, his captaincy was governed by his wife Dona Brites de Albuquerque until his son took over in 1560. Dona Brites resumed control in 1572 when her son returned to Portugal. And there were other similar examples. The careers of these formidable women have parallels on the other side of the Atlantic in the Portuguese settlements in São Tomé, Guinea and Cape Verde. What they have in common is the reality of life in the Portuguese maritime empire. Men were constantly on the move, captaining ships, taking up new appointments, serving the Crown in a variety of capacities. It was the women who often remained in one place taking control of family property and wielding local economic and political power.[3]

At first, although land was readily available, it proved difficult to attract migrants since the control which the families of the captains exerted over the territory proved a strong disincentive for settlers. As Euclides da Cunha wrote in his elegiac history of the colonising of the Brazilian backlands, the Portuguese did not approach the northern seaboard with that vital strength which comes from dense migrations, great masses of invaders capable of preserving, even when uprooted from their native soil, all those qualities acquired in the course of a long historical apprenticeship. They were scattered, parcelled out in small bands of condemned exiles or counterfeit colonists, lacking in the virile mien of conquerors. They still were dazzled by visions of the Orient. Brazil was the land of exile, a huge garrison for the intimidating of heretics and backsliders, all those victims of the sombre *let-him-die-for-it* justice of those days.[4]

The French *philosophe* Abbé Raynal put it more succinctly:

After the Court of Lisbon had had the ports, bays, rivers and coasts of Brazil explored and believed that it was certain that there was neither gold nor silver there, it showed its contempt for them to the point of sending there men condemned by the law, and lost and debauched women. Every year two or three vessels left Portugal to carry criminals from the kingdom to the New World bringing back parrots, and woods used for dyeing and marquetry.[5]

Those Portuguese migrants who did settle in Brazil in the middle years of the sixteenth century tended to come from the northern province of Minho, where landholdings were small and villages and towns had surplus population.[6] In this early phase of the diaspora, the people who left Portugal, whether as convicts, as religious exiles or simply as people seeking a better living for themselves and their families, showed a marked tendency to try to escape the control of royal government and the privileged nobility. In the same way, it had been the very informality of the *lançado* settlements in western Africa and, in the East, the opportunities to live their lives beyond the control of the viceroys that had the greatest capacity to attract emigrants.

In the last quarter of the sixteenth century the economy of Brazil began a period of rapid growth as the sugar industry became firmly established along the northern coast. Sugar-growing was dependent on supplies of labour, which was obtained from Indians, either as slaves or as wage labourers, and from African slaves. The sugar estates, usually referred to as *engenhos* (sugar mills), were owned by Portuguese of mixed social origin who soon constituted an informal aristocracy. Most lived on their estates, in contrast to the landowners of the Atlantic Islands who were frequently absentees, but the actual growing of the sugar was leased out to smallholders and sharecroppers known as *lavradores da cana*—for the most part also Portuguese immigrants. This stratification of Portuguese society meant that, over time, poor whites, free blacks (whose free status was the result of manumission and black-white cohabitation), the ubiquitous *pardo*s (people of mixed African, Indian and European descent) and Indians came to form a racially mixed lower class of artisans, smallholders, cattle men and traders. As a result the niches available for new poor white immigrants were few and their number, in consequence, less than might otherwise have been the case. However, one feature of the new colony did prove attractive to immigrants. No branch of the Inquisition was established and this meant that Brazil offered a favourable environment for New Christian settlement, though most of those who came to Brazil were merchants involved in the sugar and slave trades rather than settlers seeking a permanent home.

In 1574 the total population of European origin numbered about 17,000, and by the end of the century this had doubled to around 30,000 with probably the same number of Indians and Africans living in the Portuguese settled areas.[7] By 1625 the number of people of European origin had doubled again to 60,000, though not all of these were from Portugal, and by 1700 natural increase had pushed the total to around 100,000, rather more than those who inhabited the New England colonies at the same time.[8] Between 1532 and 1650 six cities and thirty-one towns were established in Brazil, by far the most important being Salvador de Bahia which, already in the 1580s, had a population of 15,000, and in 1620 boasted 62 churches, already well on the way to the fabled 365 churches it would one day be able to claim.[9]

The prosperity of the sugar industry in the period 1580–1660 attracted economic migrants, and when sugar went into decline in the latter part of the seventeenth century a new economy based on tobacco and gold-mining continued to bring in settlers, so that ties with Portugal remained close. As in the previous century, immigrants mostly came from the northern part of Portugal.[10] As Schwartz and Lockhart explained, 'a study of Bahia in the period 1680–1740 shows that nearly all the merchants and two thirds of the artisans were European-born … about one third of the sugar planters were born in Europe and another third were first-generation Brazilians'.[11] Merchants in particular tended to remain close to their Portuguese roots and to return home after making their money in the colony. As no university, nor even a printing press, was established in Brazil, all posts requiring an educated person had to be filled by people who had received their education in Portugal, and this helped to guarantee a continued flow of migrants in both directions, the children of the well-off going to Portugal to be educated and the educated heading for Brazil to take up posts in the church or government.

A characteristic of Portuguese emigration, which was to persist into the twentieth century, was the comparative lack of women among the migrants. Many of the men who left Portugal did so with the idea, however vaguely formulated, of returning home to their families; in the meantime they formed unofficial liaisons with Indian, African or mulatto women, leading to a significant increase in the free coloured population. Those who did take their wives with them to Brazil often sent their daughters back to Portugal rather than risk unsuitable marriages in Brazil. Although this tendency lessened in the eighteenth century when a white Portuguese population became more firmly established in the country, the social and family ties of Brazilians to the Portuguese homeland remained very strong.

As in Africa and the Estado da Índia, Portuguese society in Brazil had institutions which enabled immigrants quickly to find a place for themselves in the diasporic community. Membership of religious brotherhoods cemented social relations while at the same time upholding distinctions of status. Each Portuguese community, even quite small ones isolated from direct links with Portugal, established a Misericórdia which provided a range of social services and acted as a bank with which people could deposit money or other assets. It was a prestigious institution to which people aspired to belong and it powerfully upheld Portuguese identity and social cohesion. Local self-government was also well developed, though the formation of a Senado da Câmara depended on obtaining a charter from the king, which had the effect of restricting the spread of this particular institution. The town councils tended to represent the interests of the moneyed classes, but these interests were often closely tied up with the prosperity of the town itself, making the council an effective instrument for the welfare of the population as a whole. Where there was no council there were often informal bodies that met to represent the interests of the more important citizens.

The slave trade and the Portuguese Atlantic

Over five centuries Brazil has been the principal destination for emigrants from Portugal, leading to the dominance of the Portuguese language and the Catholic church in what is today one of the largest, most populous and economically successful countries in the world; but the immigration of Africans has been hardly less important. In no part of the world is the interdependence of these two streams of migration more clearly demonstrated.

Slaves from sub-Saharan Africa began to be obtained by the Portuguese from about the 1440s. At first they were brought to Portugal or the Atlantic Islands, but about 1520 a market began to open up in the New World, and by the seventeenth century slaves were being imported into Brazil and Spanish America in very large numbers. Although some were coming from the Cape Verde and upper Guinea region of Africa, the overwhelming majority were shipped from the Portuguese-controlled ports of Kongo and Angola. Most of the slaves were bought at fairs in the interior, though some were war captives as there was an almost unbroken series of wars in the interior during the seventeenth century. Most of the slaves shipped at Luanda or Benguela were sent directly to Brazil, and Brazilian Portuguese played a significant role in developing the trade. When the Dutch invaded Brazil and occupied the sugar-producing north of the country between 1630 and 1654, they decided that producing sugar in Brazil would be impossible without the supply of slave labour from Angola; so in 1641 an expedition was sent to occupy Luanda and São Tomé island. When the Brazilians staged a revolt against the Dutch in 1646, this was extended across the Atlantic and in 1648 an expedition organised in southern Brazil expelled the Dutch from Luanda. Brazilians now, in effect, took over the running of the slave trade in Angola. Soldiers from Brazil were sent to fight in the Angolan wars and Brazilian governors were appointed to Luanda. Increasingly also Brazilian tobacco became a commodity of choice in West African markets.

This African diaspora began and developed at the same time that the Portuguese themselves were emigrating to set up diasporic communities across the world. A comparison of the numbers involved puts both streams of migration into a context that helps to explain the forces at work in the movement of population in the early modern period. Between 1500 and 1850 around 4.67 million slaves were brought to Brazil (78 per cent in the last hundred years of the trade) while 2.9 million Portuguese emigrated (to all destinations not just Brazil) during the same period.

In considering the demographic impact on Africa and on Portugal, it is relevant that in both cases the overwhelming majority of migrants were male, while migration from Portugal certainly came from a much smaller population pool than did the slave trade from Africa.

Table 2: Numbers of Emigrants/Slaves Per Annum
(Total emigration from Portugal/export of slaves to Brazil)

Portugal	1500–1580	3,500
Slaves	1500–1575	846
Portugal	1580–1640	5,000–6,000
Slaves	1576–1650	7,464
Portugal	1640–1700	2,500
Slaves	1640–1700	9,034
Portugal	1700–1760	8,333–10,000
Slaves	1700–1750	20,222
Portugal	1760–1850	16,666
Slaves	1750–1850	36,624

Source: Magalhães Godinho, 'L'Emigration portugaise (XVe-XXe siècles), une constante structurale et les réponses aux changements du monde'; and Slave Trade Database: http://slavevoyages.org/tast/assessment/estimates.faces

The millions of African slaves landed in Brazil played a major role in developing the Brazilian economy and in the formation of Brazilian society, partly by providing the labour for the mines and plantations but also by contributing to the emergence of a free black working class. Because so few white Portuguese women migrated to Brazil in the first two centuries of settlement, their place was taken by African and Indian women, with the result that a large part of the Brazilian population, until the nineteenth century, was racially mixed and formed a distinctly creolised society. Robert Southey, writing at the beginning of the nineteenth century, thought that therein lay the vital difference between Brazil and the Spanish colonies.

The seeds of civil war had not been sown there [Brazil] by that wicked distinction of cast[e]s, which has produced so much evil in Spanish America, and must produce evil wherever it prevails. This was the result of necessity... not of wiser councils. Portugal with its limited territory and scanty population, could not pursue the unjust and jealous policy of the Spaniards, and depress the Creoles for the sake of holding them more completely in subjection. The Mameluco [person of mixed European and Indian race] was as much respected, and as eligible to all offices, as the man of whole blood, or as the native of the mother country. There are no laws to degrade the Mulatto, or the free Negro, nor were they degraded by public opinion. And thus that amalgamation of cast[e]s and colours was silently going on which will secure Brazil from the most dreadful of all civil wars, whatever other convulsions it may be fated to undergo.[12]

Robinson Crusoe in Brazil

Some Portuguese have maintained that the original idea for writing about a man stranded alone on a desert island was derived from the story of Fernão Lopes who was marooned on the island of St Helena in the sixteenth century and lived there until his death. There is no real evidence for this but it is significant that Daniel Defoe made his hero an immigrant planter in Brazil and decided to use a Portuguese character as Crusoe's saviour and patron. In marked contrast to the image, beloved of seventeenth-century travellers, of the proud, effete, luxury-loving Portuguese, ennobled simply by passing the Cape of Good Hope, Defoe drew a portrait of a simple, honest and God-fearing Portuguese captain who rescued Robinson Crusoe after his escape from slavery in Morocco and subsequently helped him regain his fortune. Much of the story of Robinson Crusoe, though the part that is seldom read, is in fact located within the Portuguese world of Brazil where the hero makes his living building up a plantation where he grows tobacco. When Crusoe returns from his lengthy exile as a castaway on the island, he meets the Portuguese captain again. From him Crusoe receives an account of the profits of his Brazilian plantation, and an offer to pay over the money that was owing.

I was too much mov'd with the Honesty and Kindness of the poor Man, to be able to bear this; and remembering what he had done for me, how he had taken me up at Sea, and how generously he had used me on all Occasions, and particularly how sincere a Friend he was now to me, I could hardly refrain Weeping at what he said to me.[13]

Robinson Crusoe was published in 1719, by which time Britain's relations with Portugal had radically altered. The suspicions and downright hostility that had sometimes marked their relations in the seventeenth century had now given way to a highly profitable commercial partnership. Portugal was rapidly becoming one of the most important markets for Britain's manufactures, with Britain providing a captive market for Portuguese wines. In the process a considerable quantity of Brazilian gold found its way to Britain to settle commercial payments. Portugal had now indeed become the 'sincere Friend' of Defoe's imagination.

The golden century

In the years 1693 to 1695 gold was found in the Brazilian interior and a gold rush was soon underway. The first large-scale emigration from Portugal and the islands had begun. Whereas, at the most, there had been net migration to the Estado da Índia during the sixteenth century of around 1,024 per annum, now many thousands of Portuguese were arriving annually in Brazil (Godinho thought that the numbers were as high as 8–10,000 per annum during the first two-thirds of the century).[14] In the first half of the eighteenth century between 500,000 and 600,000 Portuguese arrived in Brazil, and the main new centres of population were to be found no longer on the coast but in the mining regions of the interior. By 1775 20 per cent of the total population of Brazil was settled in Minas Gerais.

Most of the European immigrants, according to Schwartz, 'were young bachelors from the overcrowded northern province of Minho... [who], although of all ranks and conditions, [were] heavily weighted towards peasants and others of lower status'.[15] The Italian Jesuit Giovanni Antonio Andreoni, who published an account of Brazil in 1711, using the pseudonym Andre João Antonil, wrote that 'the insatiable thirst for gold tempts so many to leave their lands and to take to roads as hard as those of Minas that it is difficult to be able to count the number of persons who are there'. Nevertheless, he thought that already there were more than 30,000 persons working the gold mines. The mining camps were lawless and chaotic places.

Each year numbers of Portuguese and foreigners come in the fleets to pass on to Minas. From the cities, towns, reconcavos and backlands of Brazil come whites, mulattos, blacks and many Indians who are enslaved by the Paulistas. It is a mixture of persons of every condition, men and women, youths and old men, the poor and the rich, nobles and plebeians, seculars, clerics and religious of various orders, many of whom do not have a monastery or house in Brazil.[16]

The arrival of immigrants, known as Emboabas, at the mines led to extreme social tensions and eventually to civil war in which the original discoverers of the gold, the Paulistas, lost control of the mining regions. It took a decade at least for effective royal government to be imposed, and even then an open frontier continued to exist with many

Paulistas and immigrant Portuguese pushing westwards to try to find new goldfields. Eventually gold-mining began also in Goias and Cuiaba, each of these areas attracting fresh waves of migrants, in spite of the extreme hardships these encountered in arriving at the goldfields and in surviving in the interior. In 1726 Cuiaba had a population of 7,000 immigrant miners and 2,800 slaves.[17]

Whether these immigrants originated in the rural society of Portugal or the Azores, in Brazil they did not behave like peasants intent on making a living from the land. Euclides da Cunha described the destructiveness of the gold digging pioneer who

attacked the earth stoutly, disfiguring it with his surface explorations, rendering it sterile with his dredges, scarring it with the point of his pickaxe, precipitating the process of erosion by running through it streams of water from wild torrents. And he left behind him, here, there, and everywhere great melancholy and deserted *catas*, tracts forever sterile...[18]

Gold-mining peaked around 1750 with fifteen tons a year being produced. In that year the total population of Minas Gerais was estimated to be 227,000. In 1776, the year of the first Brazilian census, there were 75,800 white people in the region[19] and, although there was no overall growth in the following decade, Minas continued to attract immigrants even after the output of gold went into steep decline. Once the main deposits had been worked out, small operators known as *faiscadores* continued to work the spoil heaps and small surface veins. In a census taken in 1814 there were nearly 6,000 small-scale prospectors, two-thirds of them men of European origin and one-third slaves working on behalf of their masters.[20] For poor white immigrants and black slaves to work alongside each other was typical of some phases of the peopling of Brazil.

Few Portuguese women moved to Minas and by 1804 only a third of household heads in Vila Rica, the main town, were married. On the other hand the large number of people of mixed race, amounting to 40 per cent of the population in 1808, told a story of a century of sexual relations between whites and free or enslaved black women. As early as 1711 Andreoni had lamented that the gold obtained by successful miners enabled them 'to buy a negro trumpeter for a thousand *cruzados* and a mulata of bad conduct for double that sum in order that with her [they can] continue to multiply their scandalous sins', the gold that was mined ending up as 'hat bands, earrings and other trinkets which today you see adorning the mulatas of ill repute and the negresses rather than the ladies'.[21]

Informal empire in the backlands

As Brazil established itself, in many respects as an extension of Portugal, dominated by the church, a landowning aristocracy and the familiar institutions of metropolitan society and royal government, it also generated its own onward migration. While the sugar economy had boomed there was employment in the coastal regions, but with the decline in the prosperity of the sugar plantations after 1660 the coastal economy went into decline. This prompted pioneers to start to explore the vast tracts of the interior that extended all the way to the Andes, and to seek out the potential riches of the Amazon basin. This vast 'frontier' region attracted diverse migrants—slavers seeking Indians for service on the coast, Jesuit missionaries, prospectors looking for precious metals, contraband traders and cattlemen looking for land on which to establish cattle ranges. For these groups the *sertão*, for all its dangers and privations, offered economic opportunity and freedom from the social hierarchies of Portuguese society and the increasingly stifling dead hand of royal government. The political status of the *sertão* was uncertain. The Treaty of Tordesillas, signed with Castile in 1494, had drawn a longitudinal line between Spanish and Portuguese territory, but no one could calculate accurately where the line ran. Therefore, a treaty that should have established clearly defined frontiers and jurisdictions became instead an added source of uncertainty and confusion, presenting ideal opportunities for the entrepreneurial skills of the backwoodsman to exploit. The coastal settlements of Brazil, therefore, generated their own diaspora, their own 'informal' empire with self-governing, autonomous communities but, unlike the informal empire in Asia, on its own doorstep rather than overseas. Eventually, by the last quarter of the eighteenth century, royal government would catch up with the backwoodsmen and the *sertão* would be properly incorporated into Brazil, but not until the character of the frontier had imposed itself on Brazilian society.

São Paulo, the main town in the southern captaincy of São Vicente, was the area from which migrant backwoodsmen most persistently pushed into the interior, away from the control of captains and royal government. São Paulo was a poor settlement and, as with Portugal itself, it was poverty rather than wealth and disposable capital that was the motor of expansion. The population of São Paulo was very mixed and spoke the *lingua geral*, a creole dialect of Portuguese and Tupi-Guaraní. As sugar-growing became concentrated on the plantations in the north, the Paulistas increasingly turned for their economic survival to cattle ranching and slaving. Both activities led them into the interior and resulted in constant conflict with the Indian inhabitants of the region and their missionary protectors. The *bandeiras*, the armed expeditions which they organised, were funded by themselves and not only were they not authorised by the Crown, they were frequently undertaken in direct conflict with royal orders. The *bandeirantes* were migrants escaping the control of government, establishing their own informal communities in the interior, winning and controlling land for themselves and pushing further into the *sertão*, raiding for slaves or prospecting for precious metals. The slaving activities of the *bandeirantes* led to direct conflict with the Jesuit missionaries and also, in the years 1690–1730, to rich discoveries of gold and diamonds. It was these activities, in their eyes the successful outcome of their entrepreneurial initiatives, that prompted the government to extend its authority in order to rein back their activities. The comparison with the subsequent expansion of settlers in the United States and in South Africa is clear. Governments, often with reluctance, felt compelled to follow their frontiersmen to try to establish stability and order but also to gain a share of the wealth that was being created.

In the seventeenth century the region south of São Paulo stretching as far as the Río de la Plata, the area that would one day form the province of Rio Grande do Sul, attracted smugglers who were prepared to breach the trade monopolies of the Spanish Crown, and coastal settlements grew up to service the extensive contraband trade which used the Río de la Plata as its highway. The Portuguese Crown largely ignored these communities but in 1680 took a major initiative, establishing the Colónia do Sacramento, a formal settlement on the Río de la Plata itself. This dramatic development, uncharacteristic of a monarchy still very much on the defensive, was an attempt to establish royal control over the main contraband trade route from the Andes down the Paraguay river. Early in the eighteenth century the Crown took further measures to impose its control over the largely autonomous communities in the southern frontier region, in 1733 completing a highway to link the various coastal settlements.

In 1750, after yet another frontier war, a formal agreement with Spain laid open the vast *sertão* to the west to Portuguese settlement; and almost at the same time the control exerted by the Jesuits over their missions was finally brought to an end with the suppression of the order in Portugal in 1759. Land was now available for the pioneer who could brave the hardships of the journey into the interior. The occupation of the interior of Brazil was every bit as destructive as the expansion of Europeans in other parts of the world would prove to be. Euclides da Cunha wrote:

Those explorers who ... set out from the left bank of that river [the São Francisco], carrying with them their indispensable provisions of water in leathern pouches, made use of the same sinister pathbreaker—fire—which at once opened up and illuminated the way for them, laying bare the earth ahead of them as they went; and for months afterward, of a night, the ruddy glow of conflagrations was visible in the western skies. One can imagine what the results of such a procedure would be when carried on uninterruptedly for centuries.[22]

The planting of settlements in the interior was facilitated by the expansion of livestock farming. Cattle were raised to feed the sugar-growing areas of the coast and the mining regions, while horses and mules were bred to support the transport networks necessary in such a vast country. As N. P. Macdonald wrote:

the livestock industry ... was created and maintained by free men. Almost alone in the colonial economy this market was largely domestic and the profits remained at home; above all it had largely made possible the settlement of the colony beyond the narrow coastal fringe. The industry also provided, firstly, a framework within which one part of the colony came to some extent to depend on another and, secondly, in the shape of the horse and mule, the links with which that dependence was maintained.[23]

The nineteenth century

Although the gold rush was long over, Portuguese migration to Brazil continued in the first half of the nineteenth century, with estimates of the numbers involved ranging from 100,000 to 400,000 during that period.[24] For a brief thirteen-year period, between 1807 and 1821, the government of the kingdom of Portugal moved from Lisbon to Rio. This opened the way to the migration of substantial numbers of the Portuguese upper class, between 15,000 and 20,000 people having left with the Queen and the Prince Regent on board the fleet in November 1807—possibly the largest single departure of emigrants from Portugal ever recorded. Although Brazil broke away from Portugal in 1822 and established itself as an independent state, immigration continued as commercial and family ties remained close. However, there was no coordinated policy for attracting immigrants from Europe and, until the slave trade was finally banned in 1851, the Brazilian economy continued to depend on the import of large numbers of black slaves. As many as 500,000 may have entered Brazil in the last twenty years of the trade alone.

Incentives for Portuguese to emigrate to Brazil were strengthened by the political disruption caused by the cycle of social unrest and civil war in Portugal between 1827 and 1851. These disturbances particularly affected the Azores (in the 1830s) and northern Portugal, the areas from which traditionally most of the migrants had been drawn. Although in the 1830s Portuguese contract workers were being actively recruited to replace slave labour in the Caribbean, Brazil still remained the favourite destination for Portuguese of all classes. In colonial times Portuguese immigrants had often been officials with government appointments or people involved at some level in commerce, and after independence many Portuguese continued to look for work in retail business in Brazil. During the period 1844–48 there were frequent riots and demonstrations against Portuguese immigrants, who seemed to some Brazilians to dominate the retail trade; the Portuguese in Brazil preferred to employ their own countrymen rather than, as Gilberto Freyre put it, local youths who were 'accustomed to idleness and the easy life of the "white" or those wealthy enough to pass for white in a slave owning land'.[25]

In 1851, under pressure from Britain, the legal importation of slaves into Brazil ceased and the Brazilian authorities began actively to promote immigration from Europe, 'contributing to the spread of the idea of Brazil as a land of easy wealth, an idea that had ancient roots in the popular imagination'.[26] The nature of Portuguese migration to Brazil now underwent a marked change. Between 1850 and 1870 215,000 European immigrants arrived, probably at least half coming from metropolitan Portugal or the islands. Numbers, as usual, are very difficult to establish as at least 20 per cent of all migrants moved without passports and escaped being recorded officially, while the rates of return migration were also certainly high.[27]

Many Portuguese, often young boys, were recruited as contract labourers to work on coffee plantations. According to Caroline Brettell, 'those who went to the Brazilian *fazendas* (plantations) were badly fed, treated like slaves and punished like dogs'.[28] Many of these boys were sent abroad by their families to avoid conscription into the army and with the expectation that they would send home the wages they earned to supplement family income. The flow of remittances came to assume great importance for the families left behind, but for this to continue the illusion that the emigrant would one day return to rejoin the family was essential and had to be maintained at all costs. Although in parts of Germany, the authorities at this time banned the departure of men to Brazil under binding contracts, the Portuguese government did not stop the contracting of children and limited itself to trying to ensure that contracts of employment contained acceptable working conditions. Whenever the Portuguese government tightened the regulations covering contracts or the issue of passports, there was a corresponding rise in clandestine emigration.[29]

How was this new wave of mass migration organised? Those who travelled legally paid for passports and for their sea passage to Brazil and moved within already established networks of relations and friends. However, contractors were also at work. As early as the 1830s recruiting companies and individual *engajadores* (labour recruiters) were operating in the Azores. Recruiters specifically sought Portuguese from northern Portugal or the islands because, as the Portuguese Consul in Pernambuco explained in a letter written in 1856, with Portuguese immigrants there was 'similarity of language, religion and customs, and the natives of Minho and the Azores islands are the most suitable for rural work'.[30] These *engajadores* would often control where the emigrants went by drawing up contracts binding them to specific employers. Such contracts were particularly dubious in the case of those travelling without passports and without funds. The *engajador*, often in league with the ships' captains, many of whom were French or British, would advance the cost of the fare to Brazil. On arrival the contracted labourer would be detained on board ship until specific employers had been contacted to whom the immigrant was then delivered. The employer would pay off the *engajador* and the ship's captain (often to the tune of many times the actual cost of the passage) and the immigrant would then be bound to work off the debt, which might take many months if not years. There were cases of newly arrived immigrants being advertised in the newspapers and even being auctioned off just as slaves had been in the not too distant past.[31]

Such exploitation was made easier by the fact that immigrants were often only children of eight to fourteen years old. Minors were supposed, by law, to have guardians and only to travel with the written permission of the parents, but frequently the *engajador* was designated as guardian. For the *fazendeiros*, engaging minors was cheaper than buying slaves. Children earned little and there was no initial expenditure of capital to obtain them. Towards the end of the slave trade the cost of a slave had been around 1,500–2,000 milreis, but the payment that had to be made for the sea passage of an immigrant was only 120 milreis.[32] As the Portuguese Consul General pointed out in 1872, the Portuguese who worked on the *fazendas* were often not able to pay off the debts they owed to the ships' captains and the labour contractors and were forced to renew their contracts after three years.[33] 'Free' labour was now proven to be much cheaper than slavery!

It is one of the great ironies of history that at the very time that these poor migrants from Portugal were facing the virtual slavery of contract labour in Brazil, the Portuguese were imposing the same conditions on Africans they contracted to work on the cocoa plantations of São Tomé, a system which the international community denounced as a continuation of slavery.

The Portuguese government wished to control emigration as there were fears that the supply of labour in Portugal itself would dry up and that young men would evade their military service. However, the refusal to issue a passport was the only means of control available to the government and this was easily avoided. Clandestine migrants could travel to Spain and leave from a Spanish port, those interested in engaging contract labour having few qualms about whether the migrant had a passport of not.[34] The Portuguese government, torn as always between the desire to stop illegal emigration and protect its citizens and the concern to safeguard the lucrative flow of remittances, tried to legislate to prevent faulty contracts and to make sure that migrants signed up to acceptable working conditions. However, these measures were largely ineffectual since, in any dispute, the Brazilian authorities almost always supported the employers, while juries in Portugal seldom convicted any *engajadores* who were prosecuted. In Brazil the Associação Central de Colonização was established as an official agency to handle immigration but it acted largely outside the law, often contracting workers to non-existent enterprises and then holding them imprisoned on the island of Bom Jesus off Recife to be sold off to the highest bidder.[35]

Portuguese immigrants would often come to Brazil to join relatives or friends but, until 1888, the continued existence of slavery and an internal slave trade acted as a disincentive to non-Portuguese migrants to come to Brazil. As George Reid Andrews put it:

until the slave labor force *was* replaced, and free European workers no longer had to compete against coerced Africans and Afro-Brazilians, the immigrants were not inclined to come to Brazil, especially when they had the more attractive options of going to the United States or Argentina ... their fear was that employers who made slaves of black folks would make slaves of white folks too. And such fears were amply supported by widely publicized consular reports from European officials in São Paulo, who described working conditions for immigrants on São Paulo plantations as little better than slavery.[36]

By the 1870s it was becoming increasingly uncertain that slavery in Brazil would continue much longer and the Brazilian authorities began to take further measures to encourage the immigration of free labour to replace the slaves. As the Portuguese Consul General in Rio explained in 1871, 'it is a fact that the *fazendeiros* try by every means to obtain white people for their *fazendas*, in order, as they say, to defend themselves against any aggression by the slaves and to get them used to substituting for them'.[37] That year for the first time provincial funds in São Paulo had been set aside to subsidise European immigration, and in 1884 a Society for the Promotion of Immigration was set up in the province. Many, possibly most, of the migrants came on assisted passages, as part of a deliberate policy by Brazilian provincial and state authorities to flood the labour market with cheap labour. 'Supply and demand would now replace the violence and coercion of slavery as a means of organizing production.'[38]

After the emancipation of Brazilian slaves in 1888, their replacement by European workers was achieved rapidly and decisively. In the decade after emancipation (1890–99) 1.2 million immigrants arrived, more than half of these Italians who concentrated in the provinces south of Rio de Janeiro, while Portuguese immigrants continued to go to the long-established destinations in Rio itself and to the north. The authorities encouraged the immigration of Italian families, which added an element of stability to the labour force as well as providing a pool of even cheaper 'family' labour. Portuguese immigrants by contrast were still usually single males following the long-established pattern of migration from Portugal and the islands.[39]

The nature of Portuguese emigration to Brazil in the nineteenth and twentieth centuries

For Portuguese who planned to emigrate, Brazil was overwhelmingly the most popular destination. Between 1855 and 1960 80 per cent of

all official migrants from Portugal went to Brazil, and this figure rose
to 93 per cent during the two decades 1891–1911.[40] Only in the 1960s
did European destinations, and especially France, come to be preferred
to Brazil. Between 1872 and 1972 Brazil received a total of 5,350,889
immigrants. Of these 1,662,180 were from Portugal—a yearly average
of 16,622. However, the bulk of this emigration (62.3 per cent) took
place between 1890 and 1930. The figures are as follows:

Table 3: Portuguese Emigration to Brazil, 1872–1972

	1872–79	55,027
	1880–89	104,690
	1890–99	219,353
	1900–09	195,586
	1910–19	318,481
	1920–29	301,915
	1930–39	102,743
	1940–49	45,604
	1950–59	241,579
	1960–69	74,129
Total	1872–1972	1,662,180

Source: Merrick and Graham, *Population and Economic Development to
Brazil 1800 to the Present*, 91.

Most Portuguese who came to Brazil in the nineteenth century
headed for the capital. The 1890 census showed that 24 per cent of the
population of Rio were Portuguese.[41] 'Rio de Janeiro (both province
and city) recorded the highest relative concentration of foreign immigrants in the 1872 census, reflecting the traditional regional focus of
earlier Portuguese immigration',[42] and as late as 1920 it is estimated
that 39.8 per cent of all registered Portuguese immigrants lived in
Rio.[43] São Paulo also attracted Portuguese immigrants who constituted
11 per cent of the city's population in 1920.

Portuguese migration to Brazil had some well-marked characteristics. Throughout the nineteenth century most of the migrants were
young, single males. In the years 1835–60 60 per cent of migrants from
Alto Minho were under 20 years (48 per cent under 18), while 97 per
cent of Portuguese entering Rio between 1827 and 1829 were under
30 (50 per cent 15–19 years old).[44] Large numbers of children under
14 arrived and soon disappeared into the 'easy life of the vagabond,
filling the prisons and occupying the benches of the guilty in the law

courts'. Those who found their way into the interior were employed on the *fazendas* where they were 'subjected to hard labour which not all of them could endure'.[45] Even when an immigrant was married he seldom brought his wife with him.

In 1872 the Chamber of Deputies in Portugal arranged for the Portuguese consuls in Brazil to be sent a questionnaire covering a wide range of issues linked to emigration. Figures based on the replies recorded 49,610 migrants entering the port of Rio between 1861 and 1872. Of these, 35,740 were men, 22,500 of whom were single. Only 4,280 were women, of whom a mere 920 came with a family.[46] Most of the immigrants were illiterate. In Amazonas 98 per cent of immigrants were men, 75 per cent were minors and 87 per cent were said to be without any profession. Not more than half a dozen family units were recorded. Such figures suggest something of the dire conditions in Portugal and the islands which the emigrants were leaving behind.

In spite of the fears expressed by Portuguese consular officials that Portuguese migrants were being treated like slaves on the plantations, most Portuguese did not work in the agricultural sector. Of those who came with passports, most were looking to work in the commercial sector as *caixeiros*—employees in small family businesses—and Portuguese presence in the retail sector of the economy in the major cities remained a factor of Brazilian life which was greatly resented. A survey carried out in 1856–57 revealed that Portuguese controlled 35 per cent of all commercial establishments in Brazil.[47] The immigrants from the Azores, however, unlike their compatriots from mainland Portugal, did not go into commerce but established a tradition of working in horticulture and market gardening.[48]

Another distinguishing feature of Portuguese immigration was the high incidence of return migration. Portuguese emigrants traditionally clung to a firm belief that they would one day return to Portugal having made their fortunes, and the figure of the *Brasileiro* who returned rich to his native village was familiar in the writing of the period.[49] However, estimates of the numbers of those who actually did return vary greatly. The consuls who replied to the questionnaire in 1872 thought that very few ever returned to Portugal—the Rio consul estimating that around 400 returned annually 'because of illness or destitution'. On the other hand some estimates suggest that between 1864 and 1872 around 30–40 per cent of emigrants returned; and figures for the years 1913–14 record 55,697 returning and 88,739 leaving.[50] If such figures are anywhere near accurate, they radically alter the whole significance of migration—both its effects on Brazil and on Portugal itself. However, here as elsewhere in the story of Portuguese migration, figures quoted can differ widely and do not appear to be obtained using any consistent methodology.

The replies to the 1872 questionnaire show that urban employment ranged from being a cashier or bookkeeper to more humble artisan employment. Though some immigrants came with the tools of their trade, none of them had capital or money to cover more than the most basic expenses, and few of those on contracts ever made any savings. In answer to the question whether immigrants found it easy to find employment, the Rio consul waxed lyrical about the opportunities in Brazil: 'It is a country that is still unpopulated which possesses land among the most fertile in the world, an abundance of water and all the other conditions for the prosperity of the immigrant.'[51] But the consul in Amazonas was more measured in his reply, contrasting the great demand for unskilled agricultural and domestic labour with the scanty opportunities for artisans and skilled workers.

Immigrants suffered from severe health problems, particularly from fevers. In the coastal cities there was some charitable support but, as the Amazonas consul pointed out, 'in the interior there is nothing in the way of charitable institutions'.[52] In Ferreira do Castro's novel *Emigrantes*, the aspiring emigrant, Manuel da Bouça, expresses his fears to the agent arranging the passage:

'I always have fears about some fever...'

'What fever, man, what a story! This was formerly. Today the guarantees of health are so firm that the man who does *not* remain sound and healthy does not walk the earth.'[53]

To the question whether contract labourers were subject to corporal punishment (it is revealing that such a question was asked at all), the Amazonas consul stated that only the punishments set out in the Brazilian penal code could be administered, but that in the case of minors, as in Portugal, 'the tradition of *palmatoadas*, and sometimes of whippings with cords continues here in force in serious cases'.[54] The use of the *palmatoria* in the Portuguese African colonies was seen by many critics as one of the crimes of the colonial regime, though it seems it was a regular part of the experience of the Portuguese emigrant in Brazil.

Why were Portuguese immigrants preferred to those of other nations in Brazil, was the final question. They are preferred, said the Rio consul, echoing views commonly expressed, because they had 'identical language, religious beliefs and customs and principally because of their sobriety and love of work'.[55]

The profile of the Portuguese immigrant community in Brazil changed slowly in the course of the twentieth century. The large majority continued to be men coming from a rural background who married as far as possible with other Portuguese. Illegitimacy rates were high in the Portuguese community compared with other national groups, possibly as a result of the high proportion who settled in the cities.[56] Second- and third-generation Portuguese became more integrated, marrying more often outside their national group and gradually moving from being agricultural labourers to owning their own small coffee *fazendas*. According to Herbert Klein, a striking feature of Portuguese immigrant society in Brazil was its institutional life.

The Portuguese were the first to establish a host of voluntary institutions, going all the way from basic mutual aid societies for workers to hospitals, literary societies and libraries for the middle and upper class emigrants ... a very strong sense of community identity guaranteed that these institutions would be both among the earliest and the longest lasting voluntary institutions in modern Brazilian history.[57]

In his study of Portuguese emigration, Joel Serrão pointed out that one of the consequences of the continued emigration of so many Portuguese, even after Brazil had became independent, was the continued economic interdependence of the two countries. The Portuguese established a kind of dominance in Brazil's retail commerce, partly through the preference of Portuguese immigrants for imported Portuguese goods. This dominance was still apparent in the 1930s, while, as a result of Portuguese immigration, 'huge sums drained away to the former metropole either carried in the baggage of those emigrants who were returning as rich men or in the remittances sent to the families who had remained at home'.[58] Either way, Portugal and Brazil were locked in an economic embrace from which it was difficult to escape.

In the 1930s Portuguese emigration to Brazil declined drastically, not to recover until after the Second World War. In December 1930 the Brazilian government published Decree 19,482 banning immigration on the grounds that it had 'taken into consideration the situation of unemployment in which a large number of workers found themselves in the urban areas and that one of the causes of this situation was the uncontrolled influx of foreigners'.[59] In 1945 a quota system was introduced and the lid was lifted on further immigration only in 1946.

Conclusion

Brazil occupies exactly half the continent of South America; its population constitutes three-quarters of those who use Portuguese as their official language, and probably half of all those in the world who recognise a Portuguese origin or identity. From the seventeenth century onwards emigration to Brazil dominated the thoughts of those in Portugal and the islands who planned to emigrate. Brazil was the land of riches and opportunities, the land from which wealthy migrants returned to build ostentatious houses in Portugal and to luxuriate in their newly acquired social status. Brazil was the land to which you emigrated to make your fortune and from which you hoped to return. It was this that bound the Portuguese migrants so strongly to their mother country and strengthened the complex networks of kinship between motherland and former colony.

In the twenty-first century Brazil is a burgeoning world power, the fifth largest country in the world with an expanding economy buoyed up with oil wealth and vast territorial resources, but it is very largely the creation of the Portuguese diaspora, the planters, merchants, cattle ranchers, miners and frontiersmen who brought millions of slaves from Africa to form the lower strata of a new Lusitanian society and who maintained economic and cultural networks that linked the islands, the west coasts of Africa and the new world in what has been aptly described as the Portuguese South Atlantic.

7

PORTUGUESE EMIGRATION
IN THE TWENTIETH CENTURY

Emigration statistics—a general health warning

From around the middle of the nineteenth century until the year 2003 the numbers of people leaving Portugal with passports were fairly systematically counted and a broad pattern can be established. However, if exact figures are sought, the picture starts to go out of focus. Numbers are certainly better than no numbers but statistics about such a sensitive subject as emigration are more problematic than might at first appear. Why are emigrants so difficult to count?[1]

The first problem is that, although fairly exact figures can be calculated of those who left the country with passports, the number who left illegally, without passports, can only be guessed at, although all commentators agree that this number has always been large. Godinho, for example, thought that in the nineteenth century clandestine departures constituted a third to add to the total; that in the 1960s the proportion rose to over 60 per cent; and that overall the total number of those who emigrated illegally from Portugal should be estimated at between a quarter and a third of the number of legal emigrants.[2] Joel Serrão in his classic study of Portuguese emigration also added a third to the known total of emigrants for the whole of the period from 1855 to 1973.[3] However, when statistics are quoted by a writer it is not always clear if the figures refer to illegal as well as legal emigrants. The statis-

129

tical clarity becomes even more blurred when annual flows are calculated. For example, in 1963 the Portuguese government decided to issue passports retrospectively to certain categories of illegal emigrant. Once these passports had been issued, illegal emigrants from previous years began to appear in the annual statistics of legal emigrants, but for the year in which the passport was issued, not for the year they left the country.[4]

The second problem is that there are no exact statistics for those who returned to their homeland, although it has always been understood that one motive behind Portuguese emigration has been to return home rich and to establish a superior social position in the village from which you left. Some emigrants always returned—but how many? Estimates differ considerably.

A third problem arises when trying to account for seasonal or repeat migrations. Some emigrants left Portugal and returned many times over—a pattern of migration particularly common among those who left the Algarve to work in Spain or in Argentina. Are such migrants counted each time they leave?

A fourth problem arises if attempts are made to count the number of Portuguese entering a host country, statistics which are often used to cross-check the numbers recorded as leaving Portugal. The results can be dramatically different. In 1981, while the Portuguese Ministry of Foreign Affairs recorded 50 emigrants leaving for Switzerland, the Swiss recorded 3,200 as entering.[5] Another set of statistics, popular in some quarters and frequently quoted, purport to give the numbers of Portuguese resident in a country at any one time. Here it is not always clear what is being counted. Is it first-generation arrivals, or first-generation plus their children born since their arrival, or is some other estimate being made—for example some count of people who claim to have, or who are considered by census takers to have, a Portuguese ethnic identity? This confusion can lead to wildly different estimates of the numbers of Portuguese living outside Portugal. The General Directorate of Consular Affairs and Portuguese Communities records a total of 5,302 emigrating to Switzerland in the years 1966–90, but in 1997 the same ministry recorded 155,104 Portuguese living in Switzerland. Another example is provided by José Carlos Pina de Almeida and David Corkill who pointed out in an article published in 2010 that, 'estimates of the total number of Portuguese living in the UK range from 80,000 to 700,000 depending on the source consulted'.[6]

Such different conclusions about numbers are partly due to the advantage that some people see in inflating the figures, for instance expatriate communities seeking to enhance their influence or the Portuguese government itself using expatriate numbers as a form of leverage in international relations.

A fifth problem concerns the areas that are included in the counts and exactly which groups should be considered to be 'Portuguese'. It is not always clear if statistics for emigration refer to mainland Portugal alone, or to Portugal and the Atlantic Islands, while the status of the Portuguese overseas territories in Africa is also obscure. The Cape Verde Islands, for example, experienced large-scale emigration. Until 1975 they were an integral part of Portugal, but thereafter they were an independent country. In estimated totals of Portuguese emigrants are Cape Verdeans being counted? And what of emigration from Portugal to the African colonies in the years before 1975? The African colonies were deemed to be part of Portugal, but emigrants to the colonies were sometimes included in the emigration statistics. And after independence when many Portuguese resident in Africa left for South Africa or Australia, it is not clear whether their numbers are being counted. And what about Goa? Until 1961 Goans were Portuguese and, although Goa was incorporated into India in that year, Goans born before 1961 have recently been offered Portuguese citizenship. Finally, as previous chapters have shown, at different periods in the past all sorts of people who have never been resident in Portugal have been called, or have called themselves, 'Portuguese'. How are they to be counted?

A sixth point to note is that statistics on emigration from Portugal do not count Portuguese who move from one migration destination to another—for instance Portuguese who emigrate to France and then move from there to Canada. However, countries that record Portuguese immigrants may include such people. This probably accounts for some of the discrepancy between statistics gathered in Portugal and those gathered in the host countries.

Finally a general health warning is needed when statistics are brought into play. The fact that a large number of writers agree to use the same statistics is no guarantee of the soundness of these figures. As Philip Curtin long ago demonstrated, when discussing the numbers of slaves exported from Africa, widely accepted figures can merely be the lazy repetition of numbers that were never more than general estimates in the first place.[7]

All these caveats have to be born in mind when considering the sta-
tistical pattern of twentieth-century emigration from Portugal.

How many people left Portugal and the islands?

Because of the difficulties outlined above, there is no consensus as to
how many people left Portugal and the islands in the twentieth century—though there is broad agreement about the *pattern* of emigration. Estimates of emigrant numbers range from Cláudia Castelo who
estimates that from 1900 to 1974 3,084,597 emigrated,[8] to Jorge
Carvalho Arroteia who, in another popular book on emigration, estimated 2,270,964 for the mainland and islands.[9] So these samples show
a gap in estimates of three-quarters of a million.

These are large numbers but they need to be seen in the perspective
of emigration from Europe as a whole. A few comparisons will show
that emigration from Portugal was quite small when compared with
the numbers leaving other countries. Between 1900 and 1914 around
380,000 people left Portugal, but 9 million emigrated from Italy.
Between 1830 and 1914 some 5 million Irish emigrated to the United
States alone, from a country with a population not much larger than
that of Portugal, and around 6 million Germans. Even in Brazil, where
Portuguese had all the advantages of language, kinship and historic
cultural networks, Italians outnumbered Portuguese among immigrants in the two decades before the First World War.[10] From the sixteenth century until 1959 annual emigration from Portugal exceeded
3.5 per thousand only during the period 1901–20 (when it was 7.02
per thousand).[11] In spite of the vast literature and often heated debates
on the subject, emigration from Portugal was neither exceptional nor,
in itself, particularly large.

Global figures covering the century, even when accurate, only tell
part of the story. In the case of the Portuguese there was no even flow
of emigrants year on year; rather, historians have detected periods of
maximum emigration and other periods when there may even have
been a reverse flow. Emigration was consistently high from around
1890 to 1921, with a slight falling off during the First World War.
These were years of political turmoil, with the financial crisis of the
1890s followed by the fall of the Monarchy in 1910 and great instability in the Republican regime which followed. During that time emigration peaked in 1912 and 1913 when, according to some counts,

around 150,000 people left Portugal. There was another peak immediately after the war in 1919–20 when over 90,000 left. This was followed by a dramatic fall in emigration between 1921 and 1947, caused first by the United States introducing quotas for immigrants, followed by Brazil which closed its doors as a result of the 1930 world depression. During the 1930s some statisticians suggest there was a net return of people to Portugal; and during the Second World War emigration remained at a standstill. Emigration began again in 1947 and increased rapidly after 1951 when first Canada and then the European Common Market opened their doors to immigrants. The following twenty years were the greatest period of emigration in Portugal's history, when over a million and half people left, mostly for France and Germany, though this was also the period of peak emigration to Venezuela and Canada.

By 1970 the massive emigration of the previous decade had begun to create severe labour shortages in Portugal. The government of Marcelo Caetano tried to address this issue by encouraging Cape Verdeans to come to Portugal to fill the gaps that had opened up in the labour market. To support this policy a special bureau, CATU (Centro de Apoio aos Trabalhadores do Ultramar), was set up to help settle the new arrivals. In the short term this policy had some success. According to official figures 5,539 Cape Verdeans registered with CATU between 1971 and 1973, most of them working in construction and in the quarrying and mining sectors.[12] After the independence of Cape Verde in 1975 this recruitment was discontinued and many Cape Verdeans who had come to Portugal now used this as a springboard for on-migration, particularly to the Netherlands, Switzerland and Italy.[13]

The revolution of 1974 which overthrew the Salazarist dictatorship has rightly been seen as a turning point in modern Portuguese history, and at first sight this is confirmed by emigration statistics. Large-scale emigration that had marked the last years of the Estado Novo appeared suddenly to cease and to be replaced by a net in-migration. However, the revolution in Portugal occurred a year after the 1973 Middle East war which precipitated a sharp downturn in the world economy, and it was this as much as the revolution in Portugal that staunched the flow of emigration. The granting of independence to the former African provinces not only stopped any more migrants heading for Africa but led to a massive influx of *retornados*, Portuguese and Africans who took the opportunity to leave the chaotic world that had resulted from the unplanned Portuguese decolonisation. Not all the

Portuguese settlers returned to Portugal, for many of them preferred the shorter journey to South Africa, and not all the *retornados* were of white Portuguese descent. Portugal suddenly began to experience the unaccustomed impact of immigration.[14]

Since 1976 emigration has fluctuated with new destinations becoming popular, notably Switzerland: by 1985 21.8 per cent of all Portuguese emigrants were going to Switzerland.[15] The total of those who left Portugal between 1981 and 2003 amounted to 467,800, or 20,339 a year, substantial numbers but well below the figures experienced in the 1960s. In 1986 Portugal joined the European Union (EU). The effects of this on emigration were twofold. Free movement within the EU meant that migration in search of work became easier and visas were no longer required. On the other hand Portugal became the recipient of EU development funds. Major modernisation of Portugal's infrastructure began and the Portuguese economy enjoyed a boom, which, if not based on efficiency of production, at least led in the short term to higher wages and more employment. After the end of the Soviet Union in 1991, and still more after the accession of the former eastern European countries to the EU in 2004, Portugal began to experience large-scale immigration. Most of this immigration was from eastern Europe, but there was an influx also of Africans, Cape Verdeans and Brazilians taking advantage of the language premium they possessed to seek jobs in Portugal. From 1993 onwards to 1998 there was a net gain through immigration of 76,403.[16]

After 2003 statistics on emigration ceased to be compiled, but in 2008 the financial crisis in the Eurozone precipitated Portugal into a deep recession, causing once again a rise in emigration. Ironically a return to Africa now gathered momentum as Portuguese took advantage of a common language to seek employment in Angola and Mozambique, which were enjoying boom conditions.

Where did the emigrants come from?

The simple answer to this question is that they came overwhelmingly from the Atlantic islands and from northern Portugal, in particular from the coastal regions from Aveiro to Porto. There was also limited emigration from the Algarve to destinations in Spain and Argentina.

There are a number of factors that explain this distribution. Northern Portugal has never supported a large population, and from medieval times people have moved from a countryside that could not support them to the coastal towns. Permanent emigration from Portugal itself has been the last of a series of steps, beginning with the departure of men to seek seasonal work, followed by prolonged absences at sea or in neighbouring countries. Another reason for the concentration of emigration in the north was the long-established 'tradition of emigration' giving rise to 'chain migration', for few emigrants ever set off entirely into the unknown. Usually the decision to emigrate was made because someone from the same family or neighbourhood had already emigrated and could offer advice and support to newcomers on arrival in the host country.

In the 1950s there began to be some change. France and Germany were relatively close to Portugal and moving there was less of an adventure. As a result emigration was no longer confined to the rural poor but began to be attractive to semi-skilled and professional people from the towns and to people from other regions of Portugal. Escaping military service, for example, was not something that was of concern only to people in the north, while the increasing opportunities available in northern Europe to people with some education again served to spread the attraction of emigration. So, from 1950 onwards a rather larger percentage of emigrants began to come from the central regions of Portugal, from Lisbon and even from the Algarve. However, during the whole history of Portuguese emigration, very few migrants ever came from the Alentejo.

The Atlantic islands had always been the other major source of emigrants and this continued throughout the twentieth century. Over the period 1950 to 1979 12.23 per cent of all emigrants came from the Azores, and in the next decade the percentage rose to around 20 per cent.[17] Almost all these went to the New World, for relatively few islanders ever made the journey to northern Europe.

Where did the emigrants go?

Until the 1960s Brazil was overwhelmingly the most important emigrant destination, but Brazil was replaced by France during the period 1960–74 with a wider variety of destinations thereafter. It is these other, apparently less important, destinations that account for the diversity of the Portuguese diaspora and for the large number of countries that have active diasporic Portuguese populations.

135

In addition to the above, over the period 1943–74 251,446 Portuguese were registered as travelling to the colonies (an average of 7,858 a year), though not all these were permanent emigrants and the numbers include officials and the military on limited tours of duty. This constituted 11.8 per cent of the total number of emigrants during that period.[18]

Table 4: Destinations of Emigrants, 1900–1974

Destination	Number of migrants
Brazil	1,219,426
France	906,666
United States	307,633
Germany	183,931
Argentina, Venezuela	165,451
Canada	101,497
Other	199,993

Source: Castelo, *Passagens para África. O Povoamento de Angola e Moçambique com Naturais da Metrópole (1920–1974)*, 172.

Table 5: Destinations of Emigrants, 1900–1974 (Percentages)

	1900–50	1950–59	1960–69	1970–74
Brazil	71.5	69.5	11.3	0.85
USA	14.2	4.7	10.5	6.6
Other American	–	–	2.7	–
Argentina	2.58	2.5	0.4	–
Venezuela	–	10.3	5.7	–
Canada	–	3.3	7.7	5.9
Germany	–	–	7	18.6
France	–	4.3	50.8	62.4
South Africa	–	1.8	2.4	
Other	11.72	3.6	4.2	2.95

Sources: Engerman and Neves, 'The Bricks of Empire'; Magalhães Godinho, 'L'Emigration Portugaise (XVᵉ-XXᵉ Siècles)'; Castelo, *Passagens para África*.

Once again these broad figures hide some significant detail. Emigration from the Atlantic islands followed a very different pattern from that of mainland Portugal. Throughout the period 1955–74 the main destinations of islanders continued to be the New World, while those from the mainland went, by and large, to Europe.[19] The reasons for this difference are obvious. Emigration to the Americas remained much easier for the islanders as there were large Azorean and Madeiran communities already established there and travel was relatively simple. Moreover the American air base in the Azores inevitably attracted would-be migrants to the US. Travel to mainland Portugal and onward journeying to France or Germany were much more complicated.

Who were the emigrants?

In the nineteenth century emigration had been overwhelmingly a male phenomenon, leading to severe imbalances in the Portuguese population. In the course of the twentieth century this gradually changed. More single women began to be seen among emigrants and more families emigrated as a unit or rejoined men who had already left. The level of education of those who emigrated gradually rose, while the percentage of those who came from a rural agricultural background fell.

During the period 1961–70, which was dominated by emigration to Europe, 40.7 per cent of emigrants were women, and the overwhelming number of emigrants (91 per cent) were under 45 years of age with the age group 25–29 predominant. The numbers of men exceeded the numbers of women in all age groups except 20–24, where women formed 58.3 per cent of the total; and also, surprisingly, in the age groups 55 and upwards. The large number of women who went to take up domestic service before marriage and the liability of men of that age to do military service probably account for the proportions in the 20–24 age group. The predominance of women in the 55 and upwards group reflects the dominance of women in this older age group in the population as whole.[20]

From 1964 onwards the larger proportion was made up of married emigrants, the married rising to 58 per cent in 1965. As the 1960s advanced it became ever more common for whole families to emigrate, or for a wife and children to travel to be reunited with their family. This, of course, was only possible because of the proximity of France and Germany and the comparative ease of travel, which had not been available to earlier generations.

The biggest change in the profile of emigrants, taking the period 1955–88 as a whole, was the sharp rise in numbers of those coming from the secondary economic sector. During the first half of the century the largest group among migrants had been those from rural farming communities, as had been the case in previous centuries, but those in the secondary and tertiary sectors of the economy began to increase in numbers as the European economy opened up opportunities for skilled and semi-skilled workers. By 1988 those coming from a rural agricultural background constituted only 16.86 per cent of those who left the country. There was less change in the profile of emigrants from the islands. A survey of Portuguese immigrants in Toronto in the early 1960s (many from the Azores) found that the average schooling for men was only 3.7 years and for women 2.8 years; 50 per cent had an agricultural background.[21]

Among those embarking for the colonies in Africa a similar trend can be seen. Until 1954 people travelling alone predominated, but after 1955 there was a steady increase in those travelling as families. On the other hand, in every year from 1943 to 1973 a majority of those who embarked for Africa, whether they travelled alone or as a family, were married. For the young unmarried men and women, going to the industrial areas of Europe always proved more appealing than emigration to Africa.[22] The educational level of those emigrating to the colonies reflected the class from which most emigrants came. The figures show a slight rise in the proportion of emigrants who had secondary education, but in general the profile remained one of emigrants with primary education only and a considerable section who were classified as illiterate.[23]

How many returned?

One problem of relying on tables of statistics is the way that these appear to simplify what was often a very complex process. The number of migrants who returned to their homeland is one of the great unknowns of the emigration story.

In the nineteenth century there was a widespread belief that emigrants went abroad to earn enough money to return rich to Portugal. In Alfred Lewis's novel *Home is an Island*, the village schoolmaster tells the hero, 'Of course you will come back. Try as you will, the new land will not be your land; as you live, and perhaps love, away from your village you will for ever see it. Gradually it will acquire a new light; it will become a lovely mirage. You will return to it, if not in the physical sense, in your imagination, again and again.'[24] Some of course did return, in the physical sense, and helped to create the myth of the

Brasileiro, the man who had made his fortune in Brazil. Others returned as paupers, providing a cautionary tale exploited by those opposed to emigration. Such was poor Manuel da Bouça in Ferreira do Castro's novel *Emigrantes*, who returned poor and disillusioned. Exactly how many returned is, however, profoundly uncertain. Oliveira Martins, writing in the 1880s, thought that half of all emigrants returned, however improbable that sounds. This estimate apart, it is likely that, except for the 1930s, returns probably never exceeded 10 per cent.

More difficult to quantify are those who emigrated and returned many times over. Some of the emigrant life stories recorded by Caroline Brettell and Marcelo Borges show that many migrant workers left Portugal for a period, returned, perhaps to marry, and then left again. For them emigration may never have been a single life-changing choice but part of a way of life in which a person had to be highly mobile to find work and to survive.[25]

There are, however, periods when it can be securely stated that there was a very considerable return migration. Joel Serrão thought that nearly 10,000 'indigents' returned from Brazil in the decade 1919–30.[26] Then, in the 1930s when the world economy was suffering from the 1929 economic collapse, there was not only a sharp decline in the numbers of those leaving but some statisticians have detected a still greater number returning. According to one estimate there was a net in-migration of 103,000 between 1931 and 1940,[27] while according to Godinho, during the decade 1939–49, the low tide (*marée basse*) of emigration, 52.8 per cent returned.[28]

The second great period of return migration began in 1974 with the granting of independence to the African colonies and lasted until 1976. In those years there was a net in-migration of 898,000, amounting to nearly 10 per cent of the whole population of Portugal. Net in-migration, of course, is not the same as the total number who return—it is the number who return set off against the number who leave.

What is meant by return? The rise of migration to Europe in the 1960s made possible the seasonal return of emigrants who spent their holidays in Portugal and who retained a house in the community from which they had departed. Again, it is impossible to know how many emigrants maintained this foothold in their homeland and how many eventually retired to Portugal.

Summarising the research on this trend Maria Baganha wrote, 'after ten to fourteen years of working permanently abroad, the objectives that led a significant number of men to leave Portugal, and later to call their families to join them, apparently were attained'. As numbers of emigrants had risen sharply in the 1960s, it is only to be expected that numbers of returnees would begin to increase equally sharply by the 1980s. This, indeed, is what happened. From 7,000 a year in the 1960s, numbers of returnees rose to 13,000 in the 1970s and to 52,000 in the 1980s. After this numbers began to decline, reflecting the decline in numbers of those who had originally left in the late 1970s. Of the returnees 90 per cent returned either to work on the land or to settle in the communities from which they had departed.[29] 'For the majority of these returning migrants, emigration was a success story. A house, major appliances, a car, a small trade or restaurant, the opportunity for wives to stop working ... and a varying, but frequently reasonable, level of savings all guaranteed upward mobility.'[30]

What is clear is that for very many Portuguese emigrants, especially those going to Europe, the separation was never final and complete. They remained citizens of Portugal but living and working in another country for most of the year.

Emigration—the economic debate

Emigration loomed so large in the consciousness of the Portuguese that it was always a central issue in political debate. As with many political issues, the opposing sides were so finely balanced in their arguments that political paralysis was often the result.

Maria Baganha explains how this balance worked out in practice.

Between 1860 and 1930 the Portuguese political elites increasingly pursued an imperialistic/colonial orientation which, associated with the labor intensive character of the Portuguese economy, could have been expected to have resulted in a policy of no-exit. Such did not happen because during that same period demographic growth and economic backwardness made a substantial part of the population redundant; the chronic need for foreign currency made it advisable to trade national labor for foreign exchange. Entangled in a colonial vocation and contradictory socio-economic needs, the Portuguese elites opted for an emigratory policy aimed not to stem but rather to select the emigrant element.[31]

Nevertheless there were many who were thoroughly alarmed by the scale of emigration, which certainly reached epidemic proportions at certain periods around 1912–13 and 1919–20 and especially in the

1960s. This emigration was attributed, correctly one might say, to the backwardness of the Portuguese economy, which was neither able to absorb population growth nor even to provide a living for the existing population. Unemployment and extremely low wage levels were built into Portuguese economic life. Economic reform, including land reform, was therefore seen as the only way to resolve Portugal's underdevelopment and at the same time stem the haemorrhage of population.

Ironically, emigration appeared to others to be a cause rather than a consequence of underdevelopment—some employers complained of labour shortages caused by emigration, while others pointed to the extremely low levels of domestic consumption which held back the expansion of the internal market for goods and services, made worse by the large-scale loss of population. Against this it was argued that emigrants sustained the economy through remittances sent to their families in Portugal, remittances that actually had the effect of increasing consumption. As Maria Baganha explains, 'the restrictions on exit [that is, through the granting or withholding of passports] and the dependency on remittances are heads and tails of the same coin.... Restrictions created mechanisms that promoted family dispersion, which in turn insured the flow of remittances.'[32]

The shortage of any accurate statistics makes it very difficult to measure this inflow of money and to balance it against Portugal's chronic payments deficit and fiscal shortfalls. Moreover, as Godinho pointed out, Portugal's economic gains from emigration were not confined to remittances. To these have to be added the profits of successful emigrant businesses that were repatriated and the profits of trade between Portugal and the countries to which emigrants had gone.[33] At the end of the nineteenth century a number of economists believed that remittances and other transfers went a long way towards meeting Portugal's chronic balance of payments deficit. For example, by 1920 earnings through remittances were equal to about one quarter of earnings through exports and amounted to about 5 per cent of GNP. Godinho estimates that in the years 1924–26, the last years of the Republic, transfers covered between 40 and 60 per cent of the payments deficit.[34] Therefore, although at this time remittances never came close to covering the payments gap completely, they were very important in enabling Portugal to sustain its relatively high level of imports.[35]

During the 1930s and the war years remittances declined, but so too did Portugal's balance of payments deficit as the colonial economies started to provide Portugal with the food and raw materials that had previously been imported and to absorb more of Portugal's exports. During the 1950s remittances from the growing white population in the colonies represented 90 per cent of all remittances; but the 1960s saw a massive growth in remittances from Europe as a result of the explosion of emigration during that decade. Remittances rose from 1,868,000 contos in 1960 to 14,343,000 contos in 1970 and 26,452,000 contos in 1973, when they covered 90 per cent of the deficit in trade and represented 10 per cent of GNP.[36] Although colonial remittances ceased after the colonies became independent in 1975, remittances from emigrants in Europe continued at a very high level. In the second half of the 1970s they constituted between 6 and 12 per cent of GNP and amounted to between 20 and 46 per cent of the value of imports.[37]

The wider impact of remittances on the Portuguese economy is equally in dispute. The steady influx of money contributed substantially to inflation, but it may also have had a counter-cyclical effect when the cash continued to arrive during periods of economic downturn. It was sometimes argued that remittances helped to provide capital for investment, but most remittances went directly to the areas from which migrants had come and provided a subsidy to very poor communities that had the effect of allowing the subsistence family economy to survive and helping to keep local wages low.[38] Remittances regularly supplemented the annual income of the recipients by as much as two-thirds, and where this income was not spent on day-to-day survival it was usually spent on building houses, buying consumer goods or setting up small village-based businesses rather than on any form of direct investment.

Out of this dialectic on the profitability of emigration there gradually emerged a political synthesis. What if emigration could be diverted from the Americas to the Portuguese colonies? If only a part of those who left for Brazil or the United States could be settled in Angola or Mozambique, a major transformation of those backward colonies could be effected, the flow of remittances would continue and the expanding production and consumption in Africa would provide the economic stimulus that the Portuguese economy needed. The New State, which replaced the Republic after the military coup of 1926, tried to develop a coherent policy towards emigration along these lines after the Second World War, and during the 1950s and 1960s planned emigration to the colonies had some success.

To manage emigration more generally a Junta da Emigração was created in 1947 'to implement a quota system that defined the maximum number of departures by region and occupation, after taking into account regional labour needs and the structure of the actual population'.[39] The Junta granted passports to those seeking work abroad but refused them to people in certain key occupations. Shortly before the 1974 revolution the government took steps to remove all restrictions on emigration. As Maria Baganha explains, the policy of permitting unrestricted emigration was

capable of easing [the state's] several needs. It protected the import–export and banking groups by increasing the country's consumption power and increasing foreign exchange supply without putting in danger the country's labor supply or promoting changes that could have endangered the entrenched interests of the landowners' elite.... What in fact both emigration and remittances did was to help postpone economic change.... In sum, the removal of much of the male surplus population and the flow of remittances reduced the pressure on the Portuguese elites to favour policies which might have led to economic development and perhaps to their own displacement from power.[40]

What was the demographic impact of emigration on Portugal?

In the nineteenth and the early part of the twentieth century the vast majority of Portuguese emigrants were men—in the decade 1868–77 as much as 92 per cent, and as late as 1950 still 65 per cent—and their destinations were Brazil, South America or the United States. Some of these were single young men but many were husbands and fathers who left wives and families behind them. When these men departed there was certainly the expectation that they would at some stage return. As already explained, it was quite common for a man to emigrate, to return to Portugal to marry, and then to emigrate a second time, maybe taking his wife or children with him, before finally settling in either Brazil or back in Portugal. Such multiple comings and goings play havoc with numbers. The same persons may be counted over and over again among the statistics of those leaving and returning and they undermine the concept that all those who emigrate do so on a permanent basis. The fact that many people did come and go and live their lives in more than one country and more than one continent shows something of the part which migration played in the minds of the Portuguese. Migration—seasonal, periodic or permanent—was continually there as an option, as a career choice, or simply as a way of living life. Emigration was a means of escaping poverty, avoiding military service, restoring the family finances, finding employment, building a future; but returning to Portugal was likewise an option, a choice that was available if things did not work out, if one wanted to marry or to be reunited with a family. And to emigrate again remained an available option for the future. However, when women emigrated, it was mostly to join family already established overseas; and returning to Portugal was less likely.

The impact of emigration on Portuguese demography is a complex issue. Large-scale male emigration (like losses of men during wars) has a short-term, but very little long-term, impact on population numbers. On the other hand the departure of women or whole families has a much more significant effect. In Portugal this began to be felt once emigration switched from the Americas to Europe. From the 1960s women began to emigrate in much larger numbers (40 per cent of total emigration during the decade 1961–70), and among them were an increasing number of single women looking for work.[41] In the 1960s, therefore, Portugal for the first time experienced a net loss of population. Continental Portugal registered a small increase over the decade of just 0.4 per cent, but there was a significant loss of population in the islands. In that decade every region registered a decline except for Aveiro, Braga, Lisbon, Porto and Setúbal. The decline was due not only to large numbers of emigrants but to a noticeable decline in natural increase, presumably due to the emigration of women and children, for, as already noted, in the 20–24 age group, the key age for having children, the majority of migrants (58.3 per cent) were women.[42] However, the loss of population in the 1960s was more than made up for by the large-scale return of people from Africa in the years 1974–76, which may have added as much as 10 per cent to the population of Portugal.

Over the course of the twentieth century, the population of Portugal as a whole continued to grow (from around 5 million in 1900 to just over 9 million in 1976 and an estimated 10.69 million in 2013). At the same time the population of the rural areas of northern Portugal showed a steady decline, though much of this may have been due not to emigration as such but to the movement from rural areas to the cities, which was a phenomenon familiar in all of Mediterranean Europe.

A society of women

Maria Baganha states in her article 'Portuguese Emigration after World War II' that there is 'an assumption that Portuguese emigration is essentially an international labor flow, which has changed according to the demand for labor in the international market'. Caroline Brettell, however, has argued that migration cannot be understood except in terms of the life choices made by individuals, which are often complex and are seldom as mechanistic as phrases like 'international labour flow' would suggest.

From the middle of the nineteenth century until 1960 the large majority of emigrants were men from the rural areas of northern Portugal and the islands. The consequences of this exodus for Portuguese society and for Portuguese culture were profound. It became quite common for married women to be left to manage the rural smallholdings and to bring up families on their own—with the help, if they were lucky, of remittances from husbands or sons overseas. Even when men did not emigrate to the Americas, they often left the villages to seek work in the towns, to go as seasonal labour to Spain or Morocco or to sail with the White Fleet to the Grand Banks and the Greenland cod fisheries.

Caroline Brettell summarised the impact of this pattern of migration: 'Historically male-biased emigration can ... be linked to such phenomena as delayed marriage for women, permanent spinsterhood, high rates of illegitimacy, uxorilocal residence patterns, female heirship, and unusually lengthy birth intervals.'[43] It was quite common for many Portuguese women to remain unmarried—though this may have been due less to a shortage of men to marry than to the pressure on women not to have families and force the further division of the family farms. In Portugal in the 1860s 21 per cent of women over fifty remained unmarried, and this figure was still around 16 per cent in 1960. In some rural parishes, however, the numbers were much higher. The figures given by Caroline Brettell for the parish of Santa Eulalia in Minho show that 33.9 per cent of women over fifty in the decade 1860–69 were unmarried, with little change in the succeeding hundred years— the figure for 1950–59 being 31.2 per cent.[44]

As a result of the absence of men, women occupied a very prominent place in rural society in northern Portugal, making the important family decisions, bringing up children and managing family property. The downside of this was cultural isolation resulting from the very low level of education available for women and the various laws, particularly during the period of the Estado Novo, which prevented women from occupying positions of responsibility in the wider society. Many studies have emphasised the hardship that male emigration brought to the women left behind, reflected in the titles that Caroline Brettell gave to two of her books, *We Have Already Cried Many Tears* and *Men Who Migrate, Women Who Wait*; but few have expressed it so eloquently as Alfred Lewis. José, the hero of his novel *Home is an Island*, asks his mother if she would rather he stayed in the village. She replies,

No. you must go. Yes, you must go, as all the others before you. You can't fight the sea. The stone houses will soon be empty. Soon our streets will be without people—as soon as the old die. Yes, they will die in sorrow and will lie in our cemetery and the weeds will grow over the graves and the crosses. ... Soon the sea will call in vain, for only the old will be here....[45]

One of Wenona Giles's informants in Canada, however, gave a rather different picture.

Work was shared among women. Now looking on it, I think my mother had a lot more control over her own life without my father around, than after we came here [Canada] and started living with him. And we never felt alone—other women either single or whose husbands were away and had no children, would come over and sleep in our house. So I basically was brought up with a lot of women all around me.[46]

The rapid rise of emigration to France radically changed this situation. Increasingly women were able to migrate to join their husbands and were able to find employment for themselves in France or Germany, even if only in domestic service. Many single women also emigrated to find work and some of them settled down outside Portugal. For many women emigration was undoubtedly a liberating experience, offering for the first time life opportunities that had never been available in Portugal.

The parish and the emigrants

Emigration to western Europe rather than to the Americas brought other changes. Those who emigrated to the Americas, with some few exceptions, tended to lose touch with 'home'. Emigration to France, however, was different. Returning to Portugal was easy and many emigrants continued to maintain close contact with their 'home' village and with family members still resident there. In particular, people would return for prolonged holidays or to be present at the village festivals, usually in honour of the village's patron saint. The doings of emigrants might be recorded in parish newsletters and emigrants would be asked to contribute to fundraising events. It also became common for emigrants to build holiday homes for themselves in their 'home' villages. These houses built by the so-called *Francês* (those who had made money working in France) were often ostentatious and even garish, as had been the houses built by the *Brasileiros* in the previous century. These regular close contacts did not necessarily mean large numbers of emigrants returning on a permanent basis. Rather the contrary, as it became increasingly popular for families with homes in Portugal to remain settled in France of Germany in relatively well-paid jobs.[47] In this way the life of Portuguese communities, close-knit within Portugal itself, might come to include people resident outside Portugal altogether.

Portugal's 'fourth empire': redefining the Portuguese nation

The triumph of the idea of the nation state after the end of the First World War was never complete—even during the 1930s when some nations sought self-sufficiency to insulate themselves from the hazards of the global depression. The European colonial empires, especially those of the French and Portuguese, kept alive, in one form or another, the idea of the multi-ethnic state, even the multi-ethnic nation, existing in different parts of the world; after the end of the Second World War the multi-ethnic state has steadily become the norm in most of the industrialised countries of the world, and especially among the independent states which emerged with the end of colonial rule. In the twenty-first century there are comparatively few countries of the world which can effectively claim that they are inhabited by a single ethnicity. Nor has the pluricontinental state entirely disappeared. France still has fully integrated *départements* in the Caribbean and the Indian Ocean and *territoires* in the Pacific.

Since the end of the Estado Novo and the dissolution of the pluricontinental Portuguese state, in which Angola, Goa, Timor and Macao were all provinces of a greater Portugal, Portugal joined the EU in 1986 and successive governments have sought actively to redefine its position in the world. No longer having overseas provinces, Portugal has sought to embrace the Portuguese diaspora as an extension of the nation—rather provocatively this has sometimes been referred to as the 'fourth Portuguese empire'.[48] In 1976 a law confirmed the right of Portuguese to emigrate and to return to Portugal, and asserted that 'Portuguese citizens who are or who reside abroad enjoy the protection of the state for the exercise of their rights'.[49] In 1980 a Portuguese Communities Council was set up to advise the government on policy relating to emigrants and to promote links between various diasporic communities.[50] In 1985 a government department for overseas Portuguese communities was created and in 1992 provision was made for Portuguese emigrants to have dual nationality, a provision which allows them to vote in Portuguese elections. Following this, a raft of policies was put in place by which Portugal supported its diasporic communities. As Andrea Klimt has expressed it:

Portugal has moved increasingly to incorporate its deterritorialized population into definitions of the nation and it has become increasingly easier for the Portuguese residing abroad—even for long periods of time—to continue thinking of themselves as members of the Portuguese nation. Incorporation of dispersed populations into the national fabric has long been actively encouraged by both state and private institutions in Portugal: Portuguese banks facilitate the transfer of remittances and offer special interest rates to migrants; the Portuguese Catholic Church actively cultivates migrant congregations abroad; the state helps support Portuguese language schools for the children of migrants; and the interests of Portuguese living abroad are officially tended to by state agencies.[51]

The poet Fernando Pessoa is credited with having said, 'My nation is the Portuguese language'. As Robert Moser and António Luciano de Andrade Tosta interpret this: 'Pessoa's words captured the patriotic verve behind much of Portugal's imperial and neo-imperial discourse throughout the twentieth century.'[52] Steps have been taken to promote the study of the Portuguese language and to keep its use alive in the diasporic communities. This programme is administered now by the Instituto Camões and by Portuguese consular offices across the world. It involves very large numbers of teachers of Portuguese who follow their teaching careers in the expatriate communities—in 1977 there were 275 teachers running courses in France alone.[53] Some of these teachers move from country to country following their contracted obligations, like the scholars and churchmen of an early age.

In 1996 the CPLP (Comunidade dos Países de Língua Portuguesa) was established as a Portuguese version of the Francophonie and the (British) Commonwealth—although with the crucial difference that

Brazil rather than Portugal itself is clearly the leader of this post-imperial Lusophone world. The CPLP started out as a loose association of countries which used Portuguese as their official language. It had 'a utopic vision for a transnational community of Lusophone ... countries held together by a common language and colonial past',[54] although it did not at that time include any other country that had a large Portuguese diasporic community. However, there have been requests from Mauritius, Equatorial Guinea and Senegal for associate observer status, and Equatorial Guinea has sought full membership, even though it is officially Spanish speaking. There is a historical dimension to these requests as Senegal is the immediate neighbour of Guinea-Bissau and includes the Casamance region, which was part of Portuguese Guinea until 1886. Equatorial Guinea includes the islands of Bioko (formerly Fernando Po) and Anobom which was a Portuguese possession until 1776 and where a Portuguese creole language is still spoken. The memories of an imperial past, which so many countries have rejected in their search for independence and national identity, are now being revived in a wholly unexpected way.

With the launch of the Lusophony Games in 2006, in imitation of the Commonwealth Games, a number of countries which at one time had close links with Portugal have expressed a wish to take part. These include Morocco, India, Flores (in Indonesia), Ghana and Sri Lanka. The 2014 games are actually being held in Goa. The next move will surely be to allow diasporic Portuguese communities to take part as well and to complete the refashioning of the pluricontinental Portuguese nation.

8

THE PORTUGUESE DIASPORA IN EUROPE

Estrangeirados—*The diaspora of the upper classes*

It is a mistake to think that Portugal and the Portuguese have always looked out into the world and away from their own continent. Portugal's close proximity to Spain by land, and by sea to the maritime countries of northern Europe and the Mediterranean, has meant a regular flow of trade, of shipping and of people—a flow that has always been two-way as northern European crusaders, Italian merchants, ship owners, map makers and sugar growers, German gunners and printers and English merchants and Catholic exiles have all found their way to settle in Portugal.

As Portugal has always been a small and poor country, many ambitious and educated Portuguese have had to make careers for themselves outside their own country—indeed these exiles are in a very real sense an extension of Portugal itself, their exile enabling them to transcend the limitations of their home environment. The Portuguese have a word—*estrangeirado*—for educated Portuguese who live outside Portugal and are influenced by the culture of the countries where they work. Many of the educated and cultured Portuguese living in this often self-imposed exile have been important figures in European history, gathering round them groups of like-minded fellow countrymen, refugees from the poverty, lack of opportunity and narrow outlook of their homeland.

Like other royal dynasties, the Portuguese royal family exported princesses to marry foreign royalty and seal diplomatic alliances. Some of these Portuguese queens achieved fame and influence throughout Europe and were themselves responsible for a small diapsora of courtiers and attendants. Among the most famous of the Portuguese queens were Isabella, sister of Henry the Navigator, who married Philip the Good of Burgundy and was the mother of Charles the Bold; Leonor, daughter of Dom Duarte, who married the Holy Roman Emperor Frederick III and whose betrothal was depicted by Pinturicchio in the cathedral of Siena; another Isabella who became the wife of the Emperor Charles V and mother of Philip II of Spain; and Catherine of Braganza who married Charles II of England and Scotland.

One of the most famous of all *estrangeirados* is the fictional narrator in Thomas More's *Utopia*. In 1516 More presented the world with his fictional conceit—his imaginary land of Utopia, the Good Land and the Land of Nowhere. Utopia is described by a Portuguese navigator, called Raphael Hythloday, who had travelled with Amerigo Vespucci and had stayed behind to visit and then live in this newly discovered land where society was ordered according to rational principles. More had chosen a Portuguese to be his mouthpiece because the Portuguese were the greatest explorers of the day and accounts of their exploits were already circulating in humanist circles. Valentim Fernandes, the German printer resident in Lisbon, for example, was assembling a collection of accounts of Portuguese voyages which he was sending to his correspondent Konrad Peutinger, a friend of the Emperor Maximilian and a leading diplomat, who was also an antiquarian and humanist in his own right. By 1516 the Portuguese had already sailed to India, Indonesia and China as well as to North and South America, and from their voyages they were bringing back tales of new worlds and hitherto unknown civilisations.

There is little biographical detail about Hythloday that identifies him as typically Portuguese, but the idea that beyond Europe there were societies that operated according to different rules was already present in Portuguese narratives. The long letter written to the king of Portugal giving news of the landfall made by Cabral in Brazil in 1500 had described the Indians encountered by the Portuguese as peaceful and trusting; their absence of clothing, their lack of 'shame' and the innocence with which their naked women displayed themselves to the Portuguese were a representation of another social order, an order without the European's obsessions with guilt and shame. In their descriptions of the societies revealed by their explorations, the Portuguese were to build contrasts with their own world and to shape a social and political discourse in which alternatives to the corruption and cruelty of their own world were shown to be possible. It was to be a discourse that was to constitute a central theme of the European Enlightenment. In this way the Portuguese diaspora, beginning with the fictional Raphael Hythloday, opened up European society to critical appraisal and ultimately to revolution.

Perhaps the most famous group of Portuguese exiles of the early sixteenth century were those who gathered in Seville. Their number included the cartographer Jorge Reinel, and it was in this company that Fernão de Magalhães (Magellan), himself a Portuguese exile, found companions for his voyage to the Moluccas, which ended in the first circumnavigation of the globe.

Another group, this time of clerics and scholars, gathered around Diogo de Gouveia, the principal of the Collège de Sainte Barbe, which was part of the University of Paris. A number of notable Portuguese scholars studied there, among them Diogo de Teive, as well as Ignatius Loyola and his companions, one of whom was the Portuguese Simão Rodrigues, prior to the founding of the Society of Jesus.[1]

Damião de Góis was another sixteenth-century *estrangeirado*, who studied in Leuven and Padua, travelled widely in Europe and established a friendship with the leading humanists and reformers in northern Europe, having his likeness drawn by Albrecht Dürer. Góis was one of the first to describe the Lapps of northern Scandinavia and to publish an account of Ethiopia.

Later in the century Portuguese exiles gathered around the pretender Dom António, Prior of Crato, in his exile in France and England. After his death in 1595, this group of Portuguese, unreconciled to the government of Philip of Spain, collected in Paris, among them João de Castro, who became the principal exponent of 'Sebastianism', the idea that the dead king, Dom Sebastião, would one day return to liberate Portugal from the Spanish yoke.

Many of the leading Portuguese writers and scientists of the late sixteenth and seventeenth centuries lived abroad for much of their lives and either produced their work abroad or found in their experience of 'exile' material for their writings. Among these should be numbered the naturalist Garcia de Orta; the historian Diogo do Couto, chronicler of the Estado da Índia; Rodrigo Lopes, physician to Queen Elizabeth and possibly the model for Shakespeare's Shylock; the preacher and theologian António Vieira; Fernão Mendes Pinto and Luís de Camões himself. Later in the seventeenth century the artist Lorenzo de Castro made his career in England painting portraits and seascapes in the Dutch manner.

While the union of the Crowns of Castile and Portugal was still secure, many Portuguese nobles sought employment in the wider Spanish empire. By way of an example one might mention Francisco de Melo who commanded the Spanish army at the battles of Honnecourt and Rocroi in 1642–43.

In the eighteenth century the diplomat and writer on politics, Dom Luís da Cunha, held posts in London, The Hague, Brussels and Madrid and was Portuguese plenipotentiary at the Treaty of Utrecht, before taking up the post of ambassador in Paris where he remained until his death in 1749. At the same time a group of Portuguese gathered at the court of the Habsburgs in Vienna around the influential figure of Duke Emanuel Silva-Tarouca, who became a close adviser to Empress Maria Theresa. Silva Tarouca's circle included the Portuguese ambassador Sebastião de Carvalho e Melo, later Marquês de Pombal, who married an Austrian noblewoman and brought much of what he had learned of the Austrian Enlightenment back with him to Portugal in 1750.

José Correa da Serra, a distinguished scientist and one of the founders of the Academia das Ciências de Lisboa, having been forced to leave Portugal for political reasons, became a Fellow of the Royal Society in London and a foreign member of the Royal Swedish Academy of Sciences. He lived eleven years in Paris before moving in 1813 to the United States where he became a friend of Jefferson. He was the contemporary of the Abbé Faria, already mentioned, a Goan who lived in France and who is still recognised as one of the most important pioneers of hypnotism and psychoanalysis.

During the Napoleonic Wars a group of Francophile officers led by Gomes Freire de Andrade and the Marquês de Alorna joined Napoleon and served with the Portuguese Legion in the French army in Germany, allegedly bringing back French revolutionary principles to Portugal in 1815.

Hipolito José da Costa Pereira Furtado de Mendonça, the founder of the important periodical *Correio Braziliense*, which was published in London and appeared with 175 numbers between 1808 and 1822, was born in Colónia do Sacramento and, although he was educated at Coimbra University, was imprisoned as a freemason and then spent most of his life in exile in Britain.[2]

During the 1820s large groups of exiles, numbering many thousands, hostile to the absolutist ideas of Dom Miguel, gathered in Britain and France where they organised military expeditions to overthrow the rule of the 'pretender'. One large group of these Portuguese was located in Plymouth, among them the poet and dramatist Almeida Garrett, and it was in Plymouth that his play *Catão* was first performed. When Dom Miguel was finally dethroned and expelled from Portugal in 1834, he formed a court in exile first in Rome, then in Britain and finally in Baden.

Throughout the nineteenth century many Portuguese intellectuals made Paris their home and this tradition continued into the twentieth century. Portugal's Nobel laureate António Egas Moniz trained in Bordeaux and Paris; and its greatest nineteenth-century novelist, Eça de Queiroz, spent most of his working life in consular posts in Britain and France. It was in Germany that the famous Portuguese pianist Vianna da Mota (who had been born on São Tomé island) trained under the leading German musicians of the day. Vitorino Magalhães Godinho, possibly the leading Portuguese historian of the twentieth century, spent most of his working life in Paris and published some of his best work in French. Meanwhile Portugal's most famous twentieth-century poet, Fernando Pessoa, was brought up in South Africa, attending school in Durban and university in Cape Town. In more recent times the distinguished neurobiologist António Damásio has made his career in the United States, while Portugal's leading artist, Paula Rego, left Portugal at the age of fifteen, studied art in London and eventually became naturalised as a British subject.

One should also remember the political figures forced into exile during the Estado Novo, many of whom made careers abroad and, like their liberal predecessors in the 1820s, materially contributed to the eventual overthrow of the dictatorship—men like the poet Jorge de Sena; the journalist António de Figueiredo; the colonial administrator and member of the Cortes, turned hijacker, Henrique Galvão; and Álvaro Cunhal, the long-time leader of the Portuguese Communist Party, who lived in exile from 1960 to 1974.

These are merely examples to illustrate how the elite of Portugal have often formed their own diaspora, either driven abroad as political exiles or voluntarily seeking opportunities and a congenial environment in which to work, outside their homeland. In the lives of these individuals and their associates the Portuguese diaspora has to be seen as an extension of the cultural and political life of Portugal itself. 'In order to be a great poet, you must fall in love and be disappointed; must leave your island and go, perhaps to Africa, yes, or to war; then, after this, you may become a poet'—words placed by the Azorean writer Alfred Lewis in the mouth of the village school teacher, Professor Silva.[3]

Migrations of the povo

As has already been described, seasonal and semi-permanent migration to neighbouring countries had always been a recognised part of the way of life of the ordinary people of Portugal as well as the elite. Seasonal migration to find work during harvest time from northern Portugal to Galicia and from the Algarve to Andalucia probably extends back to Roman times and was still a feature of the life of rural Portugal in the twentieth century. Marcelo Borges has shown how seasonal migration from the Algarve to Spain, Gibraltar and Morocco was part of the life-cycle of people of the region, providing one possible explanation for the comparatively modest numbers who left the Algarve for destinations across the Atlantic. These seasonal migrations formed what Borges describes as 'distinct geographical migration systems' integrating the economy of this part of Portugal with that of its neighbour.[4]

The city of Seville was one centre of attraction and large numbers of Portuguese of all classes had always been drawn from the Algarve to work in the city and its port of San Lucar de Barrameda. Gibraltar was another destination for Portuguese, especially after it was taken over by the British in 1704 and became an important naval base. Portuguese migrant workers supplied much of the labour force for the Rock, forming a permanent Portuguese settlement in La Línea, the Spanish city located just beyond Gibraltar's border. Although, by the very nature of migrant labour, numbers fluctuated, figures for 1911 show that the Portuguese community in La Línea numbered 900 and in Gibraltar itself 364.[5] A community of Sephardic Jews also settled in Gibraltar in the eighteenth century, whose history has been researched by José Maria Abecassis.[6]

Portuguese workers also sought seasonal employment throughout Anadalucia in harvest time, the British Consul in Jerez in the late nineteenth century reporting the presence of 2,000 Portuguese workers. The worker seeking seasonal employment in Spain did not require a passport—just a simple transit permit. As a result this became a recognised route for clandestine migrants who made use of the port of Gibraltar to leave for distant destinations without a passport. After the Rio Tinto copper mines were taken over by British interests in 1873, they also employed Portuguese workers, often as strike breakers, and many of these became semi-permanent, working for as much as fifteen years in the mines and bringing their families to live with them. Portuguese were also employed in cork cutting, in fishing and fish processing and many also sought employment in the fishing industry in Morocco in the early part of the twentieth century. Marcelo Borges points out that when migrants from the Algarve began to go to Argentina, this also took the form of seasonal labourers looking for employment in the Argentinian harvest, a continuation of the historic migration patterns which had existed for centuries between Andalucia and the Algarve.[7]

An explosion of emigration

For Portuguese of all classes the neighbouring European countries to the north had always presented opportunities for those seeking temporary or long-term employment. However, in the twentieth century this migration reached unprecedented levels, overtaking the long-established movement of emigrants to Brazil and North America.

The first wave of migration across the Pyrenees occurred after the First World War when France was suffering an acute labour shortage. Between 1920 and 1925, 38,047 Portuguese went to France to work and by 1931 there were 49,000 Portuguese living in France.[8] Thereafter numbers of migrants remained small and migration ceased altogether during the Second World War. Between 1950 and 1954 official emigration figures show an average of 760 Portuguese leaving for northern European destinations each year, mostly for France. In 1955, however, there was a big change and in the five years 1955–59 3,918 left for European destinations each year (almost all of these for France). By 1959 France had over taken the US as a destination for emigration and was receiving about the same numbers as Canada. In 1960 6,434

Portuguese left for France, and this was followed during the next decade by a veritable flood of migrants.[9]

According to Francisco Carvalho, between 1961 and 1970 347,419 legal emigrants moved to France (nearly 35,000 a year).[10] The peak year was 1966 with 73,419 departures. At the same time migrants had begun to go in large numbers to Germany. Here figures disagree. According to Carvalho, between 1961 and 1970 65,249 left for Germany; but Maria Baganha gives a figure of 82,886, the peak year being 1969. Bauer *et al.* give 1975 as the peak year for workers and 1973 as the peak for family emigration.[11]

These figures are all for people leaving legally with passports. To these have to be added the very large numbers of clandestine emigrants who were leaving without passports, largely to avoid military service in Africa. Most estimates suggest that the number of emigrants who left secretly for France at least equalled the numbers leaving with passports. Joel Serrão estimated that during the years 1969–73 out of a total of 706,509 migrants who left Portugal, 56 per cent left illegally.[12] According to Baganha the single year 1970 saw a staggering 135,667 legal and illegal emigrants heading for France. These are truly extraordinary figures, the 'torrent of emigrants', as Serrão called it,[13] sweeping past the totals of those leaving for Canada, the United States and Brazil. Portugal was not just suffering a haemorrhage, it was bleeding to death.

It was not too difficult to leave Portugal without a passport, as I discovered returning by train from Portugal through Spain and France in 1964. I had a seat in a compartment full of emigrant workers. When the train stopped at the Portuguese frontier the passengers seated opposite me all got up and removed the seat while one of their number lay down in the space between the seat and floor of the compartment. The seat was then replaced and the passengers resumed their places during the passport inspection. Once safely on our way through Spain, our hidden passenger emerged none the worse for the experience.

This high tide of emigration persisted until the end of the Estado Novo, although by 1974 numbers were already falling. From 1976 onwards emigration to both France and Germany steadily declined. For the five years 1984–88 only 2,800 a year left for France, with as few as 400 in 1987. The figures for Germany were roughly the same at 2,560 per annum. During these years Portuguese also went to Belgium, the Netherlands and Luxembourg, Switzerland, Sweden, the United Kingdom and Spain. One estimate suggests that in 1973 there were 86,200 Portuguese in these countries taken together.[14] In 1986 Portugal joined the European Community and four years later the provisions for unrestricted movement of citizens within Europe came into force. This made it much easier for Portuguese of all classes to travel to Germany, and the numbers of Portuguese living there increased to around 125,000 by 1996.

What story is told by these figures? Following the creation of the EEC in 1957 the northern European economies were booming. The expanding industries of France and Germany needed large quantities of semi-skilled labour and this the Portuguese were ready to supply. Leaving for France and Germany was easy, with or without a passport, and workers felt near to home and were able to return without difficulty for holidays and visits. The incentives to work abroad were many: for men, good jobs with relatively high pay and the escape from military service; for women, the possibility to find employment and achieve a degree of economic independence; for young people, escape from the stifling cultural atmosphere of Portugal into the freer air of the Europe of the 1960s.

However, the experience of Portuguese emigrants in northern Europe depended very much on the attitude of the host country. Whereas the French encouraged family reunification and made it relatively easy for immigrants to settle and acquire French nationality, the opposite was the case in Switzerland and Germany; while the United Kingdom, with its vague and often inconsistent commitment to multiculturalism, fell somewhere between the two.

France Portugaise

For the first ten years of the massive Portuguese emigration to France, the arrival of migrant workers was unregulated and unmanaged. Around Paris informal settlements grew up in which Portuguese lived alongside North African and Spanish immigrants. One estimate suggests that there were 119 such shanty towns, some of them best described as shanty-cities. By the end of the 1960s some half a million Portuguese had settled around Paris in the so-called *bidonvilles*—the corrugated iron slums. Paris had become, in terms of population, the second biggest Portuguese city in Europe. The men sought work in factories and in construction; the women worked in catering and domestic service. People left Portugal to join neighbours or members of their

159

family who had already emigrated, the overwhelming majority coming from the north of Portugal or from Lisbon with hardly anyone coming from the islands or from Portugal south of the Tagus.

The *bidonvilles* beg comparison with the *favelas* of Brazil. Portuguese from the same region in Portugal grouped themselves in the same encampment: the *bidonville* of Conflans-Sainte Honorine, for example, was home to people from Amarante and Villa Real. It was situated at the confluence of the Seine and Oise rivers and was liable to flood. Children on their way to school had to cross a dangerous bridge and a railway line. The *bidonville* of Champigny-sur-Marne, one of the largest, housed 100,000 Portuguese. It originated with men recruited for highway construction who built their own town with the consent of the local mayor. At first living conditions were very poor with no electricity or running water. The river Marne served for washing facilities. Contractors seeking casual labour would come to recruit at the gates of the encampment, paying illegally low wages and working in conjunction with the local labour 'bosses'. The only protection to be had for the workers was the fact that they were living together in the communities where the old village life of Portugal was to some extent recreated.[15] From 1966 onwards the Parisian authorities began to clear the *bidonvilles* against the opposition of the Portuguese residents. Migrant Portuguese were now housed in apartment blocks, inevitably losing something of the communal life of the old encampments.

One striking feature of the emigration to France was the large numbers of women, often young unmarried women, who joined the exodus. Many women either came as part of whole families or married and started their own families in France. By and large the Portuguese in France were there to stay and were able to acquire French citizenship or permanent work permits.

The political and social culture of France accepts migrants who conform to the ideals of the French Republic, and Portuguese have had no difficulty settling there.

Second and third generation French Portuguese have begun to shed their traditional Portuguese identity. According to Maria do Ceu Cunha, who studied the cultural changes experienced by Portuguese in France, the first reaction of emigrants is to cling to a memory of the land they have left and to attach real value to it.

Most immigrant Portuguese had lived in the countryside in a space and time where things changed very little.... The authoritarian regime of Salazar which privileged stability, isolation and autarky, called on each and everyone to obey the old norms and had powerfully contributed to the ossification of the rural environment.

Emigration was the 'first true upheaval they [the rural migrants] had known'. The Portuguese of the next generation, however, are torn between 'two types of expectation—that of their family and their group of origin on the one hand and that of the host society on the other'. They seek to demystify the nostalgia for the 'country of origin'. They question the attempts of Portugal to maintain close relations with the emigrants, for in their eyes Portugal is simply interested in the regular payment of their remittances and welcomes them only for a one-month annual visit.[16]

This analysis, focusing on the different perspectives of different generations, has few surprises. A similar story can be told about most diasporic and emigrant communities for whom the process of emigration is indeed a cultural revolution for the first generation but not for their children and grandchildren.

Luxembourg, Switzerland and Germany—a study in contrasts

During the 1960s Portuguese emigrants sought jobs in Luxembourg, sandwiched between France and Germany, and in 1970 an agreement signed with the Duchy allowed Portuguese families to settle permanently. The 2001 census recorded 58,657 Portuguese nationals in the country. Portuguese in Luxembourg were largely employed in low-paid construction work and in domestic cleaning. In the film *História da Emigração Portuguesa: Primeiros Emigrantes, Episódio 1* made in 2006 by Jacinto Godinho, the Portuguese are described as the 'blacks of Europe'.[17] In 1970 Cape Verde was still part of Portugal, and the provisions applied to Cape Verdeans as well as Portuguese. When Cape Verde became independent, Luxembourg retained close relations with the new country, providing aid and continuing to welcome migrant workers from the islands.

Emigration to Switzerland only gathered momentum after 1980, when the slowing of demand for labour in France had greatly reduced opportunities for emigrants. Over the next thirty years Switzerland continued to admit Portuguese migrant workers until it had the largest community of Portuguese expatriates in Europe after France. By 2013, according to one estimate, there were 230,000 Portuguese in Switzerland—

a 20 per cent increase since 2008. Most Portuguese sought work in French-speaking Switzerland, because the language was easier for them to learn and because some were moving from an initial residence in France. Most came with short nine-month renewable work permits, and only after 36 months could permission be granted for a family to come to join a worker. The experience for most Portuguese was that they were welcome as workers but were not encouraged to settle or to apply for nationality. In this the Swiss behaved very much as the Germans behaved towards their *Gastarbeiter*. Once again, although there were some educated and skilled Portuguese professionals among the migrants, the vast majority came, as Rosita Fibbi wrote, to do 'the least prestigious and hardest jobs'. Following a pattern familiar in other European countries, Portuguese immigrants maintain a very low profile, almost to the extent of invisibility. 'Portuguese citizens are not widely known because as a rule they have stuck to *Gastarbeiter* rules—that is, workers who were invited to Switzerland to work and who then left to return to their original country.' First generation Portuguese have not, in general, sought Swiss nationality, and in this they are similar to the migrants who went to Germany.[18]

Alexandre Afonso, in his study of the Portuguese in Switzerland, found a number of characteristics that marked the Portuguese out from other migrants. The Portuguese, he noted, move 'within a dense network of family and friendship relations that allowed a quick diffusion of information about job opportunities, work and living conditions'.[19] The downside of this was a 'relative isolation of Portuguese immigrants with regard to the host society', with little intermarriage with other groups and very few naturalisations.[20] Moreover the average length of stay was much shorter than that of Spanish or Italian workers, as the Portuguese 'tend to return to their home country after a few years'.[21] In fact, he says, there was a 'specific ideology of return' although it was noticeable that 'most children of Portuguese emigrants do not share the return aspirations of their parents'.[22] Another notable feature was the 'low education levels of Portuguese immigrants'.[23] On a distinctly positive note, the Portuguese experienced little discrimination in the workplace and most Swiss had a 'positive or very positive image of the Portuguese'.[24]

There are distinct similarities between the Portuguese experience in Switzerland and Germany. Like the Swiss, the Germans never encouraged permanent Portuguese settlement. According to Andrea Klimt, the migration to Germany of the so-called 'guest-workers' was tightly controlled by the state and strictly linked to employment. German law during this period carefully regulated migrants' movements: only spouses of migrants and their underage children were allowed to enter the country; residence permits were time limited and linked to employment; and leaving Germany for more than three months meant forfeiting the possibility of reentry. Consequently, the migrants in Germany ... followed jobs, not friends and family.[25]

The Portuguese in Germany were *Gastarbeiter* and the option of becoming German citizens was not open to them. Germany signed a formal agreement with Portugal in 1964, and thereafter recruitment of Portuguese workers was organised by the Bundesanstalt für Arbeitvermittlung und Arbeitsloseversicherung, though it was possible for Portuguese workers to apply directly to German employers. Official recruitment was halted in 1973. In 1974 there were 80,000 Portuguese workers in Germany and a total Portuguese population there of 120,000. A decline followed, so that by 1984 only 40,000 Portuguese worked in Germany, after which there was a gradual increase again to around 55,000 in 1996 when total numbers of workers and their families peaked at 125,000.[26]

After Portugal joined the European Union in 1986, it became increasingly common for Portuguese to be employed on a totally different basis. Portuguese companies would recruit and pay workers and these companies would then work as contractors in Germany. This practice grew up as a way round German regulations respecting equal pay.[27]

Although individual Portuguese often renewed work contracts and lived in Germany for many years, it was not with any expectation of permanence. The Portuguese often experienced the same hostility as the far more numerous Turkish migrant workers. Although they formed organisations to support each other, the emergence of a Portuguese diasporic community in Germany was not possible and there were no specifically Portuguese, as there were Turkish or Yugoslav, neighbourhoods in the cities where they worked. Even second and third generation migrants remained determined at some time to return 'home'.

An incident, recalled for me by a Portuguese who had travelled by train to Germany at the height of the emigration, is illustrative of the way the Portuguese tried to ameliorate the unwelcoming atmosphere in Germany. The carriage was full of Portuguese migrants heading for Germany. During the night my informant fell asleep and did not wake until near the German frontier. She was astonished to see that the

163

Portuguese had all gone and that the carriage was filled with smartly dressed blonde-haired German women. She soon realised that these women were actually her Portuguese companions of the previous evening who had donned blonde wigs and smart German clothes in order to smooth their reception at the frontier and in the labour offices. Apocryphal or not, this story contains its own truth.

Portuguese emigration to the United Kingdom

Almost all published statistics give very small numbers of Portuguese emigrants settling in the United Kingdom. In Baganha's statistics, the United Kingdom does not feature at all; Carlos Teixeira shows numbers heading for Britain between 1966 and 1990 never rising above 783 a year, and from 1980 never even reaching three figures. Carvalho can find only three years between 1961 and 1970 when there was any emigration to the United Kingdom at all, and he estimates the numbers who went as 0.2 per cent of total Portuguese emigration.[28] However, when Olga Barradas undertook her research into the education of the Portuguese community in London, she found that 'in 1981 the Portuguese community in the United Kingdom was believed to number around 30,000 and this had doubled to 60,000 by 1997'. The Portuguese consulate in London, meanwhile, estimated the real number at around 100,000.[29] The 2001 British census came up with a figure of 36,402 Portuguese in the United Kingdom, but Martin Eaton thinks there were at least 85,000 in 2005 and possibly as many as 110,000, while the Portuguese consulate speculated that the real numbers at that time were nearer a quarter of a million.[30] Somehow large numbers of Portuguese had arrived, escaping the watchful eye of the statisticians.

The 'invisibility' of this Portuguese community was not just a matter of their absence from the statistics. As Olga Barradas observed, they 'are referred to in almost no English publications before the 1980s'. She also found that, with regard to school drop-out rates, 'there are no official data on these topics' and she concluded, 'Portuguese children in schools in Britain remain a silent and hidden minority. So far no studies are available recognising the existence of Portuguese children....'[31] Yet there are significant concentrations of Portuguese in the Ladbroke Grove and Stockwell areas of London where there are Portuguese shops, cafes, restaurants and clubs, and there are significant Portuguese communities in Northern Ireland, Norfolk, the Bournemouth conurbation, the Channel Islands and elsewhere.

It seems that from the 1950s there was a clandestine immigration, mostly from Madeira, of Portuguese taking up low-paid work as cleaners and labourers. One of the most significant areas of immigration was the Channel Islands, where unskilled labour was needed in agriculture and the hotel industry. The Jersey authorities recruited immigrant workers directly from Madeira, apparently because it was possible to find workers who already had experience of tourism and catering.[32] At first most workers came with six-month or twelve-month work permits but it is clear that many remained, renewing their permits on a regular basis. In 1975 there were around 2,000 Portuguese on the island and by 2001 this had risen to 5,500, constituting between 6 and 7 per cent of the island's population. The presence of such a large Portuguese community is all the more remarkable as residence in Jersey is considered highly desirable because of its low rates of taxation, and permission to reside in the island is jealously controlled by the authorities.

As with Portuguese communities elsewhere in the United Kingdom, this substantial minority is largely invisible. 'Although the Portuguese are now the second largest migrant community on Jersey ... they are not mentioned in any of the tourist guides, or social, political or historical writings on the Island',[33] and Jaine Beswick has commented, 'Portuguese emigration to the Island is not discussed, if alluded to at all in figures'.[34] This 'invisibility' is largely the result of a trait common in most Portuguese diasporic communities: the desire of the immigrants not to attract the attention of the authorities and to exist below the radar of public consciousness. This is no doubt a cultural trait inherited from a peasant background where evasion of taxes, feudal dues, conscription and the attention of the authorities in general was deep in the DNA of the community. It also relates more directly to the fact that so many migrants did not have 'papers' or were overstaying the terms of their work permits.

Nevertheless the Portuguese community itself, and more recently the Jersey authorities, have tried to make provision for this community.

There is a Portuguese club; a Portuguese travel and employment agency; a Portuguese football team in the Jersey football league; a special service in the main Catholic Church in Portuguese and lessons for confirmation in Portuguese. Moreover, the Jersey government [now] offers information in Portuguese, as does the hospital and the Citizens Advice Bureau ... the after-school club ... was created to allow children with a Portuguese background to be able to take qualifications in the Portuguese language at GCSE level.[35]

To this description can be added the existence of a Portuguese language press and a Portuguese Consul who presides in an avuncular manner over the expatriate community. However, as elsewhere in the Portuguese diaspora, educational achievement is conspicuous by its absence and the island's colleges have struggled to maintain the teaching of Portuguese language at secondary level.

Following Portugal's accession to the European Union, Portuguese workers arrived to fill relatively low-paid and low-status agricultural jobs in East Anglia and Northern Ireland where substantial communities of Portuguese grew up. In 2008 the Portuguese community in Northern Ireland was estimated to be 3,618, mostly to be 'found in small but highly concentrated clusters' in the small market towns of mid-Ulster.[36] The Portuguese had mostly been recruited by agencies in Portugal to work in the food processing industry. Portuguese were also recruited in large numbers to work in food processing in Norfolk, where by 2007 the local authorities estimated there were 8,000 Portuguese working in the Thetford area alone. According to José Carlos Pina Almeida and David Corkill, the term '3P migrants (referring to their predominant activities: picking, plucking and packing) is usually applied to the whole Lusophone group'.[37]

Many of the workers are temporary migrants who have come without bringing their families, and most intend at some stage to return to Portugal. However, conditions typical of the twenty-first century have added new dimensions to this traditional pattern. Among the 'Portuguese' taking advantage of the free movement of labour within the European Union are Cape Verdeans, Brazilians and Portuguese-speaking Africans—an interesting return to the sixteenth- and seventeenth-century custom of people with no direct connection with Portugal assuming a Portuguese identity. It also seems that the menial work of the '3P migrants' is now being shared by Portuguese with good secondary education and even university degrees, so meagre are the opportunities in Portugal itself—worse, apparently, than they ever were in the days of the Salazar dictatorship.[38]

The Portuguese diaspora in multicultural modern cities

The Portuguese established permanently or semi-permanently in London and Paris form part of a vast multicultural population drawn from every part of the world. London has substantial communities from virtually every major ethnic group and nationality. Typically these communities exist at two levels. At one level the educated and professionally qualified seek well-paid jobs in the modern sector of the economy, forming an international elite of high status. These are the modern version of the *estrangeirados* of an earlier century. At the same time there are the immigrants, from the same countries of origin, filling low-paid jobs in industry, agriculture and the service sector, employed as domestics, cleaners, waiters and cafe owners.

The Portuguese community illustrates this tendency perfectly. In London educated and professionally qualified Portuguese are to be found working in the arts as painters, musicians and actors, and in banking, in medicine, in the university sector, as teachers or as players and managers in the world of professional football. Glittering gatherings of these *estrangeirados* assemble at the Portuguese embassy in Belgrave Square on 10 June to celebrate Portugal's national day. To these gatherings the tens of thousands of poorer Portuguese immigrants are not invited. They have their own local *festas* and clubs, but there is little meeting between them and the diaspora of the educated.

Although all emigrant groups face similar problems of cultural and linguistic adaptation, the Portuguese stand out as among the least successful in academic achievement. This lack of educational ambition has already been noted in Jersey. In 2000, Portuguese children in the London Borough of Lambeth were amongst the bottom six ethnic groups in terms of their academic attainments.[39]

In multicultural London the various communities of the Portuguese diaspora have come together again in one city. London has communities of Cape Verdeans, Angolans, Brazilians, Mozambicans, Guineans and Timorese—united by their common official language, and many assuming a Portuguese identity in order to profit by the freedom of movement within the European Union. There is also a Goan community, part of the Asian Portuguese diaspora, the descendants of Portuguese Indians who left Goa when it was taken over by India or who were forced out of East Africa, which had been their first point of settlement, by Idi Amin. There are also Macaonese and Portuguese-speaking Ismailis who left Mozambique in the 1970s.

This modern Lusophone community has been compared to gypsies. Its members are highly mobile, moving from one part of Europe to another in search of work. Almeida and Corkill cite the example of 'Antónia, who is 39 years old, was born in Cape Verde and went to

Portugal with her parents when she was nine. She has family in Luxembourg, Italy and France.' The Portuguese consulate with its Portuguese language programmes is the only way in which this mixture of Portuguese, former Portuguese or Portuguese-speaking communities can be brought together, but this, like the cultural programmes of the Gulbenkian Foundation and the Instituto Camões, is under financial pressure. Portugal, the mother country, the linguistic homeland, the ultimate point of reference for so many people in the world, is perilously small and frail to support such a burden.

9

THE CARIBBEAN, CANADA AND SOUTH AMERICA

Portugal itself faces the Atlantic, and its islands lie part way to the New World. Constantly looking outward onto the sea, it was natural for the islanders, particularly those of the Azores, to see the Americas as a near neighbour and a desirable destination. For centuries the New World had meant only Brazil, but in the nineteenth century many Portuguese emigrants began to go to the Caribbean, to various parts of Spanish America and to the Anglophone US and Canada. Portuguese emigrants settling in English-speaking areas of the New World found a foreign language environment and a racist culture that raised barriers to settlement and integration that they did not find in Spanish America.

The Caribbean

The establishment of Portuguese communities in the Caribbean provides one of history's subtle ironies. The Portuguese had been among Europe's leading slave traders and had been the last European nation finally to abandon the trade in the 1840s. But, just as the flow of black slaves from Africa was at last reduced to a trickle and as first Britain and then France abolished slavery, so poor Portuguese found themselves substituting for the black slaves on Caribbean plantations.

The first emigrants to the Caribbean came from the Azores and were recruited privately to go to Trinidad in 1834—the very year of the abolition of slavery in the British Empire—and they arrived on board the same ships which had been used in the slave trade. The next year emigrants from Madeira were recruited for British Guiana and in the years up to 1846 12,000 arrived in that colony, escaping the famine conditions in their homeland.[1] The earliest emigrants had been recruited as contract labourers, but these contracts were forbidden by the Portuguese authorities in 1836 and subsequent emigrants went on a purely voluntary basis, encouraged by unofficial agents who received bounties on the numbers they recruited. The Madeiran authorities tried to control this outflow but their attempts merely led to a rise in clandestine emigration. In the course of the nineteenth century 86 per cent of all Madeiran emigrants went to the Caribbean and 70 per cent of those to British Guiana, so that by 1889 there were 36,724 settled there.[2] In the 1870s, however, Hawaii replaced Guiana as the preferred destination for Madeirans.[3]

One unusual feature of the emigration from Madeira to Trinidad was the number of religious refugees. Conversions to Protestantism had begun to increase in Madeira as a result of the missionary work of Dr Robert Kalley, and in 1844 a persecution began. This persuaded some hundreds of Protestant Madeirans to emigrate at first to Trinidad, from where many went subsequently to Hawaii, while others moved on to form a colony of Madeirans in Illinois.[4]

Trinidad thus acquired two separate groups of migrants from Madeira, as the Protestants and Roman Catholics formed very distinct communities. In other respects Madeiran emigration followed a familiar pattern. The first emigrants were single males, mostly poor and with little education, referred to by a local newspaper in Trinidad as 'the mere sweepings of the lanes and crossings'.[5] Many workers sent to the sugar plantations died of disease, while others soon departed to the healthier cocoa plantations or to take up urban employment. Unlike the pattern that became familiar in countries like the US, the Portuguese did not remain in a closed community but dispersed through the island, and when Tobago was joined to Trinidad in 1889 some of them settled in that island as well.

By the last decade of the century many of the earlier migrants had been joined by family members. The Madeirans ran small businesses in the island towns—typically so-called 'rum-shops', the profession of *cantineiro* being one that Portuguese found congenial in many countries where they settled. However, they were also to be found in a wide variety of other urban occupations, as shopkeepers, domestic servants, mechanics, seamstresses, petty traders, general labourers as well as clerks, barbers, drivers, overseers and managers.

Jo-Anne Ferreira describes the complexity of Trinidadian society where upper-class people of British origin occupied the highest reaches of the racial pyramid and where

the Portuguese ... are sometimes referred to as 'Trinidad white', implying that they are not fully but partially "white". For many years upper class Euro-Trinidadians did not consider the Portuguese to be "white" because of the stereotypical Mediterranean olive-skinned complexion of many. Centuries of miscegenation have produced Portuguese of a variety of descriptions, ranging from the very fair to the very dark.

Non-whites also

did not consider the Portuguese to be their social superiors and therefore felt no obligation to treat them with any deference or particular regard. Some women, however, willingly fraternised with Portuguese men in a purposeful effort to give their children a "white" father.[6]

Although some people from the islands continued to arrive throughout the twentieth century, the Portuguese became increasingly integrated with other groups. The number of people in the Portuguese community had never been large and, as there was never any concentrated Portuguese settlement, 'now, not even the descendants of these shopkeepers are recognised as "Portuguese" by most outsiders to the community, mainly because of the social and racial assimilation of members of this relatively small group'.[7] The Portuguese were last counted as a separate ethnic group in Trinidad in the 1960 census, when they numbered 2,416. By the twenty-first century a Portuguese identity had often become just a folk-memory, marked if at all by family names or by Portuguese traditions in the local cuisine. Access to the internet, however, and the increasing level of education of many descendants of Portuguese immigrants have led to a revival of interest in the Portuguese heritage and family history of many West Indians which had become almost extinct. It is possible that this rediscovery of family histories may lead to the re-establishment of active links with the wider Portuguese world.[8]

Planters in St Kitts, Antigua and St Vincent also sought to attract immigrant labour once slavery had been abolished. Between 1845 and 1848 some 2,000 Portuguese settled in St Vincent and a further 2,500 in Antigua. The immigrants mostly came from Madeira and at first were paid eight pence a day, 'less than half the first class wage of native labourers',[9] although they received free housing, land for growing food, salt meat and medical attention. There was a frighteningly high death rate—on one plantation 26 out 58 immigrants dying within a year.[10] After serving their initial contracts, the surviving Portuguese immigrants either sought work on other islands or turned to running bars or small shops. However, a description of the Portuguese as essentially small-time shop owners is not the whole story. As encumbered estates were sold up during the course of the century, some of the wealthier Portuguese invested in land and became themselves owners of plantations.

Most of the Madeiran immigrants who arrived in these islands were not indentured labourers as their Indian contemporaries were, and this left them free to move from plantation labour to other occupations, although it also meant they did not have paid return passages to their homeland. Most of them stayed in the islands but, because they were doing work that had, until very recently, been done by black slaves, as in Trinidad, they were not accepted as members of the 'white' community and were treated as a separate ethnic category somewhere between white and black.[11] This, together with the fact that most were Roman Catholic, made their integration into the existing white community a slow process. Neither did they integrate with the black population, and in the second half of the nineteenth century there were outbreaks of violence against the Portuguese by the black population in British Guiana in 1848, 1856 and 1889 and in St Vincent in 1862. This was a consequence of their success in small-scale businesses that was perceived as a form of exploitation of the black working class.

In search of fresh opportunities, and perhaps a more congenial racial environment, many Portuguese made their way from the British islands where they had first arrived to French, Spanish and Dutch Caribbean territories, and in the 1850s, as a codicil to Portugal's role in supplying the world with cheap labour, Cuba brought in 125,000 Chinese labourers using Macao, as a recruitment centre and Portuguese ships to transport the workers.[12]

Bermuda also received a number of Portuguese immigrants. Between 1815 and 1850, as the era of shipbuilding and seafaring came to a close, economic change swept over the island. Slavery was abolished in the 1830s and in 1847 the legislature voted £400 in bounties for those shipping companies that could recruit Portuguese immigrants from the Azores and Madeira to work on the farms, where it was hoped they might introduce a wine industry. The remainder of the nineteenth century saw a steady, though small, drift of Portuguese to Bermuda to work in agriculture, and by the 1870s the growing of onions by Portuguese immigrants had turned into an important export line. By 1900 the Portuguese population in Bermuda numbered 1,017. In 1922 the Immigrant Labour Board again sought to recruit agricultural labourers from the Azores and over 400 islanders arrived during the ensuing two years. In the 1930s additional recruits were obtained to work in the nascent tourist industry.[13] As a result of this continuing immigration, the Portuguese community in Bermuda has maintained its identity better than Portuguese communities in some of the other islands, and in 1997 the Portuguese Ministry of Foreign Affairs recorded distinct Portuguese populations in the Caribbean only in Bermuda, Aruba and the Dutch Antilles.[14]

British Guiana received by far the largest influx of Portuguese from Madeira and their history has been lovingly recorded by Mary Noel Menezes. At first their story followed very much the same trajectory as that of the Madeirans who went to other islands. Initially they were welcomed by the planters who saw in them the potential for a large and hard-working labour force, but within a few years problems had arisen. A large number of the new arrivals died as a result of disease exacerbated by poor living conditions. Two Commissions were actually appointed, in 1839 and 1841, to look into the causes of this mortality. The governor, Henry Light, always ambivalent about the Portuguese, wrote to London that

the Portuguese are very filthy in their habits, averse from medicine; no priest being on the coast to encourage them, they desponded at the first attacks of disease. Eager to gain money while in health, they overworked themselves in spite of the remonstrances of their employers, before they were acclimatised.[15]

As a result, official recruitment was stopped between 1842 and 1846, though by that time emigration from Madeira was self-sustaining and needed no recruitment agents.

A further problem was that many of the Madeirans rapidly left the plantations to which they had been assigned and began to earn their living either as itinerant traders or as shopkeepers. The keeping of food or rum shops was always a family business, which greatly reduced overheads, and in this the Madeirans were assisted by the close connections maintained with communities in Madeira, who supplied the emigrants with agricultural and other produce to stock their shops.

By the 1850s many Portuguese were making good money in retail trade and there were allegations that they were operating a virtual monopoly which excluded black Guianese. 'It is no common praise,' wrote *The Colonist* in 1852, 'to a race who came here scarce ten years ago destitute and penniless, that, in many instances, they are now wealthy merchants.'[16] Immigrants continued to arrive, partly because conditions in Madeira remained very hard but also because the kinship and communal networks drew ever more people to seek opportunities in what was seen as an extension of Madeira on the South American continent.

As the numbers increased and the community became more prosperous, the Madeirans took steps to create an infrastructure of institutions to support their community. First was the building of churches—the church of the Sacred Heart being erected for the Portuguese community in Georgetown in 1860—followed by schools, welfare organisations, musical groups and theatres. The first Portuguese-medium schools were opened in the 1860s and a college in 1890.[17] The Portuguese Benevolent Society was founded in 1875 with the object of providing 'relief to the sick, the elderly, the imprisoned, the unemployed, those unable to work, widows and orphans and to provide funeral and burial expenses'—a nineteenth-century reinvention of the Misericórdia of past centuries.[18] There was also a determined effort to keep the Portuguese language alive and to foster Madeiran culture in all its forms. Priests used the Portuguese language in church and the festivals were those specific to Portugal, including the celebration of 1 December, the day that commemorated Portugal's independence from Spain in 1640. The result of this was that the Madeiran community remained very separate from other communities in Guiana, marrying among themselves and not mixing with the British or with Indians or black Guianese. Some people who had made money returned to Madeira where they were known as *Demeraristas*, and the community in Guiana made a point of retaining close links with their homeland even to the extent of refusing naturalisation and, on occasions, sending petitions to the king of Portugal. As early as 1855 the Portuguese government appointed a consul in Guiana as if in recognition of the continuing Portuguese identity of the immigrants. In 1898 the Madeiran community celebrated in style the five hundredth anniversary of Vasco da Gama's voyage to India, even going so far as to name their newly founded cycling club the Vasco da Gama Club.[19]

Throughout the nineteenth century the Madeirans in Guiana suffered the same discrimination from the race-conscious society of the British Caribbean as those who went to Trinidad. Brian Moore maintained that 'on account of their racial affinity to the dominant white classes, they enjoyed a social importance out of proportion to their numerical position';[20] but they were never accepted as social equals of the British. In the censuses carried out by the British, the Portuguese were placed in a category apart from other Europeans and this has, apparently, persisted in post-independence population counts where the nationality backgrounds of the population are listed as Europe, Portugal, Africa, China and India.[21]

The Portuguese also suffered from the hostility of other ethnic groups, notably the black 'creole' Guianese. Brian Moore attributed this hostility to the commercial success of the Portuguese, which had been achieved largely at the expense of the creoles, who were ruthlessly exploited by the Portuguese store owners. In this, he claims, they were aided and abetted by the British upper classes which, even if they did not mix with the Portuguese socially, saw in them a white middle class which would provide a buffer against the vastly greater numbers of creoles and Indians. On three occasions the hostility of the creoles erupted in rioting and looting of Portuguese shops. The first occasion was in 1848, when the Portuguese had refused to join a strike of plantation workers. The second occasion occurred in 1856, following an anti-Catholic campaign orchestrated by a creole speaker known as the 'Angel Gabriel'. The third occasion in 1889 followed the murder by a Portuguese of his creole mistress.[22]

Towards the end of the century increasing numbers of young Madeirans in search of access to the professions were sent to Roman Catholic schools in Britain, notably Stonyhurst and Mount St Mary, and by 1900 people of Portuguese origin were not only practising in all the professions but had become substantial property owners and had belatedly started to seek election to political office. However, as their status rose, this, paradoxically, seemed to accelerate their disappearance as a distinct ethnic group. In spite of the large numbers of Madeirans who had gone to British Guiana in the nineteenth century, the distinct Portuguese community there shrank in size, partly through people returning to Madeira or moving on to other American destinations and partly through integration in the wider community. According to the information gathered by the Observatório da Emigração, the population in Guiana of Portuguese origin in 2002 was only 1,500.[23]

The story of the Guiana Portuguese, their exclusiveness, their passionate clinging to their Portuguese identity, their creation of institutions to support their community, are all very reminiscent of the Portuguese Sephardic Jews and the community they created in Amsterdam in the seventeenth century.

With the possible exception of Bermuda, by the last quarter of the nineteenth century Portuguese had ceased to emigrate to the Caribbean as labourers, though some family members from Madeira, who were recruited to join established Portuguese businesses, continued to settle in Trinidad as late as 1975. In the twentieth century many descendants of the original Portuguese population moved on from the Caribbean to the US and Britain. Although the Portuguese community had been well organised in the nineteenth century, supporting Portuguese language papers, Portuguese social clubs and churches, Portuguese ethnic identity and links with Portugal and Madeira weakened in the course of the twentieth century. Second and third generation Portuguese moved increasingly into the tertiary sector, aided by the available educational opportunities, and the use of the Portuguese language largely disappeared.

In the history of the Portuguese diaspora it is comparatively rare to find descendants of Portuguese immigrants playing an important role in politics. There are, however, two exceptions to this among the Caribbean Portuguese. Two men, descendants of Portuguese immigrants, have been prominent in Caribbean politics: Albert Gomes who was Trinidad's chief minister on the eve of independence, and Ralph Gonçalves who became prime minister of St Vincent and the Grenadines in 2001.

Argentina

As has been described in an earlier chapter, the period between 1580 and 1640, when the Portuguese and Spanish Crowns were united, saw large numbers of Portuguese settling in and around the major Spanish American cities, especially the settlements on the Río de la Plata. This great river seemed to many people to mark a natural boundary between Portuguese and Spanish America, and in the seventeenth century the Portuguese, eager to secure a share of the commerce with the interior, planted an outpost on the north bank of the river, which became known as Colónia do Sacramento. Portuguese soldiers garrisoned the town and settlers and traders made their way from São Paulo south to the river, in the process gradually occupying the coastal regions which became the province of Rio Grande do Sul. These settlers were not so much immigrants coming direct from Portugal as Portuguese already settled in Brazil who were migrating to find new opportunities on the frontier. Throughout the eighteenth century Colónia do Sacramento was fought over and changed hands many times before Portugal finally abandoned the town in 1776. By this time, however, large numbers of Portuguese were settled throughout the Río de la Plata basin and in 1816, six years after the effective independence of Buenos Aires from Spain, they constituted the second largest immigrant group in the city.[24] The Portuguese at this time formed a wide social spectrum, from wealthy merchants who married into local Spanish families to contraband traders and comparatively humble artisans.

Settlement in Argentina was, therefore, already woven into the tapestry of the Portuguese diaspora when large-scale migration from Portugal to ex-Spanish South America began in the late nineteenth century. This migration, from 1870 onwards, was similar in some respects to the contemporary migration to Brazil, though in Argentina there was no organised recruitment of contract workers for plantation labour. Most immigrants were young males and the employment opportunities they found as cart drivers, porters and day labourers were largely unskilled occupations.[25] As in Brazil the early immigrants usually came with the intention of returning to their families in Portugal, but in time increasing numbers of women and children crossed the Atlantic to join their families and to settle permanently in the New World.

Marcelo Borges estimates that between 1857 and 1959 around 80,000 Portuguese arrived in Argentina (averaging 800 a year)—more than half between 1910 and 1930, which was one of the peak periods for emigration from Portugal. There was a sharp rise in immigration again between 1946 and 1956, the peak year being 1951 when 2,000 Portuguese passports were issued for Argentina.[26] The vast majority of these immigrants came from two regions of Portugal: the Algarve and Guarda regions. This regional origin gave the emigration to Argentina a special character, markedly different, for example, from the emigration to the US or Canada where the principal region of origin was the Azores. By contrast the Atlantic islands only contributed an average of

3.4 per cent of Portuguese migrants to Argentina.[27] Within the areas of Algarve and Guarda there was also a high concentration in certain districts, and Borges has shown that as much as 14 per cent of all immigrants came from the single town and district of Loulé in the Algarve. Outside Buenos Aires there was a close link between places of origin and places of settlement, brought about by the operation of the networks which facilitated the migration—migrants leaving Portugal to join friends, neighbours and kin already settled abroad who could offer accommodation and general assistance to the prospective immigrant. Once again family and neighbourhood connections appear to be as important as the macro-economic conditions in the labour market in determining the patterns of migration.

According to the census of 1914, 80 per cent of the population described as Portuguese lived in the city of Buenos Aires or in the surrounding province, a distribution that had changed little by 1960. The rest were scattered widely in other provincial centres. Outside the capital 40 per cent of Portuguese lived in rural areas or worked in agricultural occupations, where the demand for labour was seasonal and therefore attracted workers looking for seasonal employment.[28] This pattern repeated itself as immigration continued, but over time a larger percentage sought work in the cities. In the rural areas around Buenos Aires the pattern was for the first Portuguese arrivals to be seasonal workers who returned to Portugal in the winter. This made good sense as the southern hemisphere summer, when demand for labour was highest, coincided with the northern hemisphere winter, and men might cross and re-cross the Atlantic two or three times. This strong tradition of seasonal migration was quite different from the patterns of emigration and settlement in North America. Eventually a man's family would join him in Argentina and he would settle permanently. This influx of migrant labour largely ceased after the 1930s and second and third generation Portuguese were less inclined to work as labourers. Many now owned land and had become independent farmers in their own right.[29]

In the western Pampas the Portuguese settled around Salliquelo and Casbas, and most came from the same limited areas of Portugal. The Portuguese who went to Patagonia, however, were not going to settlements that were already well established; they were true pioneers. The city of Comodoro Rivadavia was only founded in 1901 and Portuguese, mainly from the Algarve, were among the first settlers. When oil prospecting took off after 1907, Portuguese enrolled as workers in the oil-fields and became the largest single immigrant group in the region. Again single men predominated among the first arrivals, with family reunification becoming the established pattern after 1940.[30]

Another area where Portuguese immigrants settled in significant numbers was Villa Elisa in the Entre Ríos province. Again the Portuguese immigrants mostly came from the same region of the Algarve and concentrated in the flower growing business. As Borges wrote, 'knowing what to expect and counting on the assistance of kin and *paisanos* [fellow countrymen] gave immigrants who used those channels more possibilities of relative success'.[31] There were fewer failures and less return migration among people who had come from areas which had already provided most immigrants, suggesting that the support networks were in general very effective.

The first Portuguese Mutual Aid Associations had begun to appear around 1916, and in 2006 there were 52 Portuguese associations of one sort or another in Argentina.[32] During the 1970s a number of new ethnic associations were founded: for example the Clube Português de Esteban Echeverria founded in 1978 and the Casa de Portugal Nuestra Señora de Fatima founded in 1981 in Villa Elisa. In general the founding of associations took place a decade or so after immigration ceased and reflected the growing prosperity of the Portuguese immigrants. These associations, it has been claimed, assumed to some extent the role of 'ambassadors of Portugal in the new society'—though their image of Portugal was often far removed from the new realities of the country they had left.[33]

Given the large numbers who had emigrated to Argentina, it is surprising that the Portuguese Ministry of Foreign Affairs estimated in 1997 that there were only 16,000 Portuguese in Argentina—though this may be the number of those who still held Portuguese citizenship. In 2011 there were only 6,490 registered with the Portuguese consulate. These low numbers certainly suggest that there was an effective degree of integration by Portuguese migrants into Argentinian society.

Alongside the Portuguese, some Cape Verdeans also settled in Argentina. Most came as sailors and settled in the port towns of the Río de la Plata. Although Cape Verdeans had their own association in Ensenada as early as 1927, most of the immigration apparently took place in the 1940s and 1950s when the US was effectively closed to Cape Verdean immigration. One estimate suggests that in the first decade of the twenty-first century there were around 4,000 Cape Verdeans, or descendants of Cape Verdeans, in Argentina, but numbers are especially difficult to calculate as many Cape Verdeans have always considered themselves to be Portuguese and their descendants continue to hold on to that identity.[34]

Uruguay

Montevideo, lying opposite Buenos Aires on the Río de la Plata, was part of the same Spanish province until 1810, after which a series of confused wars led to the partial incorporation into Brazil of the Banda Oriental, as the left bank of the river was known. After further conflict, the region, which included the old Portuguese settlement of Colónia do Sacramento, became the independent state of Uruguay in 1828. As a result of the close relations with Brazil there were always a significant number of Portuguese traders, ship owners and artisans working in the country.

Although there was never any mass Portuguese immigration directly to Uruguay, settlers from southern Brazil moved in towards the end of the nineteenth century and two visible Portuguese communities grew up: in the capital and in Salto on the Uruguay River. A study made in 2007 described the Portuguese community in Salto as well-organised and very conscious of itself, though rather distant from Portugal. The Portuguese community in Uruguay is a good example of the use of a 'Portuguese' ethnic identity acting as an aid to community building rather than being a reflection of family ties with Portugal. The focus of the community was the Casa de Portugal, the heir of an old mutual aid association, the Sociedad Portuguesa de Beneficiencia, which had been founded in 1882. The main activities of the Casa were cultural and it had the responsibility of maintaining the Portuguese cemetery, but 'with rare exceptions none of these people [its members] speak Portuguese and only a few keep contact with Portugal'.[35] For many, 'Portugal became progressively a distant reality, although symbolically strong.... It is striking, the degree to which many of these people feel Portuguese even without speaking the language or having ever been to Portugal,' wrote Helena Carreiras. She described how in 2005 it was proposed to name a new school in the Salto region the Escola de Portugal. This involved consultations within the community and with parents, 'data collection on the Portuguese presence in the area, collection of old documents, photos and family stories through interviews'.

The inauguration involved preparing Portuguese food and rehearsing Portuguese dances. The national anthems of Uruguay and Portugal were to be sung and this 'forced the association to search for the music and words of the Portuguese anthem, with no guarantee that someone would be able to sing it'. A collection of books given by Portugal, she concluded, will probably be regarded 'as museum pieces with no practical utility'.[36]

The Casa de Portugal in Montevideo also grew out of earlier mutual aid societies. When surveyed in 2006, 80 per cent of its membership was made up of immigrants or the descendants of immigrants, but there was an interesting 20 per cent of people with other ethnic backgrounds who wanted to assume some kind of Portuguese identity. A description of its activities is probably typical of the activities of such organisations throughout the world:

Among the variety of activities of the Casa de Portugal there is the commemoration of the civic days of Portugal and Uruguay, the organization of Portuguese language courses, feasts, cultural events and conferences, as well as a weekly radio program *Voz Lusitana*. Although broadcast in Spanish, it disseminates news from the community and information and music from Portugal. The frequent visits of renowned Portuguese artists and intellectuals as well as public authorities are accompanied with special pride.... The Casa de Portugal also has an active folkloric group (*rancho*) of some fifty people, formed by Portuguese and youngsters of no Portuguese descent.[37]

In addition the Casa sends delegates to the Encontros das Comunidades Portuguesas e Luso-Descendentes do Cone-Sul (Meeting of the Communities of Portuguese and Descendants of Portuguese in the Southern Cone) founded in 1988.

At the end of the twentieth century it was estimated that there were possibly 10,000 people in Uruguay who could claim a Portuguese origin and 1,100 registered Portuguese. In the seventeenth century there were numerous communities, particularly in Asia, which thought of themselves as in some way 'Portuguese' but which had little connection with Portugal either direct or indirect. In spite of the activities of the Casas de Portugal, being 'Portuguese' in twenty-first-century Uruguay has something of the same flavour about it.

Venezuela

In central Venezuela there is a river called 'Río Portuguesa' which in 1909 gave its name to a separate province. However, it does not appear that this name has anything to do with the settlement of Portuguese immigrants. Tradition merely records that the river was given that name when a Portuguese woman was drowned in it.

Venezuela only became an important destination for Portuguese migrants in the 1950s at a time when emigration to the US was still difficult and Canada had barely started recruiting Portuguese workers. Between 1955 and 1974 75,211 Portuguese immigrants were recorded (an average of 4,000 a year). It was the rapid growth of Venezuela's oil industry that created the opportunities and drew in the migrants. The peak year for migration was 1965, as it was for those going to northern Europe. Venezuela was a destination which particularly attracted Madeirans and 43,992 emigrants (41.1 per cent of the total) came from that island, mostly from Funchal. Aveiro and Porto were the only areas of mainland Portugal which provided a significant number.[38] A number of political exiles also found their way to Venezuela—the most famous of them being Henrique Galvão who settled there after his notorious escape from prison in Lisbon in 1959.

Between 1975 and 1983 the numbers of immigrants remained consistently at around 2,700 a year (giving a total of 24,347), but between 1984 and 1990 immigrants numbered only 232 a year, reducing to just two recorded immigrants in 1989.[39] In 2011 the Observatório da Emigração recorded 80,029 people born in Portugal and 121,939 with Portuguese nationality. The total number of people of Portuguese origin was 268,500.

The Portuguese community, like expatriate Portuguese nationals in many other countries, forms strong communal networks, banding together in a number of cultural, sporting and mutual aid organisations. As Nancy Gomes describes it, 'the Portuguese community in Venezuela is very dynamic which is reflected in the numerous associations. There are more than fifty Portuguese or Luso-Venezuelan associations in Caracas and Valência, two of the largest cities in the country.'[40] However, in spite of this impressive array of organisations, it has proved much easier for Portuguese living in Venezuela to integrate with the native population, with whom they share many cultural similarities and a language which can be easily learned, than it is for Portuguese immigrants in Canada or the US. It is very probable that the second and third generations of Portuguese will lose their distinct Portuguese identity as so many earlier emigrants to Argentina and Uruguay have done.

Canada

The Portuguese have had a long association with Canada. Portuguese navigators, chief among them João Álvares Fagundes, were the first to explore the maritime coast, giving a Portuguese name to Labrador (supposedly named after João Fernandes '*o lavrador*'). Large numbers of Portuguese were active in the Newfoundland cod fishery in the sixteenth century, and in the seventeenth century a few Portuguese individuals, women as well as men, settled in Quebec under French auspices.[41] There was one Portuguese woman who made a dramatic intervention in the history of French Canada. In 1734 a slave woman, Marie Joseph Angélique, born in Madeira but owned by a French family in Montreal, set fire to her owner's house with the consequent destruction of a whole sector of the town. Tried as an arsonist, she was sentenced by the court to have her hand cut off and to be burned alive—a sentence commuted on appeal to torture followed by hanging.[42] It is interesting that this celebrated and much discussed case is not mentioned at all by David Higgs and Grace Anderson in their history of the Portuguese in Canada. However, it is the argument of this book that slaves, especially those born in Portugal, should be seen as part of the Portuguese diaspora and are inseparable from the currents of migration which spread Portuguese settlement around the world.

Unlike the emigration of Portuguese to Brazil or the US, the arrival of significant numbers of Portuguese in Canada only began in the 1950s and was the result of deliberate policy by the host country. In 1952 the Canadian government decided to encourage the immigration of Portuguese, initially because of an acute shortage of farm labour. The first immigrants arrived in 1953, settling in Toronto; then following the Capelinhos eruption in the Azores in 1958, a large number of displaced people left for Canada as well as the US. In 1959 the numbers arriving rose to 4,300 and in the 1960s an average of 6,500 arrived each year. According to Maria Baganha, between 1950 and 1988 138,000 Portuguese settled in Canada—accounting for 6 per cent of total emigration during that period. Numbers peaked in 1974 with 11,650 arrivals.[43] Thereafter there was a notable deceleration. About one third came from continental Portugal and the rest from the Azores, the vast majority from São Miguel, which alone accounted for more migrants than the whole of continental Portugal. According to Jorge Arroteia, many of the immigrants did not come directly from Portugal but were moving on from a previous host country.[44]

In 2006, the Canadians estimated that there were a total of 410,850 persons of Portuguese descent living in Canada, or 1.3 per cent of the nation's total population. Most Portuguese Canadians (69 per cent) were located in Ontario, primarily in Toronto, followed by Quebec with 14 per cent (mostly in Montreal) and British Columbia (8 per cent), with smaller populations in Manitoba and Alberta.[45] In spite of the regular visits of the Portuguese White Fleet to Newfoundland until 1975, there appear to have been very few Portuguese who settled in the Maritime Provinces. What is clear is that the Portuguese community in Canada, in a comparatively short time, had grown to be one of the largest in the world of the Portuguese diaspora.

Research carried out in Toronto in 1989–90 showed that 72 per cent of immigrants were sponsored by family members already settled in Canada.[46] This was the traditional pattern for migration that can be seen to have operated for hundreds of years, but in other respects Portuguese emigration to Canada reflected a major change. It was only in the 1960s that women began to leave Portugal in large numbers, and this is strikingly represented in Canadian immigration figures. Between 1962 and 1982 52 per cent of Portuguese immigrants of working age were women. Moreover, Wenona Giles, in her study of Portuguese women immigrants, concluded that women played a dominant role in the process of emigration, contacting networks of kin and organising the move.[47]

The first Portuguese immigrants who arrived in the 1950s came under contract to work on farms or on the railways. This was low-paid work which many of the immigrants found uncongenial or even impossible. There was a great deal of hardship, especially among those who did not know English, had no pre-existing network to help them and had no resources. Many drifted from one job to another, and this helped to create the stereotype of the unreliable, ignorant Portuguese immigrant.

Those who survived the early hardships gradually coalesced into compatriot communities in the main cities of Montreal, Toronto and Quebec. Here they found a variety of semi-skilled urban jobs, principally in construction, catering and cleaning. In the 1960s increasing numbers of Portuguese women came to reunite families, and with their arrival Portuguese neighbourhoods began to flourish: 'sprucing up houses, planting vegetable gardens in their small front yards, and occasionally setting out a piece of religious statuary'.[48] Carlos Teixeira quotes the description of the Portuguese neighbourhood of Kensington in Toronto by a reporter from the Toronto *Star*:

The Portuguese ... like to paint their houses bright colours, scarlet being the favourite. They will even occasionally paint the mortar between the bricks white. They often grow cabbages and other vegetables in their front yards unless the yard contains a shrine to Our Lady of Fatima, in which case flowers are preferred.... Saints and religious figures were also depicted on *azulejos* [decorative ceramic tiles]... and placed beside the main door of the house. Immigrants brought the *azulejos* representing religious figures ... as well as seeds for flowers and vegetables, directly from Portugal on their frequent trips back home.[49]

Portuguese families sought to buy houses, but to be able to do this in areas where the cost of houses was high required a great degree of cooperation within the Portuguese community, just as people would help their neighbours renovate properties. Edith Ferguson wrote about the importance of home ownership:

Owning a home is tremendously important to the rural immigrant.... In the villages of Italy and Portugal each family had its own home, even though it may have been small, poorly furnished and overcrowded. New immigrants find themselves here with no possessions, nothing but their hands. They bend every effort towards saving for a home, which gives them security, some roots and some status in the community. *Without it they are nobodies.*[50]

To help realise the dream of home ownership, it became common for Portuguese women, and even children, to try to supplement the family income by taking work in jobs that were often low paid and cash-in-hand, or they would accommodate single Portuguese in rented rooms to earn extra money.

As the Portuguese neighbourhoods grew, some Portuguese began to set up businesses to service the community. Prominent among these were the Portuguese 'travel agents' who offered a variety of services: translating, assistance with documents and financial advice, as well as helping to maintain links with Portugal or the Azores and providing assistance for other would-be immigrants. These agents have been described as mediators and, together with parish priests, the leaders of the community. As Caroline Brettell observed, 'ethnicity is partially sustained in urban areas as a good business venture'.[51]

Although some second generation Portuguese moved out of the 'ghetto', the existence of the close-knit, largely self-supporting community, with its cultural life anchored in *festas*, the church and football, had established itself as the norm for the Portuguese community.

The vast majority of Portuguese migrants who came to North America were from very poor, often rural backgrounds and had very low levels of education. They came to take up unskilled work and, at least for the first two generations, tended to live in communities often surrounded by extended family or by neighbours who had come from the same localities in Portugal or the islands. As Fernando Nunes put it in 2003,

compared to Canada's other minorities, the Portuguese–Canadian community ... includes the highest proportion of individuals with only a primary school education (less than eight years), and one of the lowest percentages of those with some form of post-secondary education.... The situation is consistent with the Portuguese being found disproportionately in low-skilled, or unskilled manufacturing, construction and service occupations.[52]

The preoccupations and priorities of these immigrant communities centred on bettering their economic position, which they sought to realise by buying their own homes and establishing small businesses, typically the small, family owned grocery store. Achieving these objectives required the effort of all family members, even children of school age, and it was soon apparent that many children from the Portuguese community were dropping out of school and taking casual work to aid their families. This became a pattern for the whole Portuguese community. The low level of academic achievement and the high drop-out rate remained an issue not only for recently arriving families but for second generation children born in the US or Canada, and gave rise to some concern among educationalists. Reports as late as the 1990s documented

the alarming fact that successive generations of Luso-Canadian children and youth in the Toronto school system dropped out of school earlier—and in greater proportions—than other students, studied and performed at significantly lower academic levels, were found in greater numbers in Remedial Reading and Special Education programs, and lagged behind other students in reading and language skills.[53]

Studies of the Portuguese Canadian community made in the first two decades of mass immigration linked low academic achievement to the preoccupations of Portuguese migrant families and the 'culture' that grew up in their communities. 'There are many requests for work permits for children between the ages of 14 and 16, and because family incomes are low, school authorities find it difficult to refuse.'[54] Another report, dated 1970, concluded:

special problems of transition are faced by a people such as the Portuguese who have moved from a largely rural class background with low educational standards and an authoritarian family, state and church life to an urban milieu speaking not only a new language, but maintaining different educational standards and expressing an often secular life style.[55]

As has already been noted, Portuguese immigrants were poor and hence very dependent on networks of kin and neighbours for survival. The immigrants took low-paid semi-skilled and unskilled work and expected their children to follow in their footsteps and contribute to the stability of the family's economic position. Having a poor education themselves, many adult Portuguese either saw little value in education or were unable to provide a supportive background for their school-age children. Ilda Januário and Manuela Marujo recorded that one of the women they interviewed told them that she would like to learn more English so that she could understand her children when they spoke to her.[56] These characteristics helped to create a stereotype of the immigrant Portuguese, and this fed into the attitudes of teachers towards immigrant children. In this way a cycle of underachievement was established to which the immigrant community, education providers and the attitudes prevalent in the wider community all contributed.

The well-intentioned multicultural policies of the Canadian governments contributed to the growth of 'ghettoes' of Portuguese immigrants. Education is, of course, the principal tool enabling people in advanced industrial societies to increase their income and social status and is the main pathway by which immigrants can become integrated into the mainstream of the population. There is some evidence that the concerns voiced about the academic achievement of Portuguese immigrants, very real for the first two generations, have become less so for the third and subsequent generations as the process of integration into Canadian life has continued, and a number of writers of distinction have now come from the Portuguese community. However, it is difficult not to contrast the experience of Portuguese immigrants in Canada with the apparently more rapid and successful integration of those who went to Argentina or Venezuela.

10

THE PORTUGUESE DIASPORA
IN THE UNITED STATES

'When I was a boy, I was already dreaming of America. A great, wonderfully rich land! So large it reaches two seas. Mountains as big as anything you've ever seen. Snow, like wheat flour, covers the mountains of America in winter....'

'What else is there in America?' the boy inquired...

'Everything, everything.'

Alfred Lewis, *Home is an Island*, 144

The beginnings

On Christmas Day 1866 a festive ball was being held at Fort Laramie in Wyoming. Around midnight a large figure clad in a buffalo skin coat with cap and boots strode into the room to give the news of a disaster that had overtaken a US force headed by Captain Fetterman. The newcomer had ridden 190 miles through hostile Indian country in appalling weather, a ride that became one of the legends of the American West. The rider, John Phillips, was in fact Portuguese. He had been born Manuel Felipe Cardoso on the island of Pico in the Azores and had come to the United States in 1850 to make his fortune on the gold diggings in the West. He later became a mail courier, rancher and hotel owner, dying in 1883.[1]

Before the nineteenth century Portuguese who found their way to North America were few and far between—in fact the only notable

189

community of Portuguese origin were Sephardic Jews who had not come from Portugal itself but from Brazil or the Caribbean. However, the Portuguese had been very active in the slave trade and in the eighteenth century slaves were often brought by Portuguese ships into Britain's North American colonies. One route was from the Cape Verde Islands, and a number of cases arose where free Cape Verdeans were treated as slaves in American ports.

The beginnings of migration from Portugal to the United States are closely linked to the American whaling industry, which began to expand from about the middle of the eighteenth century. As the industry grew, the shortage of seamen skilled in whaling led American ships to call at the Azores and Cape Verde Islands to take on experienced crews. Once communities of whalers from the islands became established in New England ports, the way was open for further migration of families and neighbours. Because whale hunting was a hard life, which attracted few native-born Americans, the Portuguese came to play a disproportionately large role in its development. According to Sandra Wolforth, by 1880 a third of the whalemen working out of New Bedford were Portuguese.[2] When whaling declined, the Portuguese remained prominent in the fishing industry based in the New England seaports until that also went into steep decline during the depression of the 1930s.

If emigration from the islands, linked often to the fishing and whaling industries, provided one stream of migrants, another stream was created by the American economy's hunger for cheap labour. During the second half of the nineteenth century Portuguese came to the United States in the same way that Italians, Irish and northern Europeans came, in search of land and employment. Although the majority of the Portuguese settled in New England, a significant number went to California, and these were to remain the two principal areas to which Portuguese would in future migrate.

Numbers of Portuguese immigrants

From the start Portuguese emigration to the United States was largely a migration of islanders, a characteristic that has marked the Portuguese American community until the present. Even during the 1960s when tens of thousands of Portuguese were emigrating to France or Germany, islanders from the Azores, Madeira and Cape Verde preferred to go to the United States or Canada. Arroteia estimated that from 1955 to 1974 56.9 per cent of Portuguese emigrants to the US came from the Azores.[3] One factor which helped to bind the Azoreans to the United States was the existence of the airbase at Lajes on the island of Terceira, which provided access for many Azoreans to the English language and to American networks that aided emigration to the United States.

With the history of the Portuguese in the United States, numbers move around as in a kaleidoscope with each author giving the data a shake. Some authors attempt to count annual immigration, others try to count the numbers of the Portuguese community in the United States at any one time, but neither set of figures attains the exactitude that statisticians desire. The United States censuses seek to record the national identity of United States residents, though the count depends on the self-description of those counted. The 1870 census recorded 8,971 Portuguese.[4] Thereafter numbers increased both by new immigration and by natural increase. In the 1880 US census there were 15,650 Portuguese, rising to 114,321 in 1920.[5] These figures are impressionistic, if only because it is not clear exactly what is being counted—whether it is people born in Portugal or whether the numbers include those born in the United States to Portuguese immigrants. Nor is it clear whether first and subsequent generations are being counted or if Portuguese emigrants and settlers in Hawaii are included, or whether the numbers always include Cape Verdeans.

If exact numbers are elusive, there are clear general trends. These show that prior to 1870 there was very little emigration to the United States, and thereafter numbers increased but only to around 1,500 a year. The big influx occurred between 1900 and 1920, continuing during the war in spite of the difficulties in obtaining passages by sea.

Maria Baganha has described the period from 1875 to 1920 as one of increasing state 'intervention and regulation'. Laws introduced during this period tried to exclude criminals, prostitutes, those carrying disease, polygamists and Asians. These measures had little impact on the numbers of Portuguese migrants, though the ban on unaccompanied children and on contract labourers might have been framed to prevent the abuses so prevalent at that time in Brazil, of which the Portuguese were very much the victims. In 1917 a regulation banned the immigration of illiterates. This may well have been intended to screen out Cape Verdean and Azorean migrants but it appears that the

Portuguese, among whom illiteracy was indeed high, found ways of evading this regulation. Maria Baganha noted that in 1915 54 per cent of the Portuguese immigrants had been classified as illiterate; but in 1920, although the numbers had grown four times, only 6 per cent were illiterate. As she points out, there had not been any dramatic improvement in Portuguese education during these five years.[6]

Table 6: Portuguese Emigration to the United States, (1820–1929)

Date	Total	% of all Port. emigration	% of total US immigration
1820–29	256		0.20
1830–39	911		0.17
1840–49	362		0.03
1850–59	4,225		0.15
1860–69	5,369	8.47	0.25
1870–79	14,265	10.52	0.52
1880–89	15,560	7.97	0.30
1890–99	26,376	8.62	0.71
1900–09	63,144	17.83	0.77
1910–19	78,413	18.16	1.24
1920–29	46,644	11.90	1.09

Source: Baganha, Portuguese Emigration to the United States 1820–1930, 256.

From the 1920s to the 1960s immigration was restricted by the American policy of national quotas, which pressed heavily on the migration from Portugal. The quotas were relaxed somewhat in 1958, following the volcanic eruption of Capelinhos in the Azores, when the Azorean Refugee Act (2 September 1958) authorised the immigration of 1,500 people from the islands. A major change took place in 1965 when quotas were reallocated and a policy of unifying families and allowing relatives to settle was adopted. This led to the second great influx of Portuguese, which lasted from 1965 till 1979, when immigration was again greatly reduced.

As these figures demonstrate, Portuguese emigration to the US was not large by comparison with other national groups. In Edward Alsworth Ross's notorious study of immigration, The Old World in the New published in 1914, are figures for foreign-born immigrants for the year 1910 which show that only Belgium, Spain, Turkey and the Balkan states had fewer than Portugal.[7] Even Finland sent a larger

Table 7: Portuguese Emigration to the United States (1930–1996)

Date	Number of immigrants	Average per annum
1930–54	16,939	678
1955–74	121,037	6,052
1975–96	89,291	4,058

Source: Peixoto, 'A Emigração', 155.

number of immigrants to the US. However, if Portuguese numbers were small, there were high concentrations of Portuguese in certain areas, which gave them a higher profile than their overall numbers would warrant. There were significant concentrations of Portuguese in Massachusetts and Rhode Island, where a substantial community of Portuguese origin settled in coastal towns and was involved in the fishing industry and the textile mills. By 1919 half the Portuguese were working, as Caroline Brettell puts it, in

unskilled mill jobs as combers, spinners, carders, and doffers, or in low wage jobs in coal yards, produce houses, slaughter houses, small grocery, fruit, fish, or bakery shops, or as farm laborers. The overwhelming majority... were from the Azores. They were young, unmarried, largely illiterate, and unskilled.[8]

This concentration of the Portuguese in New England has remained largely unchanged. According to Jerry Williams, New England in 1980 was home to 66.5 per cent of the Portuguese American population.[9] There were 190,298 'people of Portuguese ancestry' in Massachusetts, 31.5 per cent of these had been born in Portugal and 63 per cent were living in Portuguese speaking homes. 'In 1980 Rhode Island was home to 61,756 individuals of Portuguese ancestry, and continued to account for about 10 per cent of all Portuguese Americans.' Connecticut had 26,977 people of Portuguese ancestry of whom 14,525 were born outside the United States.

The Portuguese of Gloucester, Massachusetts

The port of Gloucester in Massachusetts was one of the earliest places where Azoreans settled, and the story of this community is the story in miniature of Portuguese migration to the US. In the mid nineteenth century Gloucester was one of the most important fishing ports on the east coast with some 400 schooners operating out of the port. It was easy for skilled seamen to get work, and by 1850 a dozen young Azorean men were working on Gloucester vessels. 'Their number grew tenfold over the following decade. The men worked hard, saved what they could, and even sent money home to pay for the passage of loved ones to Gloucester.' In the late 1880s 'a type of two-masted fishing schooner known as the "Gloucesterman" roamed over the western North Atlantic. These vessels, the handsomest, fastest, and strongest of their size ever built, derived their name from the port of Gloucester.'[10] These boats carried dories on board and the fishing was done from these small open boats. The hardship of this type of fishing was extreme and one Portuguese doryman was stranded at sea for ten days, surviving on a bottle of water and a haddock which he cooked by lighting a fire in the bottom of his boat.[11]

This was work at which the Azoreans excelled and many rose to become schooner captains, eventually building and owning their own boats. Most famous was Joseph Mesquita, who had arrived in the US with 50 cents in his pocket. In 1899 Mesquita commissioned his own schooner, named the *Mary P. Mesquita* after his wife. The last of the big schooners was built by the Portuguese in 1926 and thereafter the conversion to trawling began, the last schooner being converted in 1943. Some ten fishing vessels out of Gloucester were sunk by German submarines during the war; after the war fishing went into decline, and with it the prosperity of the Azorean community.

Meanwhile, however, the Azoreans had put down roots.

Over time, they bought small house lots on a rough, unsettled hill overlooking Gloucester's inner harbor known locally as Lookout Hill. Everyone was to soon call it "Portagee Hill"—the home of Gloucester's Azorean immigrants. In preparing their lots on the Hill, the men used simple tools to split rocks, prepare the ground, and frame their homes. They planted trees and vines—pears, apples, and grapes. They laid out small vegetable and flower beds: no home was complete without the morning glories, lilacs, roses, and elderberries. Chickens walked about the grounds, their coops adjoining the backyard pens for the many pigs kept on the Hill. In the fall, families slaughtered the pigs, putting up salt pork, lard and Portuguese sausages for the long New England winter.[12]

In 1893 work began on a church to be dedicated to Our Lady of Good Voyage. This church soon became the heart of the community, and when it was destroyed in a fire in 1914 money was collected and a new and much grander church was built in 1915. For the first two generations, at least, religion defined the Azorean community.

Men such as Mesquita lived in a world governed both by the Catholic Church and by traditional Azorean superstitions. Their faith was reflected in the building of the church, while their superstitions could be seen in many aspects of daily life. People attributed bad luck at sea to a bewildering assortment of superstitions. Bad luck followed if a woman set foot on a fishing vessel, or if a fisherman met a woman on the way to the ship, or even if the ship left on a Wednesday or Friday. Bad luck also befell a vessel if one of the crew mentioned the word 'priest' or 'pig' while fishing on the Banks. On the other hand, men believed that the throwing of rosary beads into rough waters could calm the raging sea.[13]

In 1900 Joseph Mesquita's newly built schooner was sunk in a collision with the liner *Saxonia*. All the crew bar one were saved, and as an act of thanksgiving Mesquita ordered a silver crown to be made in Portugal and to be sent for the performance of the ritual of crowning an 'emperor' for the traditional Azorean Holy Ghost celebrations. The crown was blessed by Pope Leo XIII and the first crowning took place in 1902, supposedly the first 'crowning' to take place in New England. Thereafter the ceremony was performed annually by different Azorean organisations. In 1931 the Fraternity Club held its first 'crowning' and the 'imperator, Manuel P. Domingos Jr, kept the magnificent silver crown on a flower-decorated altar in his home where he held open house each evening for members and friends'.[14]

Like other immigrant Portuguese communities, the Azoreans of Gloucester formed their own associations. Most important, and still in existence, was the Fraternity Club which was founded in the 1920s as a drum and bugle band and raised funds from the community to build its own premises.

The life histories of many of the Portuguese immigrants have been recorded and from them emerge tales of extreme hardship, by no means ending with their safe arrival in the US. Many continued to work long hours for very low pay and to struggle with language problems. Their survival depended on family and community solidarity. According to Filomana Dasilva,

"When they [the immigrants] come over here, the first thing they do is save money to buy a house," she said, noting that young American families do not take that approach. "They get their paycheck and that's it" and her husband added "the American dream of an easy climb up the social ladder [is] a bunch of baloney".[15]

Madeirans and Hawaii

One striking feature of the emigration to New England was the comparative absence of Madeirans. Whereas approximately 68,000 migrants left the Azores for the United States between 1955 and 1974, only 993 came from Madeira during the same period. It was not that Madeirans were not emigrating, rather that they were following their compatriots to other destinations, and among these were the Hawaiian Islands. In the 1980 census 26,447 people resident in the Hawaiian Islands claimed Portuguese descent, even though only 274 of these were actually born outside the US. Clearly Portuguese emigration to Hawaii had at one time been substantial but had run its course by 1980.

Sugar growing in the Hawaiian Islands began to develop as a commercial enterprise in the 1840s and increased dramatically in profitability during the American Civil War. As sugar was a labour-intensive crop, planters had to find labour and the Portuguese Atlantic islands were amongst the regions where they, like their counterparts in the Caribbean, sought recruits. Between 1878 and 1899 12,780 Portuguese arrived in Hawaii as contract labourers.[16] Azoreans and Madeirans were recruited by agents in roughly equal numbers but, unlike migrants to Brazil at this time, the islanders tended to emigrate as whole families. The last arrivals from Portugal came in 1909, and in 1913 it was calculated that a total of 23,578 Portuguese—7,806 men (34 per cent), 5,536 women (23 per cent) and 10,236 children (43 per cent)—had gone to Hawaii.[17]

The journey from the Atlantic islands to Hawaii involved a voyage of up to six months in a sailing ship—a journey of appalling hardship. Some migrants stowed away on board Hawaii-bound ships, one account telling of eleven stowaways on a single ship who were put to work by the captain when they were discovered. The ship took 33 days to round Cape Horn and in the course of a five-month voyage 16 people died and 16 babies were born.[18] Most Portuguese workers arrived under contracts that bound them to work for five years and as a result they had a very low social status, which placed them in a position somewhere between Asian 'coolie' immigrants and white Europeans.[19] Until 1940 the Hawaii census distinguished Portuguese from 'other Caucasians'. At the expiry of their contracts many left the sugar plantations seeking to establish themselves in low-skilled urban occupations or as smallholders. Honolulu was a favourite location and in 1898 4,000 out of a total city population of 28,000 were Portuguese.[20]

Others left the islands altogether and headed back to the American mainland, the distance of Hawaii from Europe effectively preventing any move to return to their homeland. As a result the 'Portuguese' community in Hawaii ceased to grow commensurate with the population of the islands themselves, and in 2010 people of Portuguese ancestry constituted just 4.3 per cent of the non-Hawaiian (Haole) population of the islands. Even so, this community maintained a strong ethnic identity with its own churches and its own religious *festas*. As with many other diasporic communities, there is a strong interest in family origins among Hawaiian Portuguese which can be followed on their internet sites, and it is often considered that the Portuguese made a major contribution to the culture of Hawaii by introducing the guitar, which was locally developed into the characteristic Hawaiian ukulele.

Cape Verdeans emigrating to the United States

The emigration of Cape Verdeans to the United States followed a similar trajectory to that of the Azoreans. The Cape Verde Islands lay at the crossroads of shipping lanes in the Atlantic and were regularly visited by sailing ships bound for India or Brazil. They were also used as a holding area for slaves brought from mainland Africa before being shipped across the Atlantic. The population of the islands was ethnically very mixed, and as the climate was precarious Cape Verdeans became accustomed to seek employment as crew in passing sailing ships. Like the Azoreans, the islanders also became expert hunters of whales.

In the early nineteenth century whale hunting greatly expanded in the waters round Cape Verde and visiting whaling ships, especially those from North America, made use of sheltered island anchorages and took on Cape Verdeans to supplement their crews. In the course of the nineteenth century many American whalers were largely crewed by Cape Verdeans, some of whom came to captain the whaling ships. Many of these settled permanently in the whaling ports of North America like Nantucket and New Bedford and formed communities that then acted as poles of attraction for other emigrants.

Frank Bullen (1857–1915) was one of the most prolific authors to record in memoirs and fiction the life at sea in the last days of sail. One of his best known books, *The Cruise of the 'Cachalot'*, describes life on an American whaler sailing out of New Bedford in 1875. The crew of the whaler had been assembled from a motley crowd of unem-

197

ployed, 'not only the representatives of five or six nations, but long-shoremen of all kinds, half of whom had hardly ever set eyes on a ship before!'[21] In contrast to the inexperienced 'farmers, bakers and dray-smen', the 'black portion of the crew—Portuguese natives from the Western and Canary Islands—were doing their work all right in a clumsy fashion';[22] they were the experienced part of the crew—in fact they were mostly Cape Verdeans—and were headed by the second mate, 'a Portuguese about forty years of age, with a face like one of Vandyke's cavaliers, but as I now learned, a perfect fiend when angered. He also was a first class whaleman, but an indifferent sea-man.'[23] The inexperienced landsmen were all 'allotted places in the var-ious boats intermixed with the seasoned Portuguese in such a way that the officer and harpooner in charge would not be dependent upon them entirely in case of a sudden emergency'.[24]

In the whalers the racial hierarchies that were part of normal life on land were reversed. The 'black' Portuguese were the skilled crew and were often in positions of authority over the white crew.

More than half of the total crews of the American whaling fleet are composed of these islanders. Many of them have risen to the position of captain, and still more are officers and harpooners; but though undoubtedly brave and enter-prising, they are cruel and treacherous, and in positions of authority over men of Teutonic or Anglo-Saxon origin, are apt to treat their subordinates with great cruelty.[25]

In the fo'c'sle the crew naturally separated themselves, 'the blacks [that is the Portuguese] taking the port side and the whites the star-board'. The tensions between the 'black' Portuguese who were experi-enced whalers and the white crewmen who were not was tangible until there was a prospect of the ship visiting the Cape Verde Islands.

Most of them belonged there, and although there was but the faintest prospect of their getting ashore upon any pretext whatever, the possibility of seeing their island homes again seemed to quite transform them. Hitherto they had been very moody and exclusive, never associating with us in the white side, or attempting to be at all familiar. A mutual atmosphere of suspicion, in fact, seemed to per-vade our quarters, making things already uncomfortable enough, still more so. Now, however, they fraternised with us, and in a variety of uncouth ways made havoc of the English tongue, as they tried to impress us with the beauty, fertility and general incomparability of their beloved Cape Verds.[26]

There is no sentimentality in this description. Life on a whaler was hard and to escape from the poverty of the islands to a life at sea was no easy passage or soft option. But there was a crude equality achieved where skill and endurance, not race or background, were all that mattered.

From 1900 figures for legal emigration by Cape Verdeans are available and they show that between 1901 and 1920 18,629 islanders emigrated to the United States, two thirds of them coming from the islands of Fogo and Brava, as the port of Furna in Brava was the preferred anchorage for many American whalers. In fact these emigrants were often called 'Bravas' in New England. However, during these years there was also a large clandestine emigration, particularly of men seeking to avoid military service in nearby Guinea. It was easy for emigrants to stow away on board sailing ships, many of which had Cape Verdean crews. As steamships took over more and more shipping routes, Cape Verdeans in the United States bought sailing ships that were being laid up and continued to operate them on routes to and from the archipelago. Unlike most immigrants, 'the Cape Verdeans came to have control over their own means of passage to the United States'.[27] As late as 1939 there were still old sailing ships, known as the Brava Packets, operating between the United States, the Azores and the Cape Verde Islands.[28]

Although the number of Cape Verdeans was not large in relation to the total number of Portuguese immigrants, let alone the number of immigrants entering the US as a whole, it was sufficient to cause some concern to those, like Ross, who were campaigning against unrestricted immigration, because it was apparent that many Cape Verdeans were of mixed race, and therefore were deemed to be 'black', as the term was understood in the US. In 1917 the restrictions on the entry of people deemed to be illiterate was widely assumed to be an attempt to restrict Cape Verdean immigration, and when national quotas were introduced in 1924 and revised in 1929 the regulations were framed in such a way as to make Cape Verdean immigration difficult. Visas were not to be issued by Portuguese consulates and immigrants were only to be allowed to sail from Lisbon. As a result legal emigration from Cape Verde declined to a trickle, and between 1927 and 1952 only 1,946 Cape Verdeans officially entered the US.[29]

The immigration of Cape Verdeans had led to the establishment of communities in the seaports of Massachusetts and Rhode Island that were distinct from other groups of Portuguese. Many new arrivals found employment in the cranberry bogs where they provided low-paid labour picking berries, work that native-born Americans and even most immigrants would not undertake. According to Susan Wolforth, 'in the bog areas they lived, at best, with the bare essentials of life in a semi-migratory manner'.[30] However, they soon branched out into other activities.

> Over the years we find Cape Verdeans in the United States engaged in a great variety of occupations—seeking gold in California, serving on board coast guard ships or in the coasting trade of the Fall River, as firemen on the Pacific Railway, as strawberry farmers, as field workers in the swampy area of Cape Cod and on the cotton plantations, as factory workers in the New Bedford textile industry—numbered in their thousands by the latter half of the nineteenth century.[31]

According to António Carreira, 'most of those who settled in the United States remained apart from the white community, either because the whites deliberately distanced themselves from them, or because their low socio-economic status kept them at a distance'.[32] However, in the eyes of many Americans they were 'Portuguese' and this fact helped to shape wider attitudes towards Portuguese emigration in general. The Cape Verdeans did not associate with other Portuguese communities, and as Sidney Greenfield wrote, 'in New Bedford and Providence they accepted the segregation imposed on them and restricted all but essential contacts with outsiders, speaking creole with each other, and finding meaning and satisfaction in their creole world'.[33] Some Cape Verdeans returned to the islands with their savings, bringing with them their knowledge of English, which became a widespread *lingua franca* in some of the islands, but with the continuance of periodic drought in the twentieth century there was little incentive for the majority to return to the poverty of the islands.

During the 1960s emigration from Cape Verde developed along different lines from that from the Azores. Few Azoreans emigrated to northern Europe, and after the relaxation of American immigration rules in 1965 there was a new and substantial departure from the Azores for the United States. Cape Verdeans on the other hand turned to Europe, travelling to Lisbon and then moving on from there to northern Europe in the wake of the mainland Portuguese. Then in 1975 Cape Verde became independent from Portugal, leading to a different evaluation of the Cape Verdean presence and heritage. With the establishment of a United States embassy in Praia it became easier to obtain visas and a new wave of Cape Verdean immigration began.

Between 1975 and 2005 60,000 Cape Verdeans left for the US.[34] This renewed immigration brought a whole new generation of Cape Verdeans from what was now an independent country. They often found they had little in common with the descendants of the earlier immigrants, who spoke English instead of creole and had always thought of themselves as Portuguese. Moreover the new wave of immigrants was drawn from all the islands, in contrast to the earlier immigrants who had come mainly from Brava and Fogo.

In the 2000 census 77,203 people in the United States claimed Cape Verdean descent and 87 per cent still lived in New England where the first immigrants had settled. However, this statistic means very little as it is still common for many people of Cape Verdean descent to describe their origins as Portuguese. This may be family tradition but it also helps them to create for themselves a 'white' identity that is so important in the United States.

Marilyn Halter describes the identity of the Cape Verdean community as 'always in flux, their mixed African and Portuguese heritage continues to defy rigid social classification, challenging notions of race, colour, ethnicity and identity'.[35] The retention of the creole language by the new immigrants was a device by which they established an identity different from that of Latinos or Afro-Americans. Moreover, since the independence of the Cape Verde Islands, immigrants in the United States have been able to vote in Cape Verde elections and this has also helped to set the community apart from Latinos and Brazilians with whom they might otherwise become confused, as well as from Portuguese.

California

While the large majority of Portuguese immigrants settled in New England, a sizeable minority made California their home. As with so many other nationalities, the first Portuguese arrived at the time of the gold rush in the 1840s; after a few hectic years on the goldfields, they settled as fishermen or as farmers in the fertile valleys inland from San Francisco. There they were joined by Portuguese who had originally gone as contract labourers to Hawaii and then, at the end of their contracts, came to the West Coast of the American mainland to set themselves up as independent farmers. According to Leo Pap, 2,000 Hawaiian Portuguese moved to California between 1911 and 1914.[36] While the New England Portuguese became fishermen and factory workers, the Californian Portuguese became fishermen and dairy farmers, concentrating their settlement in the San Leandro and Santa Clara counties. The high concentration of Portuguese in these areas (the population of the city of San José was at one time 60 per cent of Portuguese extraction) enabled the community to retain a high degree of individuality and some importance in spite of the relatively small numbers of immigrants.

Leo Pap was fascinated by the longevity of some of the early Portuguese pioneers who survived the hardships of migration and settlement in the west. He mentions one, 'Mrs Genevieve de Brum Vargas, born on the island of Pico in 1830, [who] arrived in Boston in 1865, soon set sail for San Francisco, from there walked (yes, on foot) down the coast to Half Moon Bay—where she was still residing in 1944, at age 114'.[37] And there were others, though their lives have to be seen in contrast to a very high level of infant and child mortality. As is so often the case, historians write the stories of those who win through and survive, not of the far greater numbers who do not.

Diane Beeson and Donald Warrin have described the lives of Portuguese women on the frontier which fit them perfectly into the mythology of the 'West'—a mythology that represented women as either 'The Forlorn Frontier Woman', the 'Sturdy Helpmate', or the 'Untamed Woman'. There were apparently many examples of the third of these since, on the frontier, the accepted norms of female behaviour counted for very little. There was, for example, Jessie, the daughter of Joe Alameda, 'who left the island of Flores in 1896 at the age of fifteen and settled in Wyoming ... and later invested his earnings in a ranch'. At the age of seven 'Jessie was riding horseback, participating in the round up of cattle, and learning to throw the lasso. She had a brief moment of fame as a young woman when it was reported in the newspapers that she had chased and lassoed a coyote.' She is quoted as having recalled, 'I did a man's work all my life, had short hair and wore pants. I just didn't like housework. To me a house is just some place to eat and sleep. I've no regrets.'[38]

What is so satisfying about this story, and the many others they record, is that they run counter to the accepted stereotypes not only of the Victorian woman in general but specifically the stereotypes of the Portuguese—home loving, obedient to their menfolk, not interested in education.

Portuguese characters inhabit the fiction of Jack London, who was born in San Francisco and died there at the early age of forty. In the poignant and semi-autobiographical novel *Martin Eden,* the eponymous hero lives in a room rented from a Portuguese woman who had come to California via Hawaii. 'Maria Silva, a virago and a widow, hard working and harsher tempered, rearing her large brood of children somehow, and drowning her sorrow and fatigue at irregular intervals in a gallon of thin wine she bought from the corner grocery and saloon for fifteen cents.' Maria makes a poor living taking in washing and pasturing two cows on wasteland and roadside verges. For her the American dream meant a life of drudgery and 'Martin grew to admire her as he observed the brave fight she made'.[39] In the end he was able to be her 'fairy prince' and spend his money on buying her a milk ranch, which is the only really happy outcome of this sad and bitter story.

In *The Valley of the Moon,* published in 1913 only three years before he died, Jack London is much more kindly disposed towards the 'American dream'. Appearing one year before Ross's poisonous denunciation of immigrants in *The Old World in the New,* the book contains a lengthy passage in which the virtues of immigrants are contrasted with the failure of native-born Americans to make their fortunes from the land. The immigrants who attract the attention of the author and his hero are the 'Porchugeeze'. The book features a working-class couple, Saxon and Billy, who become disillusioned with 'socialism' and seek land on which to earn a living by hard work. In London's eyes it was native-born Americans, not the immigrants, who had lost sight of the virtues of hard work.

'It looks as though they'd crowd our kind out,' Saxon adjudged....

'Oh, I don't know about that. I reckon the American could do what the Porchugeeze do if he wanted to. Only he don't want to, thank God. He ain't much given to livin' like a pig often leavin's.'

Billy is soon made to rethink this remark when they contemplate the wealth that 'old Silva' has made from the land.

'Forty years ago old Silva came from the Azores. Went sheep-herdin' in the mountains for a couple of years, then blew in to San Leandro. These five acres was the first land he leased. That was the beginnin'. Then he began leasin' by the hundred of acres, an' by the hundred-an'-sixties. An' his sisters an' his uncles an' his aunts begun pourin' in from the Azores—they're all related there, you know; an' pretty soon San Leandro was a regular Porchugeeze settlement.'[40]

As they contemplate the high price of land, beyond their ability to buy, Billy concludes:

'But just the same it's the Portuguese that gave it its price, and they make things go on it—send their children to school... and have them; and, as you said yourself, they're as fat as butterballs.'[41]

The early Portuguese settlers in California were very active in founding institutions to support their community. The cultural life of the Portuguese came to be focused on the Holy Ghost festivals, which had been introduced from the Azores, and the cherry festivals held in June. The first Holy Ghost festival was held in 1870 and thereafter they grew in popularity, their focus being very much on charitable work, a queen being chosen to assume the role of the queen Saint Isabel who had initiated the cult. The SPRSI (Sociedade Portuguesa Rainha Santa Isabel) was an early example of a support group organised by and for Portuguese women. The UPEC (União Portuguesa do Estado do California) was founded in 1880 as an organisation intended to provide support for those in need and to represent Portuguese interests generally. It also aimed to give the Portuguese community a high profile, for example by supporting a band and organising Portuguese participation in the Panama Pacific Exposition of 1915. It established a kind of Portuguese freemasonry that became in some ways a rival to the church for the leadership of the Portuguese community. Its annual conventions were an occasion for the elite of the Portuguese community to get together and to dine in style.[42] The impression is strong that the Portuguese communities in California were more outward going and enterprising and more willing to play an active part in local affairs than their counterparts in New England.

John Steinbeck's novels describe the struggle to survive of the dropouts, bums and poverty-stricken casual workers of America in the 1930s and 1940s. Their ethics are not those of the richer classes of society but they have a strong sense of right and wrong and a code of honour of sorts. One of their number is Joe Portagee—a classic Steinbeck anti-hero.

If he had been a hero, the Portagee would have spent a miserable time in the army. The fact that he was Big Joe Portagee, with a decent training in the Monterey gaol, not only saved him the misery of patriotism thwarted, but solidified his conviction that as a man's days are rightly devoted half to sleeping and half to waking, so a man's years are rightly spent half in gaol and half out ... he was far from satisfied with prison life in the army. In the Monterey gaol he was accustomed to ease and companionship. In the army, he found only work.[43]

Returning to his old haunts he trades in his army greatcoat for a gallon of wine, and although he does not find his friends 'he found no lack of those vile and false harpies and pimps who are ever ready to lead men into the pit. Joe, who was not very moral, had no revulsion for the pit; he liked it.' So when he was ejected he broke all the furniture and set fire to the house. He was sentenced to thirty days in gaol and 'lay luxuriously on his leather cot and slept heavily for one-tenth of his sentence.'[44] And so on. Joe Portagee is a small-time scoundrel or a gullible, trusting child, according to your point of view, and is repeatedly treated and bamboozled by his friends whom he never ceases to believe in and trust. Is this, one wonders, just another of Steinbeck's characters who live below the threshold of decency, or is he representing a view of the Portuguese commonly held by Americans?

Illinois and the Lincolns

Reference has already been made to the Madeiran Protestants who emigrated to Trinidad and then, between 1849 and 1850, moved on to Illinois where they had been offered land. About 400 Madeirans settled around Springfield and Jacksonville. It is unusual to find groups of Portuguese Protestants as the reformed church never made much impact in the Portuguese world until the latter part of the twentieth century. It is still more unexpected to find members of this community prominent in the early life of Abraham Lincoln. As Diane Beeson and Donald Warrin explain, 'Francisca Affonso was the Lincolns' cook during their last years in Springfield and prepared Lincoln's farewell banquet as he left for the White House.' She lived in the Lincoln household and the Lincolns paid for her wedding dress and bedroom furniture on the occasion of her marriage. The Lincolns had another Madeiran servant, called Mary Andrews, who entered their service at the age of sixteen and worked as a domestic and dressmaker, while two other Portuguese seamstresses are known to have worked for the Lincolns.[45] Skill with the needles is not often mentioned in connection with Madeiran emigrants, but until comparatively recent times Madeiran women produced very fine embroidery, following traditional designs, which was a product of the island as distinctive as its wines.

Integration and settling down

The massive migration of Europeans of different national backgrounds to the US in the nineteenth century created prolonged problems of adjustment. On the one hand most immigrant groups tried to cling onto some elements of their national identity, often defined in terms of religion, language, special cuisine and religious festivals. On the other hand they attempted to integrate with the broad population of the US in order to play a part in the formation of the new country and to build a future for their children. The pattern that repeated itself again and again was for the first generation to retain close ties with the culture of their country of origin but for this to become increasingly diluted in subsequent generations as those born in the New World intermarried with people from other groups, travelled and resettled, acquired an American education and in general sought much greater integration. The extent to which old ethnic identities were retained often had to do with the concentrations of settlement in one particular region and the existence of institutions deliberately created to support the old ethnic identity. As David Brookshaw has written,

diasporas of whatever ethnic origin are essentially frontier societies and cultures. Their tendency is to abolish the borderline between past (the land of origin) and the present and future (the host country): in their fluidity, they belong to both and at the same time, perhaps, to neither.[46]

In many respects the immigrant groups from mainland Portugal and the islands were no different from other immigrant groups, but there were some aspects which set them apart. Although, compared with other immigrant groups, the numbers of mainland Portuguese and islanders were not large, they showed a marked tendency to concentrate their settlements. Even after two generations had passed, most people of Portuguese origin were still to be found in the areas of original settlement in New England, parts of California, and to a lesser extent Hawaii. Andrea Klimt describes the typical Portuguese–American community:

Many first generation immigrants from Portugal as well as people of subsequent generations live in close proximity to concentrated Portuguese-American communities; shop at or own businesses that cater to a Portuguese-American clientele; belong to Portuguese-American parishes; participate in social clubs organized by people who trace their origins to the same island or region of Portugal; have access to Portuguese language newspapers and media that cover local events; can go to doctors, travel agents, lawyers, social workers who speak Portuguese and primarily serve the ethnic community; and work with and live next door to people of Portuguese heritage.[47]

In these areas of concentrated settlement the Portuguese–Americans had a high profile, establishing their own shops and restaurants and, of course, their own churches and festivals. Although some Portuguese acquired a good education and moved on and away, the large majority continued to follow semi-skilled employment in the factories, farms and fishing industries, often working alongside other Portuguese–Americans, who came originally from the same part of Portugal. The extended family was also typical of Portuguese–American communities. According to Andrea Klimt the Portuguese of New England are typically 'surrounded by extended family whose members reconvened in the United States through an extended process of chain migration'.[48]

Although Portuguese workers acquired a reputation for being willing to work at the most servile tasks and in the worst conditions, the closeness of the Portuguese community and the tendency of Portuguese to marry within the group were sometimes criticised by outsiders who thought the Portuguese 'clannish', uninterested in education and not inclined to take any part in public life.[49] This negative, and at times hostile, attitude from other groups in turn reinforced the need for the Portuguese communities to stick together, and it was this close-knit, even closed, world that encouraged further immigration from Portugal by offering security and protection for new arrivals.

This introverted world of the Portuguese–Americans appears vividly in books written by people of Portuguese descent. In Frank Gaspar's novel *Leaving Pico*, the Portuguese have created in a New England coastal town a version of the Azorean community from which they originated. There is a bitter rivalry between 'Picos' and 'Lisbons' (Azoreans and mainland Portuguese), so deeply rooted that they are barely able to talk to each other even though they live in neighbouring houses. The older generation still use the Portuguese language and dream of a romantic past based on island legends. Few non-Portuguese seem to intrude into their world and there is little indication that they are living in the multi-ethnic United States.[50]

Francisco Fagundes' autobiographical narrative, *Hard Knocks*, is typical in many ways of immigrant writing: the passage to the New World, the struggle to make your way at the same time as you are growing up, the steps towards integration and acceptance coinciding with the rites of passage from childhood to adolescence and adulthood. The old society of the islands remains ever present among the Azoreans of California, as they plan to return or to bring out relations to join them on the west coast. Like Frank Gaspar's portrait of the New England Portuguese, this also is a vivid picture of a close-knit Portuguese community—this time in the Californian dairy country—where members of the community quarrel and exploit new arrivals but in the end reluctantly support and look out for each other.[51]

If Azoreans, Cape Verdeans and mainland Portuguese tended to keep themselves separate, in the eyes of Americans they were all 'Portuguese' and therein lay a problem, particularly in the early days of immigration before the more liberal attitudes of the post-1965 era. Portuguese immigrants were frequently seen by many Americans, as they were in the Caribbean, as not truly white Europeans. The origin of this problem lay in the fact that many of the Portuguese were dark of complexion and most Cape Verdeans—who until 1975 were usually classified, and classified themselves, as Portuguese—were self-evidently of mixed race and some, especially those from the island of Santiago, were of a distinctly African phenotype. As Harney points out, as late as 1972 'Portuguese' could be classified as a separate racial category (as they were in the British Caribbean) alongside 'Negro', 'American Indian' and 'Oriental'.[52]

The claim that the Portuguese were not truly 'white' was famously given a spurious academic validity in the lengthy study published by Donald Taft in 1923 with the title *Two Portuguese Communities in New England*. In the Introduction Taft asserted that 'the Portuguese are also interesting to study because of their curious racial composition. Not only are they Southern-Europeans but also ... some of them seem to be of a semi-negroid type.' And he goes on to describe them as 'a people apparently differing somewhat in race as well as in mores, from native Americans and from other elements among the foreign-born'.[53]

Taft's disparaging conclusions about the Portuguese of New England were reflected in other writings of the time. Susan Wolforth quotes Henry Kittredge's *Cape Cod: Its People and their History* (originally written in 1930 but reissued as late as 1968) in which the Cape Verdeans are described as 'savages—a cross between exiled Portuguese criminals and the aborigines of the islands'. However, it was not just the Cape Verdeans. Estellie Smith, in a book published in 1974, 'claims that the Portuguese were "the niggers of New England"' while, according to Sandra Wolforth, there is 'an old New England saying that if you want to see a potato grow, you must speak to it in Portuguese'— an insult cleverly disguised as a compliment.[54]

The most contemptuous attacks on the Portuguese and Cape Verdeans came from Edward Alsworth Ross, a university professor who had been dismissed by Stanford University for his extreme racist views but then obtained a post at the University of Wisconsin. In 1914 he published *The Old World in the New* in which he says of the Cape Verdeans, 'they are obviously Negroid, lack foresight, and are so stupid they cannot follow a straight line'.[55] As for the Portuguese, Ross agreed that 'the standard of living of the Portuguese... is much lower than that of any other race',[56] and as Ross warms to his task, 'their moral standard is in some respects exceedingly low' and he quotes with approval a Dr Bushee who wrote, 'the idea of family morality among them is almost primitive, resembling that of the negroes of the South... what anthropologists call "sexual hospitality" is not unknown among the Portuguese'.[57]

Ross's outspoken prejudice against the Portuguese is of more than passing interest. In 1925 he was employed by the League of Nations to report on labour conditions in the Portuguese African colonies. His report entitled *Report on Employment of Native Labour in Portuguese Africa* was strongly critical of the Portuguese, whom he accused of tolerating conditions of virtual slavery in their colonies. This report has been widely used by historians as damning evidence against Portuguese colonial policy—so it is interesting to reflect on the highly prejudiced opinion of the Portuguese that Ross brought with him to his mission.

Much of the evidence adduced by Taft was reflected in the debate which was sparked off by the publication in 1933 of Gilberto Freyre's *Casa Grande e Senzala*, translated into English as *The Masters and the Slaves* in 1946. In this monumental work of cultural history Freyre emphasised the hybrid nature of Brazilian culture, which drew equally on Indian, African and European heritage. He emphasised the predisposition of the Portuguese to absorb non-European cultural traits and the sexual preference many Portuguese in Brazil demonstrated for women of African or Indian origin. Those who wanted to see the Portuguese (and Brazilians) as not truly white found in Freyre's academic study a great deal to support their views.[58]

The racist perspective of so many writers in the 1910–30 period has to be seen in the context of the much wider debate on immigration and eugenics that led to the legislation of the 1920s imposing very restricted quotas on certain categories of immigrant, including Portuguese and Cape Verdeans. Although racist attitudes of course still survive, they have been superseded by serious efforts to understand the particular nature of the Portuguese inheritance of many Americans. Important in this respect were the studies made by Sandra Wolforth and Leo Pap, which paved the way for a flood of academic and periodical publications. This interest has also given rise to a subgenre of speculation surrounding the so-called Melungeons, mixed-race groups who live in the Appalachians. A persistent legend has it that the Melungeons are descended from Portuguese who intermarried with slaves and that the name itself has an Afro-Portuguese origin. There is almost no secure evidence to support this theory, but it is nevertheless of interest as it illustrates how persistent is the idea of the Portuguese as being a group apart from the norm of European immigrant.[59]

The early pattern of Portuguese migration was for migrants to settle permanently in the United States, perhaps bringing over other family members, but eventually to take United States citizenship and not expect to return to Portugal, except for the occasional special visit. More recently it has become common for some Portuguese–Americans to buy property back in Portugal or the islands and to make more regular visits. This is undoubtedly the result of greater ease of communication and travel. Moreover there have been subtle changes in immigrant culture. Whereas in the early twentieth century it was expected that immigrants would become Americans sooner or later, towards the end of the century it was increasingly common for immigrants to think of themselves as having dual nationality. In the case of the Portuguese this was made formally possible in 1992 and coincided with the government of Portugal and the regional government of the Azores taking an active part in promoting Portuguese language and culture among emigrant communities.[60] There are four weekly newspapers published in Portuguese in the US and numerous Portuguese language radio stations. The lack of ambition in the field of education, which the early immigrant communities had displayed, is also a thing of the past. Many second and third generation Portuguese have achieved significant economic success. Others like Cardinal Humberto Medeiros have risen in the Church and immigrants, or descendants of immigrants, like George Monteiro, Francisco Fagundes and Onésimo T. Almeida have made distinguished careers in the university world. The internet has also allowed Portuguese–Americans to publicise the contribution that their community has made to public life and culture in the US, celebrating such figures as Peter Francisco, one of the heroes of the War of Independence; the writer John dos Passos, the illegitimate son of a Madeira immigrant; John Philip Sousa, famous for his military marches; and the actor Tom Hanks, whose mother was of Portuguese descent.

11

PORTUGUESE EMIGRATION TO AFRICA

Portuguese settlement on the West African mainland

The Portuguese who settled in the Cape Verde and Guinea islands in the fifteenth century early developed trading contacts with West Africa. The need to import slaves was probably the origin of this commerce, but soon other commodities were being traded, including foodstuffs, malaguetta pepper, beeswax, bark cloth, *cori* beads and currency shells, gold and ivory in exchange for horses, European manufactures, iron bars, *manilhas*, salt, rum (known locally as *grogue*) and cotton cloth woven in the Cape Verde Islands themselves and known as *panos*. Portuguese trading ships visited the river ports along the upper Guinea coast from at the latest the 1450s, and a decade later Portuguese from the islands began to settle on the African mainland. Encouraged initially by special privileges granted in 1466, trade with the Guinea coast grew so rapidly that six years later the privileges were partly rescinded in a vain attempt to limit the large numbers of Portuguese who were settling beyond the jurisdiction of the Crown and the island captains. The Portuguese who went to trade in Guinea were called *lançados*, and the hostility of the Crown towards them was aroused because their trade escaped royal taxation and control. Moreover the *lançados* were widely believed to be abandoning the church, either reverting to Jewish religious practices or mixing orthodox Catholic rites with local religious customs and beliefs.

It is not difficult to understand why so many of the Cape Verde islanders moved to the mainland. The poor prospects for agriculture in the islands was one good reason, while the society that had taken root in the islands was very hierarchical, and the grants of *morgadios* and *capelas* concentrated land and resources in the hands of a few families. Many Portuguese settlers and their mulatto offspring felt themselves excluded from owning land and from the possibility of occupying public office. Moving to the African mainland allowed them to escape the authority of Crown and captain and to trade free of restrictive official regulations. Portuguese settlement was encouraged by most African rulers, who traditionally welcomed strangers who came to trade. However, the Portuguese had to adapt to local African custom. As George Brooks wrote, they had to adopt 'different modes of barter commerce... settle ashore and travel only where their hosts gave permission; pay tolls, taxes, and gifts; [and] submit disputes to African judicial processes'.[1] In the larger, more hierarchically organised African states, the role of these strangers was very limited and they were excluded from all influence in society, except the purely commercial. In smaller African communities, however, they wielded power and influence. Once established on the mainland they were able to acquire clients and slaves and to marry (with either short- or long-term arrangements) into important African clans which gave them access to trading opportunities. Moreover escape from the close attentions of the Portuguese church hierarchy was welcomed by Jews and New Christians who had left Portugal with exactly that purpose in mind.

The *lançados* were able to maintain a high degree of independence through the freedom that their shipping gave to them. Small Portuguese vessels were very suitable for coastal trade and some *lançados* owned large fleets—Diogo Henriques de Sousa allegedly owning 22 trading vessels in the 1570s.[2] Through their auspices trade links between the African communities of coastal West Africa grew considerably.

It is impossible to estimate the numbers of the *lançado* community, but by the middle of the sixteenth century there were *lançado* towns on most of the major Guinea rivers and the numbers in the black Portuguese community had grown not only through natural increase but through the assimilation of slaves, clients and servants—known as *grumetes*—many of whom became recognised members of the Luso-African community and adopted a creolised culture. Creole culture also spread among the coastal populations—an example being the Sapi ethnic group, which adopted Christianity and was ruled by a king who took a Portuguese name. As Peter Mark expressed it, 'Luso-Africans maintained an understanding of group membership based essentially on cultural characteristics, and this facilitated assimilation into "Portuguese" society... of individual creolized African men and women.'[3]

At first there was little formal organisation among the *lançados* since they settled as individuals among the African peoples, but as their settlements grew an institutional structure became important. Some of their settlements were undoubtedly large, Cacheu in the late sixteenth century containing a Christian population of 700–800, which increased to around 1,500 by the second decade of the seventeenth century, when 500 of them were described as being '*brancos*', an honorary rather than exactly descriptive epithet since most *lançados*, whatever their skin colour, insisted on their 'white' status.[4] Cacheu unsuccessfully tried to establish its independence from the local Papel rulers. Such settlements were usually confined within a stockade and fortified by other defensive works. The communities were usually under the overall authority of an *alcaide* or *capitão-mor* whose authority would be recognised by the Portuguese authorities in Cape Verde and by the local African ruler, who would often appoint a member of the *lançado* community to hold a kind of judicial office within that community. As an example, one might take 'the *alcaide* at Cape Verde—a Luso-African named Gaspar Gonçalvo who could communicate in several European languages—[and] asserted that he was a Christian and had four wives and six children'.[5]

Other institutions of importance were provided by the church. Most settlements of *lançados* would have a church, even if this was only roughly built of wood and had no resident priest. These churches were served by itinerant mission priests from the Cape Verde Islands who spent short periods in the *lançado* communities marrying the men and baptising the children. In some communities where there was a large Jewish or New Christian population the place of the church was taken by a synagogue, though these seldom survived for very long.

Although independence from Portuguese control had been a major reason for their emigration, the members of the *lançado* community had no desire to cut themselves off from the islands. Trading links meant that there was a regular coming and going between the islands and the mainland settlements. Missionaries also visited the *lançado* communities to try to bring them back to the true faith, while many

Cape Verdeans became temporary residents on the mainland when drought was particularly severe. Moreover the *lançados* and their descendants had a strong interest in maintaining their 'Portuguese' identity. Although as Portuguese they had a privileged position within West African society, on their death their property was subject to confiscation by the ruler. Luso-Africans therefore needed to maintain links with the islands so that they could deposit some of their wealth there for their heirs to inherit. Their association with the islands and with Portugal also enabled them to access European trade goods and to benefit from the shipping and credit arrangements of island commerce.

Embedded in West Africa, but maintaining strong ties with the islands, the *lançado* community underwent a cultural transformation and creolisation. *Lançados* typically used African as well as Portuguese names and observed social and religious practices which were remarkably eclectic, customarily wearing amulets as well as crucifixes and taking offerings to prestigious local shrines. They built square houses, which were distinctive in a country where round houses were the norm, and they wore European-style clothes and hats. In many respects they became a caste of traders within West African society rather than an ethnic group based on lineage and descent. The language they used was a Portuguese creole language, related to but distinct from the creole of the Cape Verde Islands; for a long time Portuguese and Creole were the languages used in West African maritime trade, so that words such as 'palaver' and 'fetish' (from the Portuguese *palavra* and *feitiço*) passed into European and African languages.

Some of the *lançados* referred to in contemporary accounts as *tangomaos*, however, cut themselves off more completely from their Portuguese cultural heritage, 'for they wore African garments and protective amulets, underwent circumcision and scarification, [and] participated in African rituals such as divination'.[6] The term itself appears to be linked to the name given to a lineage which controlled some important shrines, raising the possibility that the Portuguese may have assumed roles of ritual importance in some African societies.[7]

By the seventeenth century visiting Europeans could see little that distinguished the *lançados* from the local African community apart from a few cultural symbols, while many of them had fallen into poverty through the operation of African inheritance laws. Richard Jobson described them as for 'the most part as blacke as the naturall inhabitants ... [but] still reserving carefully, the use of the Portingall tongue, and with a kinde of an affectionate zeale, the name of Christians, taking it in a great disdaine, be they never so blacke, to be called a Negro'.[8] The Luso-African community described themselves not only as 'Portuguese' but also as 'white'—and with good reason. The term 'white' (*branco* or *bidan*) was an indication of free status, and there is an irony in the fact that as the skin colour of the Luso-Africans came increasingly to resemble that of the Africans with whom they intermarried, so the prevalence of the slave trade made the assumption of a 'white' identity all the more important. Just as in the slave society of the US a single black ancestor, however remote, could be sufficient to give a person a 'black' identity, so in African coastal society an equally distant (and possibly imaginary) white ancestor could be enough to confer a 'white' and hence a free status.

One notable feature of the black Portuguese communities was the prominence of women in their social and economic organisation. Philip Havik explains how women from important African clans contracted 'marriages' with Portuguese traders and were able to act as intermediaries in commercial transactions:

> enjoying the confidence of both parties at the point where the interests of Africans and Europeans met, they were able to develop innovative and entrepreneurial strategies... and because of the absences, frequently prolonged, of their husbands they increasingly assumed the role of partners who looked after their husband's business affairs.[9]

The importance of women in the *lançado* community can probably be accounted for by the gradual intrusion of matrilineal structures into the traditionally patriarchal and patrilineal Portuguese community. Through their wives the *lançados* had access to commercial opportunities and became linked to West African trading lineages. Given that many *lançado* males were involved in maritime commerce, which made them temporary absentees, and that some died overseas or else failed to return, the gradual emergence of women as dominant in this community can be understood. In the seventeenth and eighteenth centuries women of the Luso-African community owned property, houses and ships and conducted their own trading expeditions. They also acted as brokers for other European traders. Peter Mark gives the example of 'the famous trader and courtesan La Belinguere [who] established a series of alliances with several European merchants of different nationalities....' According to the Frenchman Michel Jajolet de la Courbe, 'she had a noble manner and a refined tongue and she spoke good

215

Portuguese, French and English, a certain indication of the extensive commerce she had carried on with all these nations'. The term 'commerce' clearly indicated an overlap between her professional, personal and sexual life.[10]

As French, English and Dutch contacts with West Africa grew, the *lançados* clung tenaciously to their trade. However, increasingly they ceased to be principals in the trade and became interpreters and brokers facilitating commercial contacts between West African states and the visiting Europeans. There are examples of visiting Dutch and French traders taking women from the *lançado* community as local wives to assist in interpretation and commercial contacts. However, once the Luso-Africans became brokers rather than principals in the trade of the coast, their communities became more isolated and cut off from the Cape Verde Islands or any other source of Portuguese culture. By the nineteenth century Portuguese and creole had been replaced as trading languages on much of the coast by French and English. Moreover, French and English traders in Guinea had increasing problems with the self-identification of this group as 'Portuguese' because their black skin seemed to define them incontrovertibly as African.[11] Being Portuguese now became little more than using Portuguese names and claiming to be Christian rather than animist or Muslim.

In the course of the nineteenth century a number of Brazilian traders based themselves in West Africa, particularly in the region of Dahomey, making use of the moribund Portuguese trading post of Ouidah (Ajuda). These traders established important links with local African rulers, founded local families and brought about a significant revival of the influence of the black 'Portuguese', including the use of the Portuguese language in local correspondence.[12]

As well as the settlements of the *lançados*, the Portuguese Crown also established a number of official trading posts on the African coast: Arguin on the coast of Mauritania, founded around 1446; São Jorge da Mina on the coast of modern Ghana, which in 1482 was sited in a large stone-built castle; Axim in 1520 and Ajuda (Ouidah) in 1580. A permanent trading factory was also maintained at the court of the Kongo king at Mbanza, 150 miles from the coast with a linked trading port on the Zaire estuary. These permanent posts housed commercial personnel and diplomatic and religious missions—the most important being the missions that were accredited to the Obas of Benin and the kings of Kongo. The Portuguese *fidalgos*, soldiers and traders who visited Benin were expertly portrayed by Benin bronze casters who were intrigued by their dress, their firearms and their long European noses.

By the mid sixteenth century a Christian population had grown up among the people who lived around these Portuguese trading factories and forts, and this population merged with the black Portuguese from Cape Verde and São Tomé to form a substantial, partly Lusitanised population, most strikingly in the Kongo kingdom.

While São Tomé evolved as a slave-owning plantation society, drawing on the contemporaneous diasporas of European Portuguese, African slaves and Sephardic Jews, it also became a point from which migration took place to the African mainland. Using the islands as a base, a fruitful commerce grew up with the African states of the Gulf of Guinea and the Zaire region, which often deliberately flouted the commercial regulations of the Crown. Before long there were São Tomean communities settled in various coastal African states in the region. In the Kongo kingdom the São Tomeans were often in direct competition with the Portuguese Crown and, making use of their local knowledge, were able to circumvent the official embargos which tried to channel all trade through the port of Mpinda and the hands of the Kongo king and the Portuguese royal factor. During the sixteenth century the São Tomeans became a rival Portuguese presence in Kongo, frequently taking part in wars in the interior or opening up trading links with enemies of the Kongo kingdom; and it was São Tomé islanders who established the first trading station at Luanda island in order to exploit the shell fisheries there. São Tomé was the nearest sovereign Portuguese territory to the Kongo kingdom and the kings hoped that relations with the island captains would enable them to obtain military support and direct communication with Portugal. However, the islanders had no intention of acting as agents for the Kongo king and deliberately intercepted his messages. When the Kongo was invaded by the Jaga in the 1560s, the São Tomeans used the opportunity to purchase the refugee Kongolese as slaves.

The Kongo and the creolisation of an African elite

As the Portuguese settled the Atlantic islands and established an economy based on sugar and slaves, the diaspora took a direction wholly unanticipated and unimagined by the royal princes who had set the

217

EMIGRATION AND THE SEA

whole process in motion. In 1482 Dom João II had commissioned a knight of his household, Diogo Cão, to explore the coast of Africa south of the equator. Sailing into the estuary of the Zaire River, Cão came into contact with the large kingdom of Kongo. In 1491 a Portuguese embassy was despatched to establish links with the king and, somewhat unexpectedly, the ruling elite of the Kongo rapidly embraced Christianity as a new royal cult. Adopting Christianity enhanced the power of the king and cemented the alliance with Portugal from which prestigious imports would be obtained. By the early sixteenth century the Portuguese formed an influential community in Mpinda. The Portuguese community was made up of trade officials who handled the Kongo trade on behalf of the king, priests and an increasing numbers of artisans, seamen, soldiers and servants. In the capital, Mbanza, called by the Portuguese São Salvador, the Portuguese community lived in its own walled quarter within the city.

When the very survival of the Kongo kingdom was threatened by the Jaga invasion of the 1560s, a Portuguese army was sent to reinstate the Kongo king and many of the soldiers remained in the country, marrying locally and developing commercial ties with the interior. The influence of the Luso-African community in the Kongo was greatly enhanced by the adoption of a creole culture by the ruling Kongo elite. The ruling elites took Portuguese names and wore Portuguese-style clothing. Many Kongolese became literate and Christian ceremonies and customs percolated into Kongolese everyday life. Many Kongolese youths were sent to Portugal to be educated and Kongolese priests were ordained to serve the church. One son of the Kongo king, Afonso I, was made a bishop by Pope Leo X.

As the influence of the Portuguese grew, the Portuguese Crown was encouraged to try to extend this influence in the region south of the Kongo kingdom where the dominant ethnic group was the Mbundu. Embassies and missions to the Mbundu allowed commerce to develop but did not lead to the kind of alliance, underpinned by mass conversion, that had happened in the Kongo. As a result the Portuguese Crown, supported by the Jesuits, decided in 1570 to adopt a different approach. During the 1570s there was a revival of a militant approach to the spreading of the gospel which worked hand in hand with a desire to emulate the success of the Spanish conquests in the Americas and discover the gold and silver mines believed to exist in the African interior. In 1575 a 'donatary captaincy' was granted to Paulo Dias de

Novais so that he could undertake the conquest and settlement of the region that was to become Angola. Like the captaincies in the Atlantic Islands and Brazil, the Angolan captaincy had as a specific requirement the organisation of a settlement of Portuguese and the creation of a new *reino* or kingdom.

Paulo Dias began the settlement of his captaincy in 1571 by occupying Luanda. By 1579 he was meeting stiff opposition and had begun a painstaking conquest of the interior. In this he was assisted by soldiers sent from Portugal but also by the Kongo king and by the Luso-Africans settled in the Kongo kingdom. The slow conquest of the Angolan interior continued in the seventeenth century, the wars generating large numbers of captives so that Angola replaced Guinea and the Kongo as the main source of slaves for the expanding Brazilian sugar industry. Brazilian interest in Angola grew and soldiers for the wars were increasingly recruited across the Atlantic rather than in Portugal. The slaves exported through the ports of Luanda and Benguela (founded in 1616) formed the wealth of this Portuguese kingdom, but the trade was almost exclusively with Brazil not Portugal. Soldiers, governors and traders came and went between Luanda, Rio and Bahia. Convicts sent to Angola came as often from Brazil as from Portugal. The Portuguese settlements round the rim of the Atlantic had formed diasporic communities, which held strongly to their Portuguese identity but whose economic and social life was to a large extent divorced from metropolitan Portugal.

Meanwhile Angola was being organised as a new *reino* of the kings of Portugal. It was another kingdom subject to the Portuguese Crown, like the kingdoms of Portugal and the Algarve and the Estado da Índia, but although governors, convicts, missionaries and traders continued to arrive from Portugal and Brazil, the disease environment was hostile and newcomers from Europe frequently died within a short time of arrival. Increasingly the permanent Portuguese population was made up of black Portuguese—the offspring of the soldiers and traders—and the Christianised populations that lived in areas of Portuguese control. Luanda was given its own town council, and although a bishopric had been created for the Kongo in 1596, the bishops resided in Luanda which also became the site for a Jesuit mission.

During the seventeenth century the creole Luso-African community grew. Although a few Portuguese women *degredadas* were sent to Angola, most of the Portuguese there married locally with African or

Luso-African women. Many acquired land in the conquered regions which they ran as plantations with slave labour, while the frequent wars led to the recruitment of African soldiers, the *guerra preta*, who played a large part in the fighting. As the century progressed, what was essentially a Luso-African kingdom emerged, based on the twin ports of Luanda and Benguela. This Luso-African community differed from that established in Guinea and the Kongo kingdom in that it was a self-governing domain of the Crown of Portugal and not a community dependent on the goodwill of an African potentate. The Luso-African creole community of Angola not only assumed an important role in the history of the South Atlantic but became a distinctive Portuguese community in south central Africa. The local creole families controlled the port of Luanda and, in partnership with Portuguese and Brazilian interests, also controlled a slave trade which exceeded in volume even that operated by the British and French. The Luanda creoles were major landowners, organised trading caravans in the interior, controlled the church, the town government and the local militias. Inland creole towns grew up, especially along the Kwanza River and in the highlands inland of Benguela. No creole language took root but the creole families used Kimbundu as well as Portuguese for the conduct of their affairs. They were a community integrated by trade both with the world of the Atlantic and with the commerce of the African interior, while their culture derived equally from Portuguese and Brazilian and central African sources.

Since the planting of the first permanent trading posts on the African coast in the fifteenth century, the Portuguese Crown had never entirely abandoned the idea of creating thriving Portuguese communities in Africa. The creation of a 'donatary captaincy' in Angola in 1571 clearly had this intention, and in the seventeenth century there were at least two schemes for planting settler colonies in eastern Africa. The regulations surrounding the granting of *prazos* in Zambesia, whereby they were given to women on the condition that they married a Portuguese approved by the Crown, also appears to have been intended to promote settlement. In the event European Portuguese never came to Africa in sufficient numbers to establish a wholly European society. Most of the Portuguese who settled in Africa were either convicts or discharged soldiers, supplemented by a few officials, missionaries and traders. Most of these married locally and the communities that established themselves in Angola, the Kongo kingdom and Zambesia, were Afro-

Portuguese in character, owing as much to the lineages of their African mothers as to their, sometimes tenuous, links to Portuguese fathers or more distant ancestors of Portuguese of Luso-Asiatic origin.

By the nineteenth century Angola was dominated by a group of influential Afro-Portuguese families which effectively controlled the economic and political life of the colony and spoke both Portuguese and Kimbundu. In Guinea there was a creole-speaking population, who were known as Kriston, living in and around the old coastal and riverain trading settlements, and in Mozambique an important group of elite Afro-Portuguese families controlled much of the land and trade along the Zambesi and in the hinterland of the coastal towns of Sofala and Quelimane. These groups were emphatic in claiming to be 'Portuguese', a claim which frequently embarrassed the Lisbon government when British explorers reported their slaving activities and their way of life that was very far from that which the British believed should mark a European presence in Africa. The outlines were thus drawn for the image of the sinister 'half-caste' Portuguese slaver, a favourite character in Victorian novels and travelogues about Africa.[13]

Rider Haggard, John Buchan and the Portuguese as moral delinquent

In 1885 Rider Haggard published *King Solomon's Mines*, a novel which had an enormous vogue in the last years of the nineteenth century. As has already been mentioned, the Victorians interpreted Portuguese history with a particular racist slant. Portugal had had a golden age in the sixteenth century when heroic *conquistadores* performed great deeds, but this had been followed by a long period of decline brought about by moral degeneration resulting from intermarriage with Asians and Africans. Haggard bought into this interpretation. In his novel, the search for the mines originated in a document written in Portuguese by a sixteenth-century Portuguese explorer, José da Silvestra, a recognition by the author of the heroic deeds of the early Portuguese *conquistadores* and, incidentally, a recognition of Portugal's claims to prior discovery in Africa. However, this was offset by the condition of the Portuguese settlement to be met with in the late nineteenth century. 'Now I know your Delagoa Portugee well. There is no greater devil unhung in a general way, battening as he does upon human agony and flesh in the shape of slaves.'[14] The body of the old Portuguese explorer is found deep-frozen in a cave—a gaunt skeletal corpse symbolic of all that remained of Portugal's former glory, and the modern Portuguese, the descendant of Silvestra, died in his attempt to take possession of the mines discovered by his ancestor. It was left to the plucky Englishmen to win through where Portugal had failed. As such the book is a commentary on Portugal's claims made at the Berlin Conference which had concluded its deliberations in February 1885.

John Buchan acquired a great, many would think undeserved, reputation as a teller of adventure stories. The appeal of his books carried him eventually to being appointed Governor General of Canada, and no aspect of his writing was more important than the way his heroes seem to embody the mythology underpinning the British Empire. In 1910 Buchan published *Prester John*, which was to become one of his best known novels. At the time the British colonies in South Africa, newly united by the Act of Union, were trying to establish a satisfactory relationship with the Portuguese who had emerged from the partition of Africa in control of a third of the coastline of eastern Africa, including Delagoa Bay, the best port of access to the southern African interior. Although a working relationship had been established in the Mozambique–Transvaal Convention of 1908, the desire of South African politicians to gain possession of the bay was frequently expressed and helped to fuel the campaign to vilify the Portuguese which had been, and still was, the stock in trade of much English writing on imperial topics.

John Buchan's *Prester John* is set in South Africa and is a tale of a charismatic black leader, Laputa, who raises a rebellion against the whites. In this story the African leader is the noble savage representing all that is finest in native African culture. Alongside him, as the personification of moral corruption, is the Portuguese Henriques. Buchan is using the clichés popular at the time which represented the Portuguese, who ruled the nearby colony of Mozambique, as decadent, cruel and thoroughly unrepresentative of the civilising mission of the white race. For many writers, to be Portuguese was considered as being synonymous with being a slaver, and the epithet 'half-caste' was often attached to them to emphasise that they were not really white Europeans at all. Here one might recall the separate status accorded to the Portuguese immigrants in the British Caribbean islands.

Henriques was first met by the hero, David Crawfurd, on his voyage out to South Africa:

he... was a little man... and in looks the most atrocious villain I have ever clapped eyes on. He had a face the colour of French mustard—a sort of dirty green—and bloodshot, beady eyes with the whites all yellowed with fever. He had waxed moustaches, and a curious, furtive way of walking and looking about him.[15]

This passage is almost a textbook example of racism in which a man's complexion, hinting at racial mixture, is taken as a sure indication of moral turpitude. Henriques is a dapper dresser but wears yellow shoes 'to match his complexion'—a thing only a cad would do! '"I'll wager that fellow has been a slave driver in his time," I told Mr Wardlaw, who said, "God pity his slaves then".'[16]

Later, trying to find out more about Henriques, Crawfurd consults a Scot called Aiken: 'Tut, my man, most of the subjects of his Majesty the King of Portugal would answer to that description. If he's a rascal, as you think, you may be certain he's in the I.D.B. [Illicit Diamond Buying] business.' And Aiken is correct, Henriques is in the business of selling the diamonds that had been smuggled to Laputa who was to head the rising. But worse, Henriques had been responsible for the death of some Boer farmers and, overhearing this, Crawfurd says, 'My fingers itched to get at the Portugoose—that double-dyed traitor to his race.'[17]

Henriques, it transpires, is a traitor even to Laputa, his collaborator and the leader of the black rebellion, and wants to get possession of the necklace of rubies which is the talisman of the rising. Crawfurd determines he must at all costs find 'a means of spoiling the Portugoose's game'.[18] As treachery of the blackest kind is revealed, Crawfurd finds himself in the company of Laputa who thus describes Henriques rather perceptively: 'The Portuguese is what you call a 'mean white'. His only safety is among us.... You are too hard on Henriques. You and your friends have treated him as a Kaffir, and a Kaffir he is in everything but Kaffir virtues.'[19]

Once again a character in a story, one might say a caricature rather than a character, is a metonym for the relations of one nation with another. Henriques and Crawfurd stand for Portugal and Britain, rivals in the colonial field and standing for opposed moral principles. Henriques, the 'mean white', has a full house of the vices of his nation; while Crawfurd is the honest, upright Britisher and, by implication, the representative of the force making for civilisation, justice and morality in the world. It is significant that when the two finally meet, Henriques is laid out not by a bullet but by a good straight left to the jaw.

Portugal's dilemma in Africa

The Portuguese were well aware of the way they were perceived and represented to the Victorian public. The Lisbon government knew that it depended on the private armies and local networks of the creoles to maintain its presence in Africa while, at the same time, it wanted to free itself from the accusations which the behaviour of these elites brought on it. To do this it seemed necessary to increase white settlement in the colonies, so experiments in planting settlers were begun almost immediately after Brazil declared its independence from Portugal in 1822. Before long the idea began to take shape in official circles that Africa might become a 'new Brazil', bringing economic benefits to the mother country and leading to the growth of a new society that would resemble that of Brazil.

Most of these early experiments proved unsuccessful. Plans for settlements in eastern Africa came to nothing, but in Angola the establishment of the coastal settlement of Mossamedes in the south of the colony began to attract some settlers, particularly fishermen from Madeira and some Portuguese who left Pernambuco during the anti-Portuguese riots there in the 1840s. Behind Mossamedes lay the healthy Huila highlands, and some Portuguese settled there to ranch cattle. However, these new settlements were modest and did little to divert the flood of emigration bound for the Americas.[20] For most Portuguese, Africa still conjured up images of slavery, witchcraft, warfare, disease and famine, and this, added to the lack of amenities and its undeveloped economy, proved profoundly unattractive to would-be emigrants who were easily able to access long-standing networks in Brazil.

In the last years of the nineteenth century there was intense debate about emigration, and almost everyone of note in Portugal had something to say about it. As Portugal's position in Africa became increasingly threatened by Britain, it was argued that the only way to achieve effective occupation of the colonies was to promote white settlement. This alone would secure Portugal's status as a colonial power and with it the country's very survival. However, here opinions differed with some arguing that the object should be to recreate Portuguese society in Africa through colonisation by farming families. The settlement of whole families was deemed necessary because if men came alone to Africa, following the pattern of emigration to the Americas, the result would be a population of mulattos which, in the context of the race-conscious world of the end of the nineteenth century, was seen as highly undesirable. Others argued that Africa should be exploited through capital investment, allowing the Africans to provide the labour force. In this case the existence of the large African population would, it was claimed, leave no room for unskilled Portuguese immigrants.[21]

Most colonial governors expressed reservations about encouraging the settlement of poor Portuguese families. They would have no skills to help in the development of the colonies and would be a burden on the colonial exchequer. Two twentieth-century High Commissioners in Angola, Norton de Matos and Vicente Ferreira, however, were exceptions and tried in various ways to increase Portuguese settlement. Norton was opposed to Portuguese settlers living off African labour and envisaged largely segregated communities.[22] Although he persisted with subsidised passages to Angola for would-be immigrants, his policy had little success.

Meanwhile, the Portuguese government continued with the policy of establishing settlements for convicts. Convicts had been sent to Angola and Mozambique since the sixteenth century and the idea persisted that these forced settlers could be made to form thriving agricultural communities in the interior. The reality was invariably disastrous as there was no support provided and the convicts either starved or deserted. Those who survived did so by slaving or carrying on petty trade, while others drifted to the towns and lived as vagabonds and paupers. The convicts helped to confirm the evil reputation that Angola had in the eyes of would-be immigrants, but the practice continued until 1934 when the 1,500 remaining convicts were repatriated.[23]

According to Cláudia Castelo, the white Portuguese population of Angola in 1900 stood at around 9,000 and that of Mozambique at under 3,000.[24] These figures, however, only tell part of the story of the Portuguese presence, as they do not include the members of the long-standing Portuguese creole communities. Nor do they accurately represent all the non-African elements in the population, people who remained closely allied to the Portuguese even if they did not have a 'Portuguese' identity—for example, the Boers who had migrated to Huila in the 1880s or the Indians who had come to Mozambique to trade and the Goans who worked in the administration. Moreover, as the South African economy developed rapidly in the 1870s, a large and very diverse population was to be found in the seaports of the Mozambique coast, which provided the ports of entry to the Transvaal.

Settlement policy 1926–74

Portuguese settlement in Africa grew only slowly in the first two decades of the twentieth century, and was mostly made up of civil servants, demobilised soldiers and men working for the large companies that had begun operations—companies like the Benguela Railway or Diamang in Angola, Sena Sugar and the Mozambique Company in Mozambique. As Cláudia Castelo observes, the Portuguese who came to Africa at this time were few in number when compared with the masses who were leaving for the New World, but among them were people with some education or professional skill who were rather different from the poor and often illiterate emigrants leaving Portugal at this time for the US, Brazil or Argentina.

During the 1930s the government of Salazar stopped sending convicts to Africa and brought the various schemes for assisted passages to an end. Salazar did not want poor Portuguese to go to Africa where they would prove a burden on the local exchequers and would bring Portugal's 'civilising mission' into disrepute. Instead it was held that, as the economy of the colonies gradually expanded, there would be a natural increase in the white population.[25] There was, indeed, a slow growth in the numbers of Portuguese in the colonies, mostly due to the increase in the numbers of civil servants and technocrats sent to carry out Salazar's development policies. By 1940 there were 44,083 whites in Angola and 27,438 in Mozambique, not all of them Portuguese. The census of that year also recorded the people of mixed race, whose numbers were rather more than half that of the whites. Their numbers are almost certainly only a rough figure, as there were very many descendants of the old creole population of uncertain racial status.

During the Second World War Portugal took the first steps towards the industrialisation of the colonies, and this policy was pursued more vigorously after the war as a range of food processing and consumer industries were created.[26] These were also the years of the coffee boom in Angola. With the rapid expansion of the colonial economies, the employment opportunities for Portuguese immigrants greatly increased and substantial numbers now set off for Angola and Mozambique. This coincided with both Brazil and the US strictly limiting the numbers of immigrants. In 1951 a Junta da Emigração was created to regulate emigration to the colonies in an attempt to weed out the poor and illiterate.[27] From 1950 to 1960 there was a net immigration of over 10,000 a year, and during the 1962–72 period numbers ranged between 14,326 in 1965 and 3,260 in 1971. The year 1961 was exceptional as the outbreak of rebellion in Angola in that year led to a net departure from Angola of 4,971, most of whom returned the following year. Altogether between 1943 and 1974 there was net migration to Africa of 251,446. Although these numbers are not as high as the numbers going to France, they are comparable with emigration to most other destinations during this period. At the end of the colonial period there were 324,000 whites in Angola and 190,000 in Mozambique, 35 per cent of whom had been born in Africa.[28] These numbers were higher than the number of British settlers who went to Central Africa and Kenya during the same period.

During the 1950s and 1960s the government invested heavily in creating agricultural settlements on irrigated land. The largest of these, Cela in Angola, was established in 1953–54. These so-called *colonatos* were supposed to showcase the regime's policy of creating multi-racial rural communities, and some African farmers were allocated land within the settlements alongside Portuguese immigrants. However, the *colonatos* never attracted very many people and do not account for the large Portuguese immigration during these years.

Cláudia Castelo has emphasised that the Portuguese who settled in Africa were relatively skilled and well educated when compared with migrants to other destinations. In 1973 I had the evidence of my own eyes when I travelled to Mozambique on board the liner *Infante Dom Henrique*. There were three classes of passenger on the liner, which represented vividly the Portuguese experience of empire. The very luxurious first class was the domain of governors, generals, senior clerics and the rich; there was a comfortable second class for the professional classes and administrators; and a third class was crowded with poorer emigrants. There women sat all day on deck busy with knitting and crochet work, the men in groups playing cards, with no suspicion of how short their stay in Africa would be.

The typical migrant community, writes Cláudia Castelo, was 'mostly urban, not too mixed racially, and fairly balanced in gender terms, with a high percentage of young people, schooling levels above the national average, and people working mainly in the service sector'.[29] The Angolan Portuguese she describes as entrepreneurial people, attracted by the commercial possibilities of the country, who enjoyed a society that was freer and more open than that of Portugal. Settlers who went to Mozambique were more likely to be in government service. In 1948 10.88 per cent had secondary education or higher and only 6.3 per cent were deemed illiterate. By 1973 16.14 per cent had secondary education or above.[30]

The settlers in Africa always tended to be resentful of Lisbon, and during the war there had been stirrings of opposition in the colonies that had been prompted by the possibility that Portugal would be occupied by the Axis and the colonies would be left to 'go it alone'.[31] Then in 1958 resentment at the control of Lisbon had found expression in the presidential election when the voters in the colonies heavily backed the opposition candidate Humberto Delgado. The vote for Delgado, Castelo writes, 'did not represent an anti-colonial stance but an anti-centralist one, following a "Brazilian" path. The small white bourgeoisie was becoming autonomist.'[32]

After independence

Portugal's decolonisation, following the April 1974 revolution, led to a rapid departure of more than 90 per cent of the Portuguese who had settled in Africa. This created a new large-scale dispersal which took place in a very short time and can probably find a parallel only in the departure of the Portuguese Jews at the end of the fifteenth century. Around three quarters of a million people are thought to have moved back to Portugal, many of them Africans and Indians as well as white Portuguese, but significant numbers also left for Australia and South Africa.

Although most of the recent immigrants departed from the colonies once they became independent, this was not the end of the story of the Portuguese presence in Africa. Left behind were a high proportion of the creoles, descendants of the Afro-Portuguese, who had lost their power and social status during the high colonial period but who formed the core of the liberation movements and aspired once more to take control of the countries where they had once ruled. The ruling elites of the PAIGC, Frelimo and MPLA were largely made up of members of old Afro-Portuguese families (like the Van Dunems in Angola), and Africans like Agostinho Neto and Eduardo Mondlane who had been educated in Portugal and had married white wives, or Amílcar Cabral and his brother Luís who were creoles from Cape Verde. Independence was very much a transfer of power from the white European Portuguese to the black Afro-Portuguese creoles.

Moreover the successor regimes were in many respects very Portuguese in character, not only sharing a language with the colonial power and taking over its highly bureaucratised legal system and administrative culture, but also inheriting the contacts and networks that had bound the former Portuguese state together. The elites of the newly independent Lusophone states still went to Lisbon for medical treatment, sent their children there for university education or their wives on shopping trips. Angolans and Mozambicans continued to follow the fortunes of Benfica, Sporting and FC Porto. Politicians who fell out of favour went into exile in Lisbon and politicians in favour deposited their money there. Moreover the links between the former colonies that had been created in colonial times, and strengthened during the liberation struggle, survived in the semi-formal PALOP (Países Africanos de Língua Portuguesa) organisation which met regularly and which allowed Angola to act as the patron for little São Tomé and to intervene to resolve political crises in the island. When the CPLP was formed in 1996, the Lusophone African states all joined, reconnecting with the wider Lusophone world.

While Portugal enjoyed the benefits of new European Union membership, large numbers of Angolans and Guineans (and Brazilians) moved to Lisbon to work, and when the downturn of the European economy hit Portugal after 2008, equally large numbers of Portuguese began to return to Africa seeking professional and managerial posts in the expanding, even booming, economies of oil-rich Angola and coal- and gas-rich Mozambique. By 2012 estimates were putting the numbers of Portuguese in Angola at over 100,000 and growing—a number soon to approach the numbers that had settled there in the colonial era.

Cape Verdeans in Africa

As early as the fifteenth century the Portuguese settlers in the Cape Verde Islands began to establish trading settlements on the coast of upper Guinea. These grew into permanent towns during the sixteenth and seventeenth centuries, and the interaction of the Portuguese influence stemming from the islands and the African influences of the mainland helped to create the creole language and culture of the Kriston creole population. Cape Verdean links with Portuguese Guinea continued throughout the colonial period, and members of the Cape Verdean elite formed the PAIGC which brought Guinea (as well as Cape Verde) to independence in 1975.

However, Portuguese Guinea was not the only part of Africa to which Cape Verdeans migrated and where they settled. In one respect the story of the Cape Verdeans in Africa reflects the character of the wider Portuguese diaspora. Emigration from the islands affected all classes, both the educated and the poor and destitute. In the 1930s the Salazar government began to expand the colonial civil service and to give it fresh duties in the promotion of agricultural production. There was a marked shortage of suitable recruits and the government increasingly turned to the Cape Verde Islands to fill the gaps in government service. Cape Verdeans were employed in all the African colonies as teachers or administrators, and some joined the important and prestigious Colonial Inspectorate. As Alexander Keese has pointed out, although these people were for the most part very loyal to the regime and 'would fully embrace the rhetoric of the *Estado Novo*',[33] some of them were to be found among the strongest critics of official policy, particularly as it affected the islands themselves'. When Cape Verde became independent in 1975, many of those who had worked for the Portuguese colonial regime found a return to their homeland to be problematic. 'A majority of those officials would after April 1974 migrate to Lisbon, into a sometimes inevitable, sometimes self-chosen exile.'[34]

As well as the elite of colonial officials, thousands of ordinary Cape Verdeans also found their way to Africa. António Carreira found the first evidence of labourers being recruited in Cape Verde for work in Africa in the eighteenth century when 'successive levies of people from Santiago' were sent to Guinea between 1765 and 1773 to build the fortress of São José in Bissau.[35] This proved to be a precedent, for when the crippling cycle of droughts struck the islands after 1855, a cycle that was to last for the next hundred years, contracting the destitute islanders for work in the African colonies was seen as a way of providing famine relief. The cocoa and coffee *roças* (plantations) of São Tomé and Príncipe were just beginning to become profitable and required large quantities of labour. Cape Verdeans were offered contracts to work there alongside contracted labourers from Angola. Emigration was certainly seen by the islanders as an option when faced by famine, but they preferred to obtain passages to the US or South America, while many made the short sea crossing to seek work in Dakar or The Gambia. São Tomé and Príncipe were not popular destinations owing to the reputation the islands had for disease and for ill treatment of the workforce.

Early in the twentieth century the Portuguese authorities took steps to prevent emigration to Dakar and enacted measures to steer emigrants to São Tomé and Príncipe. Between 1902 and 1922 22,671 Cape Verdeans were recruited under contract and figures show a further 14,845 recruited between 1941 and 1949—years that included the severe famines of 1941–42 and 1947—and 34,530 between 1950 and 1970. In addition some Cape Verdeans were recruited for work in Angola and Mozambique.[36]

Mortality in São Tomé and Príncipe was high and there was some repatriation—Carreira records 12,150 Cape Verdeans repatriated between 1906 and 1936—but in the course of three-quarters of a century a permanent population of Cape Verdean plantation workers was established. Its position in the islands was anomalous in a number of respects. The inhabitants of the Cape Verde Islands were deemed to be *civilisados*, that is, they were not subject to the *indigenato*, the laws governing African natives (*indígenas*). They had the same legal status as European Portuguese, yet they were performing work contracts alongside the African labourers (*serviçais*). Cape Verdeans acquired a reputation with the *roça* managers of being 'difficult' and even unruly as some of them had levels of education better than the white overseers. Augusto Nascimento even records that 'some Cape Verdeans were actually asked to write letters for the white illiterate employers'.[37] At the same time there was no love lost between them and the *serviçais*, and during the disturbances of 1953 the Cape Verdeans sided with the white population.

At independence in 1975 there were around 15,000 Cape Verdeans still in São Tomé and Príncipe, including 6,500 children. They were marginalised by the new ruling elite and in 1990 even lost the right to vote in elections. According to Nascimento they have remained a group 'impoverished and aged [with] little political leverage',[38] a fragment of the Portuguese diaspora left stranded by the receding tide of empire.

Portuguese settlement in South Africa

The Frelimo leaders who took over the Mozambique government in 1975 made little or no effort to persuade the white population to stay. The nationalisation of businesses, housing, education and health sent a message that the privileged white standard of living was no longer sustainable. The scramble to leave the colony followed rapidly. The easiest means of departure was to drive to the South African border, and the Portuguese troops still in Mozambique apparently provided escorts for these convoys. Once in South Africa the refugees were received in temporary camps before being permanently resettled in the country. Since many of the refugees were professional people or skilled workers, their incorporation into the industrial economy of South Africa was not difficult. According to official figures, 33,000 Mozambican whites and 4,000 Angolans entered South Africa between 1974 and 1980—though the real number is likely to have been higher.[39]

The Portuguese who arrived from the former colonies found Portuguese communities already well-established in South Africa. The most numerous were Madeirans who had begun to come to South Africa at the end of the nineteenth century when many of their compatriots were emigrating to Angola. Many of the Madeirans established themselves as fishermen, while others made a living from market gardening. One factor which made the migration of Madeirans to South Africa relatively easy was the regular stops at Madeira made by Union Castle liners en route to South Africa. By 1904 there were said to be 1,000 Madeirans in Cape Colony.[40] Once communities had been established, the process of chain migration took effect and there was a steady flow of new arrivals from the island throughout most of the twentieth century, at around 200 a year. Another estimate shows 14,000 Madeirans entering South Africa between 1940 and 1981.[41] Like the Atlantic islanders who settled in Canada or the US, the Madeirans tended to form closed communities, to marry among themselves and to maintain a low profile. The Madeirans also adopted a lifestyle rather different from other white South Africans. The 'Madeiran pioneer filled the space around his dwelling, through the small trellis, the backyard with kale and other vegetables, often with a hencoop and sometimes even a pigsty', as Victor Pereira da Rosa and Salvato Trigo rather patronisingly put it.[42] However, although a lack of education held back the social advancement of this group, as it did in Jersey and elsewhere, many of them did very well in their businesses. The same authors calculated that people of Madeiran descent controlled 75–80 per cent of the horticultural market of Johannesburg and 80 per cent of the fruit market.

Although they shared a religious affiliation in common, the Madeiran community remained to a large extent isolated from other Portuguese immigrants. The Madeirans also suffered from the strong prejudices current in racially divided South Africa, particularly in the 1960s and 1970s when the tide of Afrikaner nationalism was running strongly. They were openly reviled as an undesirable element and were even described as 'white kaffirs'.[43] A survey conducted in 1977 showed that between 40 and 45 per cent of Afrikaners thought that all Portuguese immigration should be stopped.[44]

There was a third group of Portuguese in South Africa: direct immigrants from mainland Portugal. Many of these came with assisted passages to the colony of Mozambique, making their way from Lourenço Marques to South Africa in search of better jobs. Most of these were skilled people responding to the high demand for skilled white labour in segregated South Africa.

As usual with Portuguese migrations, there are widely differing estimates of the size of the Portuguese population in South Africa. As da Rosa and Trigo put it,

we would not dare to estimate their numbers, in the manner of some political and community heads, who state that the Madeirans in the country number 300,000. The data supplied by the South African Statistics Branch on white, especially Portuguese, immigration are both arbitrary and inconsistent'

They go on to quote some estimates that claim 'that there are 600,000 Portuguese in South Africa, or just as readily that there are 700,000 ... The inflation of numbers by some Portuguese living in Johannesburg even borders on the simplistic, when they try to convince us and to convince themselves that they are a million.'[45]

The more sober statisticians who compile the *Observatório da Emigração* have arrived at much more modest figures. In 2011 the Portuguese consulate had 70,171 registered, of whom 34,913 had been born in Portugal, though many of these had dual nationality. These figures do not count people with a Portuguese ancestry who are South African citizens, who were estimated in 2008 to be 200,000.[46] Whatever the absolute numbers, in terms of proportions it is thought that around 50 per cent are Madeirans or their descendants, 35 per cent refugees from Mozambique and Angola and 15 per cent from continental Portugal.[47]

The Portuguese community in Johannesburg funded the building of two cathedrals, maintains a number of social clubs and since 1963 Portuguese language newspapers, but the community identity has been weakened by marriages outside the group and by dispersal from the original points of settlement, like 'Little Portugal' in Johannesburg.

According to Glaser they 'lacked the kind of cohesion we see in other immigrant groups such as Jews and Greeks', while 'most were comfortable with their Portuguese origins [they] were eager to become ordinary white South Africans'. Like Portuguese communities elsewhere, they have kept a low profile and 'have become a diverse, mobile, transnational group, with often hybrid fluid identities'.[48]

12

THE PORTUGUESE AND THE SEA

The inhabitants of coastal Portugal and the Atlantic islands have always lived in close proximity to the sea, which both imprisoned them in their small world but also offered them the means to escape from it. It was through their activity as seamen, whalers and fishermen that so many islanders discovered the desire and also the means to emigrate, and it was the spirit of cooperation and interdependence, so essential for survival at sea, which determined that their emigration, historically so closely linked with seafaring, would be a family and community affair not just dependent on the decision of an individual.

Two intimate portraits of seafaring Portuguese show them at home on the ocean, no longer setting out as discoverers and *conquistadores* but seeking a livelihood beyond the limited horizons of their homeland.

Rudyard Kipling had never been to sea, but his book *Captains Courageous* (published in 1897), a rite-of-passage novel written as a children's story but from an adult's perspective, idealised the life of fishing schooners working on the Grand Banks off Newfoundland. The hero of the story, Hervey Cheyne, is washed overboard from a liner but is fished out of the sea by Manuel, a Portuguese seaman linefishing from a dory based on the schooner *We're Here*. Hervey's first sight of Manuel as he comes round is of a figure 'showing a pair of little gold rings half hidden in curly black hair'.[1] Manuel cheerfully informs him, '"I think you cut into baits by the screw, but you dreeft—you dreeft to me, and I make a big fish of you."'

Harvey's companion, Dan, explains that Manuel 'rows Portugoosey; ye can't mistake him'.[2] Manuel talks in a sort of all-purpose 'Dago' dialect, which doesn't sound very Portuguese, but this must be put down to Kipling's irrepressible habit, not always successful, of trying to reproduce the language of ordinary working men and ordinary soldiers and sailors. 'There is no to be thankful for to *me*!' he says. 'How shall I leave you dreeft, dreeft all around the Banks?'[3] Manuel came originally from Madeira and had brought with him a banjo—one thinks of the Portuguese bringing the guitar to Hawaii. He had also, in traditional sailor fashion, made a model: 'After supper I show you a little schooner I make with all her ropes. So we shall learn.'[4] To Hervey he says,

'We make you fisherman, these days. If I was you, when I come to Gloucester, I would give two, three big candles for my good luck.'

'Give who?'

'To be sure—the Virgin of our Church on the Hill [Our Lady of Good Voyage in Gloucester]. She is very good to fishermen all the time. That is why so few of us Portugee men ever are drowned.'

'You're a Roman Catholic then?'

'I am a Madeira man. I am not a Porto-Pico [Azorean] boy. Shall I be Baptist then? ... I always give candles—two, three more when I come to Gloucester. The good Virgin, she never forgets me, Manuel.'[5]

Manuel's talk was slow and gentle—all about pretty girls in Madeira washing clothes in the dry beds of streams, by moonlight, under waving bananas; legends of saints, and tales of queer dances or fights away in the cold Newfoundland baiting-ports.[6]

Like so many Portuguese in exile, Manuel expressed himself in music, playing 'the jangling, jarring little *machete* to a queer tune, and sang something in Portuguese about "*Nina*, innocente" ending with a full-handed sweep that brought the song up with a jerk.[7]

The Portuguese fisherman, for so many writers the pioneer of Portuguese emigration who opened up the route to the New World, also embodies the virtues implicit in a pre-industrial way of life. The life aboard the ocean-going fishing schooners, which made up the Portuguese White Fleet, required endurance, discipline and dedication. The schooner was the archetypal community in which every person's life rested on the skill of the captain and the support that each member of the crew gave to his fellow. It was the perfect metaphor for society and was idealised by those who saw in the common life of the ordinary

Portuguese seamen virtues that had been nearly lost in the more prosperous societies of the West.

In 1951 Alan Villiers described this ideal world, sailing with the Portuguese cod fishing fleet—the so-called White Fleet, which continued to sail from Portugal to the seas off Newfoundland and Greenland until the revolution of 1974 put a final end to the days of sail.

The Portuguese Bankers had formed the last sailing convoys. There were usually two each way every season; the older, slower schooners to the Grand Banks, and the bigger schooners, with the motor-ships, direct to Davis Straits. Each group went back to Portugal in its own convoy as it had sailed. Station-keeping was managed by sail-handling, particularly by means of the large fishermen's stay sails set between the masts. Usually the sailing convoys kept to themselves, all the ships clearly marked with the Portuguese colour painted on their sides, bows, and counters; and all burning their navigation lights by night, unlike the great hurrying crowds of ordered steamers, deepladen and silent.[8]

The White Fleet was in many ways anachronistic—the schooners maintained by Portugal still powered by the wind when other fishing fleets had fully mechanised. The White Fleet was protected by the Salazar government to support the old way of life of the sea, just as it idealised and tried to preserve the life of the rural peasant on the land. 'Here was a sailing ship,' Villiers wrote, 'a schooner in the old tradition, a vessel designed to be moved by the wind. Magellan could have stepped aboard, or Queiros, or Corte Real, Cabral, da Gama—any of them....'[9]

Villiers' book, *The Quest of the Schooner Argus*, was a romantic farewell to a vanishing way of life, the life of the migrant labourer of the sea. 'There was a democracy fore-and-aft,' he wrote, and the ship's community ran efficiently and without the conflict that Bullen, for example, found on the whalers. Many of the men were related and had sailed with the captain on previous voyages. They were in many respects a family. The schooner's crew was divided between Azoreans and mainlanders, each of them taking separate watches, though Villiers pointed out that 'this marked no schism between the Islanders and the mainland Portuguese, who were the best of friends'.[10]

The dangers of the doryman's life are traditional and remain unchanged—the dangers of swamping, of being overwhelmed in the sea, lost in fog, run down by shipping, smashed against his own ship in a seaway. Alone upon the North Atlantic, often out of sight of his mother-ship and a hundred miles and more from the nearest land, his boat a little thing of fragile planks without power of any kind and without even a rudder, with a home-made sail and an oar or two his only means of making headway through the water, compelled to overload if he is to fish usefully at all, and forced to remain habitually upon the turbulent water of the fog-bound Banks or the stormy shallow seas off Greenland, never knowing when he leaves his ship in the morning that he will come safely back again at night, his food in the dory always cold, his dory without shelter and as exposed as a raft or a piece of driftwood, it is certain that if he were not sustained by his religion and his long traditions, he could never venture to be a doryman.[11]

The skills and endurance of the doryman were legendary.

A small Algarvian *caique* [a single-masted sailing boat] had once sailed to Rio de Janeiro. This had happened in 1807, at the beginning of the Peninsular War, when the Algarvians were among the first to fight. This they did—against heavy odds—with such success at Olhao... that the townspeople decided to send the good news....[12]

Six months at sea and away from friends and family, the fishermen nevertheless kept in touch with home, just as emigrants would try to do.

Once a week there was a special programme broadcast from Portugal for the men on the Banks.... A recording unit went round to each of the principal fishing ports in turn, and recorded brief messages from wives and children at home....These programmes were called the *Hora de Saudade*, the hour of longing: they were the only relaxation the dorymen knew, and they were tremendously appreciated. They were arranged by the Gremio [the fishermen's association] at Lisbon, and have been a feature of the Portuguese Banks fishing for more than a decade.[13]

The mother ship of the fleet was the hospital and supply boat *Gil Eanes*.

The arrival of the *Gil Eanes*, with Captain Tavares de Almeida as the representative of the Gremio and a sort of Portuguese admiral of the Grand Banks and Greenland, was an important event.... The ancient *Gil Eanes*, which was nothing but a little 2,000 tonner built as a short haul tramp, was the only hospital ship on the Banks or, indeed, in the North Atlantic and she was a most useful vessel.[14]

The old ship was replaced in 1955 by a brand new hospital ship which was given the same name and which is preserved today in the port of Viana do Castelo.

The men who manned the schooners and fished from the little dories gave Villiers an insight into what governed the lives of migrant workers and turned many of them into permanent emigrants.

She [the schooner *Vaz*] had as mate an ancient codhunter who had long been master in his own right, and then retired, only to sicken of what seemed to him the aimless life ashore at Ilhavo, and seek a berth afloat again. He did not care for the responsibility of being master, though he had several sons who were masters in the fleet. It may be (as was hinted more than once, though never by Ilhavans) that Ilhavo was something of a matriarchy. Certainly the women there had been left to their own devices while their menfolk were at sea for six to nine months of the year, for at least four and a half centuries. The seafaring traditions of Ilhavo, indeed, went back a good deal further than that, for it had always been noted for its sailors and its fishermen. There were critics who declared that the women of Ilhavo were so accustomed to the undisputed command of their homes and everything in sight, that they now ran Ilhavo and the menfolk too, and the only retreat a man knew was a ship. Whether this was so or not I don't know, but there were fishing communities in which such conditions appeared to prevail. At Nazare, for instance, it was said the women took the fish from the men as they landed, sold them, and only doled out to the fishermen a few niggardly centavos of tobacco.[15]

Villiers saw in the Portuguese fishermen of the White Fleet the virtues and strength of character which he thought were only to be found at sea, and these he set out in a series of pen portraits. They are portraits of the sort of men who in earlier times had been the pioneers, founding the emigrant Portuguese communities throughout the world.

Consider, for example, such a man as Francisco Emilio Battista … First Fisher of the *Argus* since she was built…. He was a lithe, slight man, without an ounce of superfluous fat, with a strong, dark face, and fierce, imperious eyes. He had strong wrists, great hands and a ready smile despite the hardships of his chosen life. Above all he had an infinite capacity for thoroughness in all he did or thought of doing, singleness of purpose and the ability to go straight for what he aimed at, and to keep going despite all difficulties. His energy was boundless, and his strength of will indomitable…. His father Jose fished for forty campaigns upon the Banks and died in the Algarve at the age of seventy.[16]

Francisco Emilio Battista was a simple man, an illiterate, and consequently debarred from entry to the USA and… Australia. Yet he was a man whose knowledge was his own, gained and secure in his own mind, a man educated by life and not misled by nonsense, a man who knew and got on with the job for which he was fitted, a man untroubled by political slogans, uninhibited by any confusion of besetting doubts, unhampered by theories, complacent or destructive. His way of life was set, and for him and his happy kind it was enough: his feet were upon the earth though half the year they trod the frail planks of an arctic dory. He was a man—I thought—very close to God—he, and all dorymen. Down upon the sea, his life in his hands, he knew the way of the sea and the way of the Lord. And, knowing these things, he was fortunate.[17]

239

Francisco Martins ... was a handsome young man, a born fisherman.... His father was a Banker before him: fishing was the only life the family knew.... He had had to swim several times, and he knew he had been lucky to survive. He did not want to expose his children to those risks, though he accepted them cheerfully himself. He would like them to go to America, or perhaps South Africa, or Australia, for there were too many people in the Azores. It was not good to remain crowded upon an island, even so lovely an island as St Michael's [Sao Miguel]. As for himself, he was happy enough at his work—he certainly always gave that impression.... But six months was a long time to be gone from home.[18]

The Portuguese who fished on the Grand Banks, like the rural peasants who set out from the Minho or the Azores to the New World, clung to the 'old ways' with a kind of conservatism which gave them a sense of security against the dangers of life at sea or the unknown hazards of life in the Americas.

The truth was that they were as conservative as they were courageous. New ideas for the ship—yes: they were acceptable and the dorymen could see their great advantages. But new ideas in the dories were entirely different, and not to be tolerated. The ship was something in which they lived and slept and cleaned and salted fish; but their dories—why, they were their lives.[19]

NOTES

FOREWORD

1. Caroline Brettell, 'The Emigrant, the Nation, and Twentieth-century Portugal: An Anthropological Approach', *Portuguese Studies Review*, 2, no. 2 (1993), 51.

1. EMIGRATIONS, DIASPORAS AND PEOPLE ON THE MOVE

1. Toby Green, *The Rise of the Trans-Atlantic Slave Trade in Western Africa, 1300–1589*, Cambridge University Press (Cambridge, 2012).
2. William H. McNeill, 'Human Migration: A Historical Overview', in W. H. McNeill and Ruth S. Adams, *Human Migration Patterns and Policies*, Indiana University Press (Bloomington, 1978), 3–19.
3. James H. Sweet, *Recreating Africa*, University of North Carolina Press (Chapel Hill, NC, 2003).
4. Miriam Halpern Pereira, *A Política Portuguesa de Emigração 1850–1930*, A Regra do Jogo (Lisbon, 1981), 7.
5. Joel Serrão, *A Emigração Portuguesa. Sondagem Histórica*, 2nd edn, Livros Horizonte (Lisbon, 1974), 86–7.
6. This point is concisely argued in Suner Åkerman, 'Towards an Understanding of Emigrational Processes', in W. H. McNeill and Ruth S. Adams, *Human Migration Patterns and Policies*, 287–306.
7. Ibid., 287–8; see discussion in Brettell, 'The Emigrant, the Nation, and Twentieth-century Portugal: An Anthropological Approach', 52.
8. John Darwin, 'Decolonisation and Diaspora', in Eric Morier-Genoud and Michel Cahen, *Imperial Migrations. Colonial Communities and Diaspora in the Portuguese World*, Palgrave Macmillan (Basingstoke, 2012), 316–26; quotation from 322.
9. Linda Colley, *Britons. Forging the Nation 1707–1837*, 2nd edn, Yale University Press (New Haven and London, 2005).
10. Edward Shils, 'Roots—The Sense of Place and Past: The Cultural Gains and

Losses of Migration', in McNeill and Adams, *Human Migration Patterns and Policies*, 411.

11. Helena Carreiras, Diego Bussola, Maria Xavier, Beatriz Padilla and Andrés Malamud, 'Portuguese *Gauchos*: Associations, Social Integration and Collective Identity in Twenty-first Century Argentina, Uruguay and Southern Brazil', *Portuguese Studies Review*, 14, no. 2 (2006–7), 290–1.

12. An excellent introduction to the vast literature on the Portuguese diaspora is Edward A. Alpers and Molly Ball, '"Portuguese" Diasporas: a Survey of the Scholarly Literature', in Eric Morier-Genoud and Michel Cahen, *Imperial Migrations. Colonial Communities and Diaspora in the Portuguese World*, Palgrave Macmillan (Basingstoke, 2012), 31–71.

13. A. J. R. Russell-Wood, *A World on the Move*, Carcanet (Manchester, 1992).

14. Stefan Halikowski-Smith, *Creolization and Diaspora in the Portuguese Indies. The Social World of Ayutthaya 1640–1720*, Brill (Leiden, 2011), 2.

15. Green, *The Rise of the Trans-Atlantic Slave Trade in Western Africa, 1300–1589*, 263.

16. Ibid., 143.

17. Priscilla Doel, 'The White Fleet and the Iconography of Control', in Carlos Teixeira and Victor M. P. Da Rosa, *The Portuguese in Canada*, University of Toronto Press (Toronto, 2000), 37–52. Quotation from page 43.

18. Carreiras *et al.*, 'Portuguese *Gauchos*: Associations, Social Integration and Collective Identity in Twenty-first Century Argentina, Uruguay and Southern Brazil', 288.

19. Shils, 'Roots—The Sense of Place and Past: The Cultural Gains and Losses of Migration', 408.

20. See ch. 4 of Malyn Newitt, *Portugal in European and World History*, Reaktion Books (London, 2009).

2. POINTS OF DEPARTURE: PORTUGAL FROM THE FIFTEENTH TO THE NINETEENTH CENTURY

1. José Maria Ferreira de Castro, *Emigrantes*, first published 1928, Guimarães (Lisbon, 1946), 30.

2. For the Portuguese military nobility, see J. G. Monteiro, *A Guerra em Portugal nos Finais da Idade Média*, Editorial Notícias (Lisbon, 1998), and discussion in Malyn Newitt, 'The Portuguese Nobility and the Rise and Decline of Portuguese Military Power 1400–1650', in D. J. B. Trim, ed., *The Chivalric Ethos and the Development of Military Professionalism*, Brill (Leiden, 2003), 89–116.

3. A. H. de Oliveira Marques, *A Expansão Quatrocentista*, vol. 2 of *Nova História da Expansão Portuguesa*, Joel Serrão and A. H. de Oliveira Marques, eds, Editorial Estampa (Lisbon, 1998), 203.

4. Ibid., 300–1.

5. 'Letter of João de Meneses to Dom Manuel, 1514', in Pierre de Cenival, ed., *Les sources inédites de l'histoire du Maroc: archives et bibliothèques de Portugal*, Tome 1 (1486–1516), Geuthner (Paris, 1934), 545–8. Translation in M. Newitt,

The Portuguese in West Africa 1415–670, Cambridge University Press (New York, 2010), 37–40.

6. Oliveira Marques, *A Expansão Quatrocentista*, 298.

7. 'O vector social dinâmico é o cavaleiro-mercador', quoted in Alberto Vieira, 'A Emigração portuguesa nos Descobrimentos: Do Littoral às Ilhas', *Portuguese Studies Review*, 15, nos. 1–2 (2007), 69.

8. François Pyrard, *The Voyage of François Pyrard*, A. Gray, ed., 2 vols., Hakluyt Society (London, 1887–90), 86.

9. Alan Villiers, *The Quest of the Schooner Argus*, Hodder and Stoughton (London, 1951).

10. Caroline Brettell, *Anthropology and Migration*, Altamira (Oxford, 2003), 14–15.

11. Richard Robinson, *Contemporary Portugal*, George Allen and Unwin (London, 1979), 153.

12. For a good summary of Ericeira's policies see A. R. Disney, *A History of Portugal and the Portuguese Empire*, Cambridge University Press (Cambridge, 2009), vol. 1, 245–8.

13. Figures from A. H. de Oliveira Marques, *History of Portugal*, Columbia University Press (New York, 1972), vol. 1, 387–92.

14. António Costa Pinto, 'Elites, Single Parties and Political Decision-making in Fascist-era Dictatorships', *Contemporary European History*, II (2002), 434.

15. Oliveira Marques, *A Expansão Quatrocentista*, 305.

16. Pyrard, *The Voyage of François Pyrard*, 122.

17. Oliveira Marques, *A Expansão Quatrocentista*, 302–3; Vitor Luís Pinto Gaspar da Conceição Rodrigues, 'A Guiné nas Cartas de Perdão (1463–1500)', in *Congresso Internacional Bartolomeu Dias e a sua Época*, Comissão Nacional para as Comemorações dos Descobrimentos Portugueses (Porto, 1989), vol. IV, 397–412.

18. Timothy J. Coates, *Convicts and Orphans. Forced and State-Sponsored Colonizers in the Portuguese Empire, 1550–1755*, Stanford University Press (Stanford, CA, 2001), 25.

19. Malyn Newitt, *History of Mozambique*, Hurst & Co. (London, 1995), pp. 22, 24, 54.

20. Figures from Coates, *Convicts and Orphans*, 40.

21. Adolfo Coelho, *Os Ciganos de Portugal*, Publicações Dom Quixote (Lisbon, 1995); Coates, *Convicts and Orphans*, 45–6.

22. Pyrard, *The Voyage of François Pyrard*, 80.

23. Maria Helena Vilas-Boas e Alvim, 'A Mulher e a Expansão na Perspectiva de alguns Cronistas e Historiadores seus Coevos', in *O Rosto Feminino da Expansão Portuguesa*, 2 vols., Comissão para a Igualdade e para os Direitos das Mulheres (Lisbon, 1995), vol. 1, 265; Coates, *Convicts and Orphans*, 141–77.

3. POINTS OF DEPARTURE: THE ATLANTIC ISLANDS

1. Rinaldo Caddeo, ed., *Le Navigazioni Atlantiche di Alvise da Cá da Mosto*

(Milan, 1929), printed in *Viagens de Luís de Cadamosto e de Pedro de Sintra*, Academia Portuguesa de História (Lisbon, 1948), 9–13.

2. John Barrow, *A Voyage to Cochinchina in the Years 1792 and 1793*, Cadell and Davies (London, 1806), 23.

3. Ibid., 15.

4. Numbers from T. Bentley Duncan, *Atlantic Islands. Madeira, the Azores and the Cape Verdes in Seventeenth-Century Commerce and Navigation*, Chicago University Press (Chicago, 1972), 255.

5. Alberto Vieira, 'Emigration from the Portuguese Islands in the Second Half of the Nineteenth Century: the Case of Madeira', in David Higgs, ed., *Portuguese Migration in Global Perspective*, Multicultural History Society of Ontario (Toronto, 1990), 47.

6. Jo-Anne S. Ferreira, 'Madeiran Portuguese Migration to Guyana, St Vincent, Antigua and Trinidad: A Comparative View', *Portuguese Studies Review*, 14, 2 (2009), 67–8.

7. Vieira, 'Emigration from the Portuguese Islands in the Second Half of the Nineteenth Century: the Case of Madeira', 42–60.

8. Victor Pereira da Rosa and Salvato Trigo, *Azorean Emigration. A Preliminary Overview*, Fernando Pessoa University Press (Porto, 1994), 68.

9. Oliveira Marques, *History of Portugal*, 371; Francis M. Rogers, *Atlantic Islanders of the Azores and Madeira*, Christopher Publishing House (North Quincy, MA, 1979), 30.

10. Luís Mendonça and José Ávila, *Emigração Açoriana (sécs. XVIII a XX)* (Lisbon, 2002), 13.

11. Victor Pereira da Rosa and Salvato Trigo, *Azorean Emigration. A preliminary overview*, Fernando Pessoa University Press (Porto, 1994), 69.

12. Ibid., 14.

13. Ibid., 24–7.

14. Luís da Silva Mouzinho de Albuquerque, 'Observações sobre a Ilha de S. Miguel', quoted in Mendonça and Ávila, *Emigração Açoriana (sécs. XVIII a XX)*, 20.

15. Ibid., 20–21.

16. Ibid., 32.

17. José Carlos Garcia, *O Museu dos Baleeiros e a Cultura da Baleação*, O Museu do Ilha do Pico (Lajes do Pico, 2002), 13.

18. Jerry Williams, 'Azorean Migration Patterns in the United States', in Higgs, ed., *Portuguese Migration in Global Perspective*, 145–57; quotation from p. 146.

19. Francisco Soares de Lacerda Machado, *História do Concelho das Lages*, Tipografia Popular (Figueira da Foz, 1936). Facsimile edition 1991, 127–34.

20. Mendonça and Ávila, *Emigração Açoriana (sécs. XVIII a XX)*, 35.

21. Pereira da Rosa and Trigo, *Azorean Emigration. A Preliminary Overview*, 67.

22. Alfred Lewis, *Home is an Island*, first published 1951, Tagus Press (Dartmouth, MA, 2012), 124.

23. Maria Emília Madeira Santos, ed., *História Geral de Cabo Verde*, 3 vols.,

Centro de Estudos de História e Cartografia Antiga and Instituto de Investigação Científica Tropical (Lisbon, 1991–2002); quotation from vol. 2, 229–30.

24. Ibid., 231–2.
25. Ibid., 240–44.
26. Arquivo Histórico Nacional (Cabo Verde), *Descoberta das Ilhas de Cabo Verde/Découverte des Îles du Cap-Vert*, AHN Praia and Sépia Paris (Praia) (1998), 58/54.
27. Elisa Silva Andrade, *Les Îles du Cap-Vert de la découverte à l'Indépendance Nationale (1460–1975)*, L'Harmattan (Paris, 1996), 45.
28. C. R. Boxer, *Race Relations in the Portuguese Colonial Empire 1415–1825*, Clarendon Press (Oxford, 1963), 14.
29. Ibid.
30. 'The Voyage of M. George Fenner to Guinie, and the Islands of Cape Verde, in the yeere of 1566…', in Richard Hakluyt, *The Principal Navigations, Voyage Traffiques & Discoveries of the English Nation*, 8 vols., J. M. Dent (London, 1907), vol. 4, 147.
31. *Linhas Gerais da História do Desenvolvimento Urbano da Cidade de Mindelo*, República de Cabo Verde (Lisbon, 1984), 13.
32. António Carreira, *The People of the Cape Verde Islands*, Christopher Fyfe trans., Hurst & Co. (London, 1962), 8.
33. Barrow, *A Voyage to Cochinchina in the Years 1792 and 1793*, 65–6.
34. Ibid., 70–71.
35. Ibid., 67–8.
36. Ibid., 70.
37. Carreira, *The People of the Cape Verde Islands*, 52, 77.
38. Vieira, 'A Emigração portuguesa nos Descobrimentos: Do Littoral às Ilhas', 75.
39. Ibid., 72.
40. Ibid., 78.
41. Ibid., 79.
42. Rogers, *Atlantic Islanders of the Azores and Madeira*, 48–9.
43. Augusto Reis Machado, ed., *Viagem de Lisboa à Ilha de S.Tomé. Escrita por um pilôto Português (século XVI)*, Portugália (Lisbon, n.d.), 51.
44. Francisco Tenreiro, *A Ilha de São Tomé*, Junta de Investigações do Ultramar (Lisbon, 1961), 63.
45. Machado, ed., *Viagem de Lisboa à Ilha de S.Tomé*, 52.
46. Ibid., 51.

4. THE DIASPORA OF THE SEPHARDIC JEWS

1. Miriam Bodian, '"Men of the Nation": the Shaping of *Converso* Identity in Early Modern Europe', *Past and Present*, 143 (1994), 54–6.
2. Quoted in Yosef Yerushalmi, 'Exile and Expulsion in Jewish History', in Benjamin R. Gampel, *Crisis and Creativity in the Sephardic World 1391–1648*, Columbia University Press (New York, 1997), 22.

3. António José Saraiva, *A Inquisição Portuguesa*, 3rd ed, Europa-América (Lisbon, 1964) and *Inquisição e Cristãos-Novos*, Editorial Nova (Porto, 1969).

4. Daviken Studnicki-Gizbert, *A Nation upon the Open Sea. Portugal's Atlantic Diaspora and the Crisis of the Spanish Empire, 1492–1640*, Oxford University Press (Oxford, 2007), 25–6.

5. Ibid., 44; Daniel Swetschinski, *Reluctant Cosmopolitans. The Portuguese Jews of Seventeenth Century Amsterdam*, Littman Library of Jewish Civilization (Oxford, 2000), 64.

6. Studnicki-Gizbert, *A Nation upon the Open Sea. Portugal's Atlantic Diaspora and the Crisis of the Spanish Empire*, 43.

7. Ibid., 72.

8. George E. Brooks, *Eurafricans in Western Africa*, Oxford University Press (Oxford, 2003), 93.

9. Green, *The Rise of the Trans-Atlantic Slave Trade in Western Africa, 1300–1589*, 134.

10. Malyn Newitt, 'Portugal, the Inquisition and the Triumph of English Merchant Capitalism', ch. 7 in *Portugal in European and World History*, Reaktion Books (London, 2009).

11. See discussion in Newitt, *Portugal in European and World History*, ch. 7.

12. Swetschinski, *Reluctant Cosmopolitans. The Portuguese Jews of Seventeenth Century Amsterdam*, 115.

13. Linda Rupert, 'Trading Globally, Speaking Locally: Curaçao's Sephardim in the Making of a Caribbean Creole', 109–22, and Francesca Trivellato, 'The Port Jews of Livorno and their Global Networks of Trade in the Early Modern Period,' 31–48, in David Cesarini and Gemma Romain, eds, *Jews and Port Cities 1590–1990*, Vallentine Mitchell (London, 2006).

14. Renata Segre, 'Sephardic Refugees in Ferrara: Two Notable Families', in Gampel, ed., *Crisis and Creativity in the Sephardic World 1391–1648*, 164.

15. Trivellato, 'The Port Jews of Livorno and their Global Networks of Trade in the Early Modern Period', 33.

16. Yosef Kaplan, 'The Self-definition of the Sephardic Jews of Western Europe and their Relation to the Alien and the Stranger', in Gampel, ed., *Crisis and Creativity in the Sephardic World 1391–1648*, 121.

17. Miriam Bodian, *Hebrews of the Portuguese Nation: Conversos and Community in Early Modern Amsterdam*, Indiana University Press (Bloomington, 1997), 45.

18. Ibid., 61.

19. Ibid., 134.

20. Ibid., 50–51.

21. Ibid., 75.

22. Ibid., 142.

23. Adam Sutcliffe, 'Identity, Space and Intercultural Contact in the Urban Entrepôt: The Sephardic Bounding of Community in Early Modern Amsterdam and London', in Cesarini and Romain, eds, *Jews and Port Cities 1590–1990*, 105.

24. Kaplan, 'The Self-definition of the Sephardic Jews of Western Europe and their Relation to the Alien and the Stranger', 122.
25. Judith C. E. Belinfante *et al.*, *The Esnoga. A Monument to Portuguese–Jewish Culture*, D'Arts (Amsterdam, 1991).
26. Kaplan, 'The Self-definition of the Sephardic Jews of Western Europe and their Relation to the Alien and the Stranger', 123, 125, 127, 144.
27. Evelyne Oliel-Grausz, 'Networks and Communication in the Sephardi Diaspora: An Added Dimension to the Concept of Port Jews and Port Jewries', in Cesarini and Romain, eds, *Jews and Port Cities 1590–1990*, 66.
28. Bodian, *Hebrews of the Portuguese Nation: Conversos and Community in Early Modern Amsterdam*, 160; Kaplan, 'The Self-definition of the Sephardic Jews of Western Europe and their Relation to the Alien and the Stranger', 141.
29. Klaus Weber, 'Were Merchants more Tolerant? "Patrons of the Jews" and the Decline of the Sephardi Community in Late Seventeenth Century Hamburg', in David Cesarini and Gemma Romain, eds, *Jews and Port Cities 1590–1990*, Vallentine Mitchell (London, 2006), 77, 79, 80.
30. Swetschinski, *Reluctant Cosmopolitans. The Portuguese Jews of Seventeenth Century Amsterdam*, 95.
31. Todd M. Endelman, *The Jews of Georgian England 1714–1830*, University of Michigan Press (Ann Arbor, MI, 1999), 168.
32. Ibid.
33. Yerushalmi, 'Exile and Expulsion in Jewish History', 11.
34. Bodian, *Hebrews of the Portuguese Nation: Conversos and Community in Early Modern Amsterdam*, 75.
35. Swetschinski, *Reluctant Cosmopolitans. The Portuguese Jews of Seventeenth Century Amsterdam*, 312.
36. Bodian, *Hebrews of the Portuguese Nation: Conversos and Community in Early Modern Amsterdam*, 37.
37. Swetschinski, *Reluctant Cosmopolitans. The Portuguese Jews of Seventeenth Century Amsterdam*, 119.
38. Ibid., 88.
39. Lois C. Dubin, '"Wings on their Feet…and Wings on their Head": Reflections on the Study of Port Jews', Cesarini and Romain, eds, *Jews and Port Cities 1590–1990*, 23.
40. Bodian, *Hebrews of the Portuguese Nation: Conversos and Community in Early Modern Amsterdam*, 95.
41. Segre, 'Sephardic Refugees in Ferrara: Two Notable Families', 182.
42. Dubin, '"Wings on their Feet…and Wings on their Head": Reflections on the Study of Port Jews', 21.
43. Segre, 'Sephardic Refugees in Ferrara: Two Notable Families', 161.
44. Dubin, '"Wings on their Feet…and Wings on their Head": Reflections on the Study of Port Jews', 25.
45. Swetschinski, *Reluctant Cosmopolitans. The Portuguese Jews of Seventeenth Century Amsterdam*, 113.

5. PORTUGUESE MIGRATION AND SETTLEMENT IN ASIA

1. C. R. Boxer, *The Portuguese Seaborne Empire, 1415–1825*, Hutchinson (London, 1969), 52.

2. Figures from T. Bentley Duncan, 'Navigation between Portugal and Asia in the Sixteenth and Seventeenth Centuries', in C. K. Pullapilly and E. J. Van Kley, eds, *Asia and the West. Encounters and Exchanges from the Age of Explorations*, Cross Cultural Publications (Notre Dame, IN, 1986), 24.

3. Boxer, *The Portuguese Seaborne Empire, 1415–1825*, 53.

4. John Villiers, 'The Estado da India in Southeast Asia', in Malyn Newitt, ed., *The First Portuguese Colonial Empire*, University of Exeter Press (Exeter, 1986), 50.

5. Francesco Carletti, *My Voyage Round the World*, ed. Herbert Weinstock, Methuen (London, 1964), 208–9.

6. Jan Huyghen van Linschoten, *The Voyage of Jan Huyghen van Linschoten to the East Indies*, A. C. Burnell, ed., 2 vols., Hakluyt Society (London, 1885), especially chapters 28–32, pages 175–222.

7. Pyrard, *The Voyage of François Pyrard*, 74.

8. Ibid., 121.

9. Ibid.

10. Jean Baptiste Tavernier, *Travels in India by Jean Baptiste Tavernier*, V. Ball, ed., Macmillan (London, 1889), vol. 1, 188.

11. Ibid.

12. R. S. Whiteway, *The Rise of Portuguese Power in India, 1497–1550*, 1st edn 1899, reprinted Susil Gupta, Augustus Kelley (New York, 1967), 25.

13. Ibid., 136.

14. Carletti, *My Voyage Round the World*, 128.

15. Ibid., 210.

16. M. H. Goonatilleka, 'A Portuguese Creole in Sri Lanka. A Brief Socio-linguistic Survey', in Teotonio R. de Souza, ed., *Indo-Portuguese History. Old Issues, New Questions*, Concept Publishing Company (New Delhi, 1984), 149.

17. Cesar Fedrici, 'The Voyage and Travell of M. Caesar Fredericke, Marchant of Venice, into the East India and beyond the Indies', in Richard Hakluyt, ed., *The Principal Navigations Voyages, Traffiques & Discoveries of the English Nation*, 8 vols., Dent (London, 1927), vol. 3, 198–269; quotes from 24–43.

18. Maurice Collis, *The Land of the Great Image*, New Directions (New York, 1985), 109–11; Alexandra Pelúcia, *Corsários e Piratas Portugueses*, A Esfera dos Livros (Lisbon, 2010).

19. António Pinto da França, *A Influência Portuguesa na Indonésia*, 3rd edn, Prefácio (Lisbon, 2003), 28.

20. Abbé Carré, *The Travels of the Abbé Carré in India and the Near East, 1672 to 1674*, Charles Fawcett, ed., 3 vols., Hakluyt Society (London, 1947), 521–2.

21. Ibid., 731–47.

22. Stefan Halikowski-Smith, *Creolization and Diaspora in the Portuguese Indies. The Social World of Ayutthaya 1640–1720*, Brill (Leiden, 2011), 2.

23. Shihan de Silva Jayasuriya, *The Portuguese in the East*, Tauris Academic Studies (London, 2008), 6.

24. Goonatilleka, 'A Portuguese Creole in Sri Lanka. A Brief Socio-linguistic Survey', 149.

25. Halikowski-Smith, *Creolization and Diaspora in the Portuguese Indies*, 10.

26. Ibid., 6.

27. Jayasuriya, *The Portuguese in the East*, 12.

28. For these events and their aftermath see C. R. Boxer, *Francisco Vieira de Figueiredo: A Portuguese Merchant-Adventurer in South East Asia, 1624–1667*, Martinus Nijhoff (The Hague, 1967).

29. Goonatilleka, 'A Portuguese Creole in Sri Lanka. A Brief Socio-linguistic Survey', 152.

30. Carré, *The Travels of the Abbé Carré in India and the Near East, 1672 to 1674*, 445.

31. William Dampier, *A Voyage to New Holland in the Year 1699*, Argonaut Press (London, 1939), 171–2.

32. Gervase Clarence Smith, *The Third Portuguese Empire 1825–1975*, Manchester University Press (Manchester, 1985), 30.

33. Pinto da França, *A Influência Portuguesa na Indonésia*.

34. Joseph Conrad, *An Outcast of the Islands*, first published 1896, Collins Classics (London, 1955), 19.

35. Ibid., 19.

36. Ibid.

37. Ibid., 19–20.

38. Ibid., 20.

39. Ibid., 22.

40. Clarence Smith, *The Third Portuguese Empire 1825–1975*, 28.

41. Ibid., 71.

42. Maria Beatriz Rocha-Trindade, 'The Portuguese Diaspora', in Carlos Teixeira and Victor M. P. Da Rosa, eds, *The Portuguese in Canada*, University of Toronto Press (Toronto, 2000), 21.

43. M. N. Pearson, *The New Cambridge History of India. I.1. The Portuguese in India*, Cambridge University Press (Cambridge, 1967), 149.

44. 'Abbé Faria (1746–1819)' at http://www.durbinhypnosis.com/abbe%20faria. htm. (Faria's dates are actually 1756–1819); Chirly dos Santos-Stubbe, 'Abade Faria (1756–1819) in Scientific and Fine Arts Literature', in Charles Borges, Óscar Pereira and Hannes Stubbe, *Goa and Portugal History and Development*, Concept Publishing (New Delhi, 2000), 336–45.

45. Alexandre Dumas, *The Count of Monte Cristo*, Harper Perennial (London, 2008), 149.

46. Ibid., 150, 152.

47. Ibid., 163.

48. Ibid., 167.

49. Margret Frenz, 'Representing the Portuguese Empire: Goan Consuls in British Africa, *c*.1910–1963', in Eric Morier-Genoud and Michel Cahen, *Imperial Migrations. Colonial Communities and Diaspora in the Portuguese World*, Palgrave Macmillan (Basingstoke, 2012), 201.

50. See for example Pedro Machado, 'Without Scales and Balances. Gujerati Merchants in Mozambique, *c*.1680–1800', *Portuguese Studies Review*, 9, nos. 1–2 (2001), 254–80.

51. Caroline Brettell, 'Portugal's First Post-Colonials: Citizenship, Identity, and the Repatriation of Goans', *Portuguese Studies*, 14, no. 2 (2006–7), 48–9.

52. Ibid., 157.

53. Ibid.

54. Rupa Chanda and Sriparna Ghosh, 'Goans in Portugal: Role of History and Identity in Shaping Diaspora Linkages', Working Paper 368, Indian Institute of Management (Bangalore, July 2012): ttp://www.iimb.ernet.in/research/working-papers/goans-portugal-role-history-and-identity-shaping-diaspora-linkages, 6.

55. Rocha-Trindade, 'The Portuguese Diaspora', 21.

56. 'Observatório da Emigração' produced by CIES Centro de Investigação de Estudos de Sociologia, http://www.observatorioemigracao.secomunidades.pt/np4/paises.html?id=14

6. THE PORTUGUESE IN BRAZIL

1. Guilhermino César, O '*Brasileiro' na Ficção Portuguesa*, Parceria A. M. Pereira (Lisbon, 1969), 25.

2. Mendonça and Ávila, *Emigração Açoriana (sécs. XVIII a XX)*, 44.

3. Janina Klawe, 'O Papel das Mulheres nos Descobrimentos e na Expansão Portuguesa', in *O Rosto Feminino da Expansão Portuguesa*, 2 vols., Comissão para a Igualdade e para os Direitos das Mulheres (Lisbon, 1995) vol. 1, 254–5.

4. Euclides da Cunha, *Rebellion in the Backlands*, Samuel Putnam trans., University of Chicago Press (Chicago, 1964), 68–9.

5. Guillaume-Thomas Raynal, *Histoire Philosophique et Politique des Etablissements et de Commerce des Européens dans les deuz Indes*, first published 1770, 10 vols., Jean-Leonard Pellet (Geneva, 1782), vol. 5, 6.

6. James Lockhart and Stuart Schwartz, *Early Latin America: a Short History of Spanish America and Brazil*, Cambridge University Press (Cambridge, 1983), 188–9.

7. N. P. Macdonald, *The Making of Brazil: Portuguese Roots 1500–1822*, Book Guild (Lewes, 1996), 188–9.

8. Fréderic Mauro, O *Império Luso-Brasilero 1620–1750*, Estampa (Lisbon, 1991), 212.

9. Lockhart and Schwartz, *Early Latin America: a Short History of Spanish America and Brazil*, 228; Macdonald, *The Making of Brazil: Portuguese Roots 1500–1822*, 193.

10. Mauro, *O Império Luso-Brasilero 1620–1750*, 214.
11. Lockhart and Schwartz, *Early Latin America: a Short History of Spanish America and Brazil*, 234.
12. Robert Southey, *History of Brazil*, 1st edn 1817, Longman, Hurst, Rees and Orme (London, 1910), 691.
13. Daniel Defoe, *The Life and Strange Surprizing Adventures of Robinson Crusoe of York, Mariner*, first published 1719, Oxford University Press (Oxford, 1999), 282.
14. Magalhães Godinho, 'L'Emigration Portugaise (XVᶜ-XXᵉ Siècles)', 9.
15. Lockhart and Schwartz, *Early Latin America: a Short History of Spanish America and Brazil*, 370.
16. André João Antonil, *Cultura e opulência do Brasil por suas drogas e minas*, André Mansuy Diniz Silva, ed., Comissão Nacional para as Comemorações dos Descobrimentos Portugueses (Lisbon, 2001), 243–4.
17. Macdonald, *The Making of Brazil: Portuguese Roots 1500–1822*, 318.
18. Cunha, *Rebellion in the Backlands*, 44.
19. Laird Bergad, *Slavery and the Demographic and Economic History of Minas Gerais, Brazil, 1720–1888*, Cambridge University Press (Cambridge, 1999), 91.
20. Macdonald, *The Making of Brazil: Portuguese Roots 1500–1822*, 349.
21. Antonil, *Cultura e opulência do Brasil por suas drogas e minas*, 310, 311.
22. Cunha, *Rebellion in the Backlands*, 44.
23. Macdonald, *The Making of Brazil: Portuguese Roots 1500–1822*, 361–2.
24. Thomas Merrick and Douglas Graham, *Population and Economic Development in Brazil 1800 to the Present*, Johns Hopkins University Press (Baltimore and London, 1979), 34.
25. Marcus Carvalho, 'O Antilusitanismo e a questão social em Pernambuco, 1822–1848', in *Emigração/Imigração em Portugal*, Actas do Coloquio Internacional sobre Emigração e Imigração em Portugal (sec xix-xx), Fragmentos (Alges, 1993), 145, 150.
26. Pereira, *A Política Portuguesa de Emigração 1850–1930*, (Lisbon, 1981), 7.
27. Ibid., 21.
28. Brettell, *Anthropology and Migration*, 12.
29. Pereira, *A Política Portuguesa de Emigração 1850–1930*, 16–17, 49.
30. Quoted in Pereira, *A Política Portuguesa de Emigração 1850–1930*, 65–6.
31. Ibid., 18, 23–5.
32. Ibid., 28, 31.
33. Ibid., 165.
34. Ibid., 22.
35. Ibid., 26.
36. George Reid Andrews, *Blacks and Whites in São Paulo, Brazil, 1888–1988*, University of Wisconsin Press (Madison, 1991), 97.
37. Quoted in Pereira, *A Política Portuguesa de Emigração 1850–1930*, 155.
38. Andrews, *Blacks and Whites in São Paulo, Brazil, 1888–1988*, 88.
39. Ibid., 111.

40. Rosana Barbosa Nunes, 'Portuguese Immigrants in Brazil: an Overview', *Portuguese Studies Review*, 8, no. 2 (2000), 27.

41. Herbert S. Klein, 'The Social and Economic Integration of Portuguese Immigrants in Brazil in the Late Nineteenth and Twentieth Centuries', *Journal of Latin American Studies*, 23 (1991), 318.

42. Merrick and Graham, *Population and Economic Development in Brazil 1800 to the Present*, 93.

43. Nunes, 'Portuguese Immigrants in Brazil: an Overview', 27–44; figure from p. 38.

44. Ibid., 31.

45. 'Resposta ao questionário', António de Almeida Campos to João de Andrade Corvo, 30 July 1872, in Pereira, *A Política Portuguesa de Emigração*, 164–9.

46. Ibid.

47. Klein, 'The Social and Economic Integration of Portuguese Immigrants in Brazil in the Late Nineteenth and Twentieth Centuries', *Journal of Latin American Studies*: 23, (1991), 317.

48. Pereira, *A Política Portuguesa de Emigração*, 31.

49. César, O *'Brasileiro' na Ficção Portuguesa*.

50. Pereira, *A Política Portuguesa de Emigração*, 34–5.

51. 'Resposta ao questionário', António de Almeida Campos to João de Andrade Corvo, 30 July 1872, in Pereira, *A Política Portuguesa de Emigração*, 167.

52. Ibid., 199.

53. Ferreira do Castro, *Emigrantes*, 49.

54. 'Resposta ao questionário', António de Almeida Campos to João de Andrade Corvo, 30 July 1872, in Pereira, *A Política Portuguesa de Emigração*, 200.

55. Ibid., 169.

56. Klein, 'The Social and Economic Integration of Portuguese Immigrants in Brazil in the Late Nineteenth and Twentieth Centuries', 323–7.

57. Ibid., 327.

58. Serrão, *A Emigração Portuguesa. Sondagem Histórica*, 52–3.

59. Quoted in Cecilia Maria Westphalen and Altiva Pilatti Balhana, 'Politica Legislação Imigratórias Brasileiras e a Imigração Portuguesa', in *Emigração/ Imigração em Portugal*, Actas do Coloquio Internacional sobre Emigração e Imigração em Portugal (sec xix-xx), Fragmentos (Alges, 1993), 22.

7. PORTUGUESE EMIGRATION IN THE TWENTIETH CENTURY

1. A general discussion of the problem as it affects Portuguese emigration to the UK can be found in José Carlos Pina Almeida, 'Citizens of the World: Migration and Citizenship of the Portuguese in the UK', *Portuguese Studies*, 23 (2007), 214–17.

2. Magalhães Godinho, 'L'Emigration portugaise (XVᵉ-XXᵉ siècles), une constante structurale et les réponses aux changements du monde', 12.

3. Serrão, *A Emigração Portuguesa. Sondagem Histórica*, 37.

4. Francisco Carvalho, *A Emigração Portuguesa nos anos 60 do século XX. Porque*

não revisitá-la hoje? CPES Centro de Pesquisa e Estudos Sociais (Lisbon, 2011), 22.

5. Maria Ioannis Baganha, 'Portuguese Emigration after World War II', 19; Maria Beatriz Rocha-Trindade, 'The Portuguese Diaspora', in Carlos Teixeira and Victor M. P. Da Rosa, eds, *The Portuguese in Canada*, University of Toronto Press (Toronto, 2000), 20.

6. José Carlos Pina Almeida and David Corkill, 'Portuguese Migrant Workers in the UK: A Case Study of Thetford, Norfolk', *Portuguese Studies*, 26, no. 1 (2010), 29.

7. Philip Curtin, *The Atlantic Slave Trade: a Census*, University of Wisconsin Press (Madison, 1969), ch. 1.

8. Cláudia Castelo, *Passagens para África. O Povoamento de Angola e Moçambique com Naturais da Metrópole (1920–1974)*, Edições Afrontamento (Porto, 2007), 172.

9. Jorge Carvalho Arroteia, *A emigração portuguesa—suas origens e distribuição*, Biblioteca Breve (Lisbon, 1983), 77, 101.

10. Merrick and Graham, *Population and Economic Development in Brazil 1800 to the Present*, 91, 94.

11. Engerman and Neves, 'The Bricks of Empire 1415–1999: 585 Years of Portuguese Emigration', 485.

12. Carreira, *The People of the Cape Verde Islands*, 205–6.

13. Valdimir Nobre Monteiro, *Portugal/Crioulo*, ICL Estudos e Ensaios (Mindelo, 1995), 129–34.

14. This estimate comes from Nunes, Bela, Mata and Valério, 'Portuguese Economic Growth 1833–1985', 326.

15. Alessandra Venturini, *Postwar Migration in Southern Europe 1950–2000*, Cambridge University Press (Cambridge, 2004), 17.

16. Venturini, *Postwar Migration in Southern Europe 1950–2000*, 10.

17. Baganha, 'Portuguese Emigration after World War II', 10.

18. Castelo, *Passagens para África. O Povoamento de Angola e Moçambique com Naturais da Metrópole (1920–1974)*, 180.

19. Arroteia, *A emigração portuguesa—suas origens e distribuição*, 99.

20. Carvalho, *A Emigração Portuguesa nos anos 60 do século XX*, 88–9.

21. David Higgs and Grace M. Anderson, *A Future to Inherit. The Portuguese Communities of Canada*, McClelland and Stewart (Toronto, 1976), 71–2.

22. Castelo, *Passagens para África. O Povoamento de Angola e Moçambique com Naturais da Metrópole (1920–1974)*, 188, 199.

23. Ibid., 189–90.

24. Lewis, *Home is an Island*, 177.

25. For example the case of António José Rodrigues described in Caroline Brettell, *Men Who Migrate, Women Who Wait. Population and History in a Portuguese Parish*, Princeton University Press (Princeton, 1986), 70–72.

26. Serrão, *A Emigração Portuguesa. Sondagem Histórica*, 38.

27. Nunes, Mata and Valério, 'Portuguese Economic Growth 1833–1985', 325–6.

28. Magalhães Godinho, 'L'Emigration portugaise (XVᵉ-XXᵉ Siècles)', 19.
29. Peixoto, 'A Emigração', 177.
30. Baganha, 'Portuguese Emigration after World War II', 13–14.
31. Maria Ioannis Baganha, *Portuguese Emigration to the United States 1820–1930*, Garland Publishing (New York, 1990), 94.
32. Baganha, *Portuguese Emigration to the United States 1820–1930*, 95–6; for a discussion see Brettell, 'The Emigrant, the Nation, and Twentieth-century Portugal: An Anthropological Approach'.
33. Magalhães Godinho, 'L'Emigration Portugaise (XVᵉ-XXᵉ Siècles)', 28.
34. Ibid.
35. Helen Graham, 'Money and Migration in Modern Portugal: an Economist's View', in David Higgs, ed., *Portuguese Migration in Global Perspective*, The Multicultural History Society of Ontario (Toronto, 1990), 83.
36. Magalhães Godinho, 'L'Emigration portugaise (XVᵉ-XXᵉ siècles)', 29; Carvalho, *A Emigração Portuguesa nos anos 60 do século XX*, 123; Stephen Syrett, *Contemporary Portugal. Dimensions of Economic and Political Change*, Ashgate (Aldershot, 2002), 28.
37. Graham, 'Money and Migration in Modern Portugal', 84.
38. Caroline Brettell, 'Leaving, Remaining and Returning: Some Thoughts on the Multifaceted Portuguese Migratory System', in David Higgs, ed., *Portuguese Migration in Global Perspective*, The Multicultural History Society of Ontario (Toronto, 1990), 71.
39. Baganha, 'Portuguese Emigration after World War II', 4.
40. Baganha, *Portuguese Emigration to the United States 1820–1930*, 96, 103.
41. Carvalho, *A Emigração Portuguesa nos anos 60 do século XX*, 87.
42. Arroteia, *A emigração portuguesa—suas origens e distribuição*, 121, 128; Carvalho, *A Emigração Portuguesa nos anos 60 do século XX*, 93, 117.
43. Brettell, 'Leaving, Remaining and Returning: Some Thoughts on the Multifaceted Portuguese Migratory System', 69.
44. Caroline Brettell, *We Have Already Cried Many Tears*, Schenkman Books (Rochester, VT, 1982), 73.
45. Lewis, *Home is an Island*, 180.
46. Wenona Giles, 'The Gender Relations of Nationalism, Remittance, and Return among Portuguese Immigrants Women in Canada: an Era of Transformation—the 1960s-1980s', *Portuguese Studies Review*, 11, no. 2 (2003–4), 25–40; quotation from 39.
47. Brettell, *Anthropology and Migration*, 80–92.
48. For example, Stanley L. Engerman, and João César da Neves, 'The Bricks of Empire 1415–1999: 585 Years of Portuguese Emigration', *European Journal of Economics*, 26 (1997), 476.
49. Quoted in Giles, 'The Gender Relations of Nationalism, Remittance, and Return among Portuguese Immigrants Women in Canada: an Era of Transformation—the 1960s-1980s', 11, no. 2 (2003–4), 34.
50. Manuela Aguiar, *Emigration Policy and Portuguese Communities*, Secretaria

de Estado das Comunidades Portuguesas Centro de Estudos (SECP) (Lisbon, 1987), 28–30.

51. Andrea Klimt, 'Divergent Trajectories: Identity and Community among Portuguese in Germany and the United States', *Portuguese Studies Review*, 14, no. 2 (2006–7), 233.

52. Robert Henry Moser and Antonio Luciano de Andrade Tosta, *Luso-American Literature. Writings by Portuguese-speaking Authors in North America*, Rutgers University Press (New Jersey, 2011), xxiv.

53. Rogers, *Atlantic Islanders of the Azores and Madeira*, 362.

54. Moser and Tosta, *Luso-American Literature. Writings by Portuguese-speaking Authors in North America*, xxiv.

8. THE PORTUGUESE DIASPORA IN EUROPE

1. For the Collège Sainte-Barbe see Agnès Pellerin, *Les Portugais à Paris au fil des siècles et des arrondissements*, Chandeigne (Paris, 2009), 46–9.

2. João Pedro Rosa Ferreira, *O Jornalismo na Emigração*, Instituto Nacional de Investigação Científica (Lisbon, 1992).

3. Lewis, *Home is an Island*, 112.

4. Marcelo Borges, 'Migration Systems in Southern Portugal: Regional and Transatlantic Circuits of Labor Migration in the Algarve (18th to 20th Centuries)', *International Review of Social History*, 45 (2000), 173.

5. Ibid., 181, 184.

6. José Maria Abecassis, *Genealogia hebraica: Portugal e Gibraltar, Sécs. XVII a XX*, Sociedade Industrial Gráfica Telles da Silva (Lisbon, 1990–91).

7. Borges, 'Migration Systems in Southern Portugal: Regional and Transatlantic Circuits of Labor Migration in the Algarve (18th to 20th centuries)', 191–202.

8. Serrão, *A Emigração Portuguesa*, 56, 59.

9. The above figures calculated from Baganha, 'Portuguese Emigration after World War II', 19.

10. Carvalho, *A Emigração Portuguesa nos anos 60 do século XX*, 79. Baganha gives 350,000 for the whole period 1950–88.

11. Thomas Bauer, Pedro T. Pereira, Michael Vogler and Klaus F. Zimmerman, 'Portuguese Migrants in the German Labor Market: Selection and Performance', *International Migration Review*, 36 (2002), 470.

12. Serrão, *A Emigração Portuguesa*, 64.

13. Ibid., 35.

14. Ibid., 66.

15. Pellerin, *Les Portugais à Paris au fil des siècles et des arrondissements*, 201–2, 214–17.

16. Quotations from Maria do Ceu Cunha, *Portugais de France*, CIEMI L'Harmattan (Paris, 1988), 79, 80, 33.

17. Film made by Jacinto Godinho, *História da Emigração Portuguesa: Primeiros Emigrantes, Episódio 1* can be seen on YouTube. The film was also presented in Oxford and London by the Instituto Camões.

18. swissinfo.ch 'Why Portuguese Seek Work in Switzerland' http://www.swissinfo.ch/eng/swiss_news/Why_Portuguese_seek_work_in_Switzerland.html?cid=34262848. Interview with Rosita Fibbi.
19. Alexandre Afonso, 'History, Facts and Figures of Portuguese Immigration in Switzerland', http://papers.ssrn.com/sol3/papers.cfm?abstract_id=947727, 5.
20. Ibid., 7.
21. Ibid., 6.
22. Ibid., 9, 10.
23. Ibid., 9.
24. Ibid., 7.
25. Klimt, 'Divergent Trajectories: Identity and Community among Portuguese in Germany and the United States', 215.
26. Bauer *et al.*, 'Portuguese Migrants in the German Labor Market: Selection and Performance', 470–71.
27. Ibid., 471.
28. Carvalho, *A Emigração Portuguesa nos anos 60 do século XX*, 59, 60.
29. Olga Barradas, 'Now You See Them, Now You Don't: Portuguese Students, Social Inclusion and Academic Attainment', *Goldsmiths Journal of Education*, 3, no. 1 (2000), 2.
30. Martin Eaton, 'Portuguese Migrant Worker Experiences in Northern Ireland's Market Town Economy', *Portuguese Studies*, 26, no. 1 (2010), 13.
31. Quotations from Barradas, 'Now You See Them, Now You Don't: Portuguese Students, Social Inclusion and Academic Attainment', 1, 7, 10.
32. Vanessa Mar-Molinero, 'Family and Transmission: Collective Memory in Identification Practices of Madeirans on Jersey', *Portuguese Studies*, 26, no. 1 (2010), 97.
33. Ibid., 98.
34. Quoted in ibid., 98.
35. Ibid., 99.
36. Eaton, 'Portuguese Migrant Worker Experiences in Northern Ireland's Market Town Economy', 14–15.
37. José Carlos Pina Almeida and David Corkill, 'Portuguese Migrant Workers in the UK: A Case Study of Thetford, Norfolk', *Portuguese Studies*, 26, no. 1 (2010), 33.
38. Pina Almeida and Corkill, 'Portuguese Migrant Workers in the UK: A Case Study of Thetford, Norfolk', 37.
39. Barradas, 'Now You See Them, Now You Don't: Portuguese Students, Social Inclusion and Academic Attainment', 7.

9. THE CARIBBEAN, CANADA AND SOUTH AMERICA

1. Jo-Anne S. Ferreira, 'Madeiran Portuguese Migration to Guyana, St Vincent, Antigua and Trinidad: a Comparative Overview', *Portuguese Studies Review*, 14, no. 2 (2006–7), 65.
2. Ferreira, 'Madeiran Portuguese Migration to Guyana, St Vincent, Antigua and

Trinidad: a Comparative Overview', 70; Vieira, 'Emigration from the Portuguese Islands in the Second Half of the Nineteenth Century: the Case of Madeira', 47.

3. Vieira, 'Emigration from the Portuguese Islands in the Second Half of the Nineteenth Century: the Case of Madeira', 47.

4. Ibid., 45.

5. Quoted in Jo-Anne Ferreira, *The Portuguese of Trinidad and Tobago*, University of the West Indies (St Augustine, 1994), 19.

6. Ferreira, *The Portuguese of Trinidad and Tobago*, 49–50.

7. Ibid., 1.

8. For example, http://freepages.genealogy.rootsweb.ancestry.com/~portwestind/general/index.htm

9. Arnold Thomas, 'Portuguese and Indian Immigration to St Vincent (1885–1890)', *Journal of Caribbean Studies*, 14, 1&2 (1999–2000), 43.

10. Ibid., 44.

11. Ferreira, 'Madeiran Portuguese Migration to Guyana, St Vincent, Antigua and Trinidad: a Comparative Overview', 72–3.

12. K. O. Laurence, *Immigration into the West Indies in the 19ᵗʰ Century*, Caribbean Universities Press (St Lawrence, Barbados, 1971), 31.

13. 'The story of Portuguese Bermudans', http://www.rootsweb.ancestry.com/~bmuwgw/portuguese.htm

14. Quoted in Rocha-Trindade, 'The Portuguese Diaspora', 21.

15. Quoted in Mary Noel Menezes, *The Portuguese of Guyana: a Study in Culture and Conflict*, self-published (1993), 24.

16. Quoted in Menezes, *The Portuguese of Guyana: a Study in Culture and Conflict*, 31.

17. Ibid., 111–13.

18. Quoted in ibid., 72.

19. Ibid., 76–7.

20. Brian L. Moore, 'The Social Impact of Portuguese Immigration into British Guiana after Emancipation', *Boletin de Estudios Latinoamericanos e Caribe*, 19 (1975), 3.

21. Kathleen J. Mundell de Calado, 'At Odds and against all Odds: a Glimpse into the Portuguese Experience in British Guiana, through the Eyes of Edward Jenkins', *Revista de Estudos Anglo-Portugueses*, 19 (2010), 241.

22. Moore, 'The Social Impact of Portuguese Immigration into British Guiana after Emancipation', 10–15.

23. *Observatório da Emigração*, http://www.observatorioemigracao.secomuni-dades.pt/np4/paises.html?id=244

24. Marcelo J. Borges, 'Portuguese Migration in Argentina: Transatlantic Networks and Local Experiences', *Portuguese Studies Review*, 14, no. 2 (2006–7), 90.

25. Ibid., 90.

26. Helena Carreiras, Diego Bussola, Maria Xavier, Beatriz Padilla and Andrés Malamud, 'Portuguese *Gauchos*: Associations, Social Integration and

Collective Identity in Twenty-first Century Argentina, Uruguay and Southern Brazil', *Portuguese Studies Review*, 14, no. 2 (2006–7), 275.

27. Borges, 'Portuguese Migration in Argentina: Transatlantic Networks and Local Experiences', 95.
28. Ibid., 99, 106.
29. Ibid., 102.
30. Ibid., 112.
31. Ibid., 123.
32. Carreiras, Bussola, Xavier, Padilla and Malamud, 'Portuguese *Gauchos*: Associations, Social Integration and Collective Identity in Twenty-first Century Argentina, Uruguay and Southern Brazil', 271.
33. Ibid., 275–8.
34. Marta Maffia, 'Cape Verdeans in Argentina', in Luís Batalha and Jørgen Carling, *Transnational Archipelago. Perspectives on Cape Verdean Migration and Diaspora*, Amsterdam University Press (Amsterdam, 2008), 47–8.
35. Carreiras, Bussola, Xavier, Padilla and Malamud, 'Portuguese *Gauchos*: Associations, Social Integration and Collective Identity in Twenty-first Century Argentina, Uruguay and Southern Brazil', 287.
36. For the description of this event see ibid., 288.
37. Ibid., 285.
38. Arroteia, *A emigração portuguesa—suas origens e distribuição*, 39–40.
39. Rocha-Trindade, 'The Portuguese Diaspora', 20.
40. Nancy Gomes, 'Os portugueses na Venezuela', *Relações Internacionais*, 24 (2009) http://www.scielo.oces.mctes.pt/scielo.php?pid=S1645-9199200900040 0010&script=sci_arttext
41. Higgs and Anderson, *A Future to Inherit. The Portuguese Communities of Canada*, chs. 1 and 2.
42. Afua Cooper, *The Hanging of Angélique*, University of Georgia Press (Athens, 2006).
43. Brettell, *Anthropology and Migration*, 110; Baganha, 'Portuguese Emigration after World War II', 7.
44. Arroteia, *A emigração portuguesa—suas origens e distribuição*, 41–5.
45. Canadian Census 2006 summarised in Wikipedia; the same number is to be found in *Observatório da Emigração*.
46. Carlos Teixeira, 'On the Move: Portuguese in Toronto', in Carlos Teixeira and Victor M. P. Da Rosa, eds, *The Portuguese in Canada*, University of Toronto Press (Toronto, 2000), 207–20; quotation from p. 212.
47. Giles, 'The Gender Relations of Nationalism, Remittance, and Return among Portuguese Immigrants Women in Canada', 28.
48. Brettell, *Anthropology and Migration*, 102.
49. Teixeira, 'On the Move: Portuguese in Toronto', 211–12.
50. Quoted in Higgs and Anderson, *A Future to Inherit. The Portuguese Communities of Canada*, 71.
51. Brettell, *Anthropology and Migration*, 130–32, 136.
52. Fernando Nunes, 'Portuguese–Canadian Youth and their Academic

Underachievment: a Literature Review', *Portuguese Studies Review*, 11, no. 2 (2003–4), 41–87; quotation from p. 42.
53. Ibid., 42–3.
54. Ibid., 50.
55. Ibid., 52.
56. Ilda Januario and Manuele Marujo, 'Voices of Portuguese Immigrant Women', in Carlos Teixeira and Victor M. P. Da Rosa, eds, *The Portuguese in Canada*, University of Toronto Press (Toronto, 2000), 107.

10. THE PORTUGUESE DIASPORA IN THE UNITED STATES

1. John D. McDermott, 'The Famous Ride of John 'Portuguese' Phillips, http://www.philkearny.vcn.com/phillips.htm
2. Sandra Wolforth, *The Portuguese in America*, R&E Research Associates (San Francisco, 1978), 33.
3. Arroteia, *A emigração portuguesa—suas origens e distribuição*, 35.
4. Brettell, *Anthropology and Migration*, xii.
5. Ibid.
6. Baganha, *Portuguese Emigration to the United States 1820–1930*, 55, 67, 91.
7. Edward Alsworth Ross, *The Old World and the New*, T. Fisher Unwin (London, 1914), 311–12.
8. Brettell, *Anthropology and Migration*, xii.
9. Figures from Jerry Williams, 'Azorean Migration Patterns in the United States', in David Higgs, ed., *Portuguese Migration in Global Perspective*, Multicultural History Society of Ontario (Toronto, 1990), 149, 156.
10. Gordon Thomas, 'The Portuguese "Gloucesterman"', *Gloucester, the Magazine of the New England Coast*, 2, no. 3 (1978), 4–7.
11. Ibid.
12. John N. Morris, *Alone at Sea: Gloucester in the Age of the Dorymen (1623–1939)*, Commonwealth Editions (Beverly, MA, 2010), 84.
13. Ibid., 86.
14. Marilyn Myett, 'Men from Azores marched into heart of Gloucester', *Gloucester Daily Times*, 12 February 1967.
15. John Laidler, 'Many Portuguese still chasing the American dream', *Boston Sunday Globe*, 4 December 1991.
16. Williams, 'Azorean Migration Patterns in the United States', 151.
17. Vieira, 'Emigration from the Portuguese Islands in the Second Half of the Nineteenth Century: the Case of Madeira', 48.
18. Recorded in Leo Pap, *The Portuguese-Americans*, Twayne Publishers (Boston, MA, 1981), 75.
19. Robert F. Harney, '"Portygees and Other Caucasians": Portuguese Migrants and the Racialism of the English-speaking World', in David Higgs, ed., *Portuguese Migration in Global Perspective*, Multicultural History Society of Ontario (Toronto, 1990), 115.
20. Pap, *The Portuguese-Americans*, 78.

21. F. T. Bullen, *The Cruise of the 'Cachalot'*, first published 1899, Collins (London, 1953), 20.

22. Ibid., 21.

23. Ibid., 25.

24. Ibid., 27.

25. Ibid., 32.

26. Ibid., 36.

27. Marilyn Halter, 'Cape Verdians in the United States', in Batalha and Carling, *Transnational Archipelago. Perspectives on Cape Verdean Migration and Diaspora*, 36.

28. Wolforth, *The Portuguese in America*, 24.

29. Figures from Carreira, *The People of the Cape Verde Islands*, 80.

30. Wolforth, *The Portuguese in America*, 80.

31. Carreira, *The People of the Cape Verde Islands*, 48.

32. Ibid., 47.

33. Sidney Greenfield, 'The Cape Verde Islands: Their Settlement, the Emergence of their Creole Culture, and the Subsequent Migrations of their People', in David Higgs, ed., *Portuguese Migration in Global Perspective*, Multicultural History Society of Ontario (Toronto, 1990), 173.

34. Halter, 'Cape Verdians in the United States', 37.

35. Ibid., 45.

36. Pap, *The Portuguese-Americans*, 68.

37. Ibid., 109.

38. Diane Beeson and Donald Warrin, 'Portuguese Women on the American Frontier', in *O Rosto Feminino da Expansão Portuguesa*, 2 vols., Comissão para a Igualdade e para os Direitos das Mulheres (Lisbon, 1995), vol. 2, 78.

39. Jack London, *Martin Eden*, first published 1909, Penguin Books (London, 1993), 241.

40. Jack London, *The Valley of the Moon*, first published 1913, The Echo Library (Teddington, 2008), 194.

41. Ibid., 200.

42. For details of the Portuguese communities in California see Meg Rogers, *The Portuguese in San Leandro*, Arcadia Publishing (San Francisco, 2008) and *Portuguese in San Jose*, Arcadia Publishing (San Francisco, 2007).

43. John Steinbeck, 'Tortilla Flat', in *The Steinbeck Omnibus*, Heinemann (London, 1950), 93–136; quotation from p. 116.

44. Ibid., 117.

45. Beeson and Warrin, 'Portuguese Women on the American Frontier', 81.

46. David Brookshaw, 'Unwriting American History: Frank X. Gaspar's *Leaving Pico*', in John Kinsella and Carmen Ramos Villar, *Mid-Atlantic Margins, Transatlantic Identities: Azorean Literature in Context*, Department of Hispanic, Portuguese and Latin American Studies, University of Bristol, *Lusophone Studies*, 5 (Bristol, 2007), 140.

47. Klimt, 'Divergent Trajectories: Identity and Community among Portuguese in Germany and the United States', 226.

48. Ibid., 227.
49. See discussion in Harney, '"Portygees and Other Caucasians": Portuguese Migrants and the Racialism of the English-speaking World', 118, 128.
50. Frank X. Gaspar, *Leaving Pico*, University Press of New England (Hanover, NH, 1999). For a discussion of the novel see Brookshaw, 'Unwriting American History: Frank X. Gaspar's *Leaving Pico*.'
51. Francisco Cota Fagundes, *Hard Knocks: An Azorean-American Odyssey*, Gávea-Brown (Providence, RI, 2000).
52. Harney, '"Portygees and Other Caucasians": Portuguese Migrants and the Racialism of the English-speaking World', 113, 117.
53. Donald R. Taft, *Two Portuguese Communities in New England*, Columbia University Press (New York, 1923), 18–19.
54. Wolforth, *The Portuguese in America*, 46, 17.
55. Ross, *The Old World and the New*, 179.
56. Ibid., 180.
57. Ibid., 180–81.
58. Gilberto Freyre, *Casa Grande e Senzala* (1933), translated as *The Masters and the Slaves*, Alfred Knopf (New York, 1946).
59. For an elaborate defence of this legend see Manuel Mira, *The Forgotten Portuguese. The Melungeons and other Groups. The Portuguese Making of America*, Portuguese American Historical Research Foundation (Franklin, NC, 1998).
60. Klimt, 'Divergent Trajectories: Identity and Community among Portuguese in Germany and the United States', 233.

11. PORTUGUESE EMIGRATION TO AFRICA

1. George E. Brooks, *Eurafricans in Western Africa*, Oxford University Press (Oxford, 2003), 49.
2. Ibid., 78.
3. Peter Mark, *'Portuguese Style' and Luso-African Identity*, Indiana University Press (Bloomington, 2002), 22.
4. Brooks, *Eurafricans in Western Africa*, 77.
5. Ibid., 84.
6. Ibid., 50.
7. José Lingna Nafafé, *Colonial Encounters: Issues of Culture, Hybridity and Creolisation. Portuguese Mercantile Settlers in West Africa*, Peter Lang (Frankfurt am Main, 2007), ch. 5, especially 169–70.
8. Quoted in Brooks, *Eurafricans in Western Africa*, 89.
9. Philip Havik, 'Sóciais, Intermediárias e Empresárias: o Género e a Expansão Colonial na Guiné', in *O Rosto Feminino da Expansão Portuguesa*, 2 vols., Comissão para a Igualdade e para os Direitos das Mulheres (Lisbon, 1995), vol. 2, 87.
10. Mark, *'Portuguese Style' and Luso-African Identity*, 89–90.
11. Ibid., 24–5.

12. Bruce Chatwin, *The Viceroy of Ouidah*, Picador Pan (London, 1982); Robin Law, 'The Evolution of the Brazilian Community in Ouidah', in Kristin Mann and Edna G. Bay, *Rethinking the African Diaspora*, Cass (London, 2001), 22–41.

13. Malyn Newitt, 'British Travellers' Accounts of Portuguese Africa in the Nineteenth Century', *Revista de Estudos Anglo-Portugueses*, 11 (2002), 102–29.

14. H. Rider Haggard, *King Solomon's Mines*, first published 1885, Cassell and Co. (London, 1893), 23.

15. John Buchan, *Prester John*, first published 1910, Nelson (London and Edinburgh, 1912), 26.

16. Ibid., 27.

17. Ibid., 121.

18. Ibid., 157.

19. Ibid., 210.

20. For the founding of Mossamedes see W. G. Clarence-Smith, *Slaves, Peasants and Capitalists in Southern Angola 1840–1926*.

21. For these debates see Castelo, *Passagens para África. O Povoamento de Angola e Moçambique com Naturais da Metrópole (1920–1974)*, 50–55.

22. Ibid., 81, 82, 88.

23. G. Bender, *Angola under the Portuguese: the Myth and the Reality*, Heinemann (London, 1978).

24. Cláudia Castelo, 'Colonial Migration to Angola and Mozambique: Constraints and Illusions', in Eric Morier-Genoud and Michel Cahen, *Imperial Migrations. Colonial Communities and Diaspora in the Portuguese World*, Palgrave Macmillan (Basingstoke, 2012), 113.

25. Ibid., 76–9.

26. For the Portuguese colonies during the Second World War see Malyn Newitt, 'The Portuguese African Colonies during the Second World War', in Judith Byfield, ed., *Africa in World War Two*, Cambridge University Press, forthcoming.

27. Ibid., 133–4.

28. Numbers from Castelo, 'Colonial Migration to Angola and Mozambique: Constraints and Illusions', 116–17, 120.

29. Ibid., 120.

30. Castelo, *Passagens para África. O Povoamento de Angola e Moçambique com Naturais da Metrópole (1920–1974)*, 189–90.

31. Newitt, 'The Portuguese African Colonies during the Second World War', and the sources quoted.

32. Castelo, 'Colonial Migration to Angola and Mozambique: Constraints and Illusions', 122.

33. Alexander Keese, 'Managing the Prospect of Famine. Cape Verdean Officials, Subsistence Emergencies, and the Change of Elite Attitudes during Portugal's Late Colonial Phase, 1939–1961', *Itinerario*, 36, no. 1 (2012), 53.

34. Ibid., 62.

35. Carreira, *The People of the Cape Verde Islands*, 101.

36. Figures from ibid., 201–14.

37. Augusto Nascimento, 'Cape Verdeans in São Tomé and Príncipe', in Luís Batalha and Jørgen Carling, *Transnational Archipelago. Perspectives on Cape Verdean Migration and Diaspora*, Amsterdam University Press (Amsterdam, 2008), 56.

38. Ibid., 59.

39. Clive Glaser, 'The Making of a Portuguese Community in South Africa, 1900–1994', in Eric Morier-Genoud and Michel Cahen, *Imperial Migrations. Colonial Communities and Diaspora in the Portuguese World*, Palgrave Macmillan (Basingstoke, 2012), 222–3.

40. Victor Pereira da Rosa and Salvato Trigo, 'Islands in a Segregated Land: Portuguese in South Africa', in David Higgs, ed., *Portuguese Migration in Global Perspective*, Multicultural History Society of Ontario (Toronto, 1990), 183.

41. Glaser, 'The Making of a Portuguese Community in South Africa, 1900–1994', 217.

42. Pereira da Rosa and Trigo, 'Islands in a Segregated Land: Portuguese in South Africa', 185.

43. Ibid., 191.

44. Ibid., 194.

45. Ibid., 185–6.

46. *Observatório da Emigração*, http://www.observatorioemigracao.secomuni-dades.pt/np4/paises.html?id=244

47. Pereira da Rosa and Trigo, 'Islands in a Segregated Land: Portuguese in South Africa', 184.

48. Glaser, 'The Making of a Portuguese Community in South Africa, 1900–1994', 231–2.

12. THE PORTUGUESE AND THE SEA

1. Rudyard Kipling, *Captains Courageous*, first published 1897, Macmillan (London, 1932), 13.

2. Ibid., 38.

3. Ibid., 41.

4. Ibid., 81.

5. Ibid., 95.

6. Ibid., 139.

7. Ibid., 103–4.

8. Alan Villiers, *The Quest of the Schooner Argus*, Hodder and Stoughton (London, 1951), 185.

9. Ibid., 84–5.

10. Ibid., 45.

11. Ibid., 81.

12. Ibid., 143.

13. Ibid., 84–5.
14. Ibid., 107.
15. Ibid., 113.
16. Ibid., 142.
17. Ibid., 148.
18. Ibid., 152.
19. Ibid., 153.

BIBLIOGRAPHY

'Abbe Faria (1746–1819)', http://www.durbinhypnosis.com/abbe%20faria.htm (Faria's dates are actually 1756–1819).

Abecassis, José Maria, *Genealogia hebraica: Portugal e Gibraltar, Sécs. XVII a XX*, Sociedade Industrial Gráfica Telles da Silva (Lisbon, 1990–91).

Afonso, Alexandre, 'History, Facts and Figures of Portuguese Immigration in Switzerland', http://papers.ssrn.com/sol3/papers.cfm?abstract_id=947727.

Aguiar, Manuela, *Emigration Policy and Portuguese Communities*, Secretaria de Estado das Comunidades Portuguesas Centro de Estudos (SECP) (Lisbon, 1987).

Åkerman, Suner, 'Towards an Understanding of Emigrational Processes', in W. H. McNeill and Ruth S. Adams, *Human Migration Patterns and Policies*, Indiana University Press (Bloomington, 1978), 287–306.

Alpers, Edward A. and Molly Ball, '"Portuguese" Diasporas: a Survey of the Scholarly Literature', in Eric Morier-Genoud and Michel Cahen, *Imperial Migrations. Colonial Communities and Diaspora in the Portuguese World*, Palgrave Macmillan (Basingstoke, 2012), 31–71.

Andrade, Elisa Silva, *Les Îles du Cap-Vert de la découverte à l'Indépendance Nationale (1460–1975)*, L'Harmattan (Paris, 1996).

Andrews, George Reid, *Blacks and Whites in São Paulo, Brazil, 1888–1988*, University of Wisconsin Press (Madison, 1991).

Antonil, André João, *Cultura e opulência do Brasil por suas drogas e minas*, André Mansuy Diniz Silva, ed., Comissão Nacional para as Comemorações dos Descobrimentos Portugueses (Lisbon, 2001).

Arquivo Histórico Nacional (Cabo Verde), *Descoberta das Ilhas de Cabo Verde/ Découverte des Îles du Cap-Vert*, AHN Praia and Sépia Paris (Praia) (1998).

Arroteia, Jorge Carvalho, *A emigração portuguesa—suas origens e distribuição*, Biblioteca Breve (Lisbon, 1983).

Baganha, Maria Ioannis, 'Portuguese Emigration after World War II', http://ies.berkeley.edu/research/files/CP02/CP02-Port_Emigration.pdf.

——— *Portuguese Emigration to the United States 1820–1930*, Garland Publishing (New York, 1990).

BIBLIOGRAPHY

Barradas, Olga, 'Now You See Them, Now You Don't: Portuguese Students, Social Inclusion and Academic Attainment', *Goldsmiths Journal of Education*, 3, no. 1 (2000).

Barrow, John, *A Voyage to Cochinchina in the Years 1792 and 1793*, Cadell and Davies (London, 1806).

Bauer, Thomas, Pedro T. Pereira, Michael Vogler and Klaus F. Zimmerman, 'Portuguese Migrants in the German Labor Market: Selection and Performance', *International Migration Review*, 36 (2002), 467–91.

Beeson, Diane and Donald Warrin, 'Portuguese Women on the American Frontier', in *O Rosto Feminino da Expansão Portuguesa*, 2 vols., Comissão para a Igualdade e para os Direitos das Mulheres (Lisbon, 1995), vol. 2, 75–85.

Belinfante, Judith C. E. *et al.*, *The Esnoga. A Monument to Portuguese-Jewish Culture*, D'Arts (Amsterdam, 1991).

Bender, G., *Angola under the Portuguese: the Myth and the Reality*, Heinemann (London, 1978).

Bergad, Laird, *Slavery and the Demographic and Economic History of Minas Gerais, Brazil, 1720–1888*, Cambridge University Press (Cambridge, 2006).

Bodian, Miriam, '"Men of the Nation": the Shaping of *Converso* Identity in Early Modern Europe', *Past and Present*, 143 (1994), 48–76.

—— *Hebrews of the Portuguese Nation: Conversos and Community in Early Modern Amsterdam*, Indiana University Press (Bloomington, 1997).

Borges, Marcelo, 'Migration Systems in Southern Portugal: Regional and Transatlantic Circuits of Labor Migration in the Algarve (18th to 20th Centuries)', *International Review of Social History*, 45 (2000), 171–208.

—— 'Portuguese Migration in Argentina: Transatlantic Networks and Local Experiences', *Portuguese Studies Review*, 14, no. 2 (2006–07), 87–125.

Boxer, C. R., *Race Relations in the Portuguese Colonial Empire 1415–1825*, Clarendon Press (Oxford, 1963).

—— *Francisco Vieira de Figueiredo: A Portuguese Merchant-Adventurer in South East Asia, 1624–1667*, Martinus Nijhoff (The Hague, 1967).

—— *The Portuguese Seaborne Empire, 1415–1825*, Hutchinson (London, 1969).

Brettell, Caroline, *We Have Already Cried Many Tears*, Schenkman Books (Rochester, VT, 1982).

—— *Men Who Migrate, Women Who Wait. Population and History in a Portuguese Parish*, Princeton University Press (Princeton, NJ, 1986).

—— 'Leaving, Remaining and Returning: Some Thoughts on the Multifaceted Portuguese Migratory System', in David Higgs, ed., *Portuguese Migration in Global Perspective*, The Multicultural History Society of Ontario (Toronto, 1990), 61–80.

—— 'The Emigrant, the Nation, and Twentieth-century Portugal: An Anthropological Approach', *Portuguese Studies Review*, 2, no. 2 (1993).

—— *Anthropology and Migration*, Altamira (Oxford, 2003).

—— 'Portugal's First Post-Colonials: Citizenship, Identity, and the Repatriation of Goans', *Portuguese Studies*, 14, no. 2 (2006–7), 143–70.

BIBLIOGRAPHY

Brooks, George E., *Eurafricans in Western Africa*, Oxford University Press (Oxford, 2003).

Brookshaw, David, 'Unwriting American History: Frank X. Gaspar's *Leaving Pico*', in John Kinsella and Carmen Ramos Villar, *Mid-Atlantic Margins, Transatlantic Identities: Azorean Literature in Context*, Department of Hispanic, Portuguese and Latin American Studies, University of Bristol, *Lusophone Studies*, 5 (Bristol, 2007), 139–49.

Buchan, John, *Prester John*, first published 1910, Nelson (London and Edinburgh, 1912).

Bullen, F. T., *The Cruise of the 'Cachalot'*, first published 1899, Collins (London, 1953).

Caddeo, Rinaldo, ed., *Le Navigazioni Atlantiche di Alvise da Cá da Mosto* (Milan, 1929), printed in *Viagens de Luís de Cadamosto e de Pedro de Sintra*, Academia Portuguesa de História (Lisbon, 1948).

Carletti, Francesco, *My Voyage Round the World*, ed. Herbert Weinstock, Methuen (London, 1964).

Carré, Abbé, *The Travels of the Abbé Carré in India and the Near East, 1672 to 1674*, Charles Fawcett, ed., 3 vols., Hakluyt Society (London, 1947).

Carreira, António, *The People of the Cape Verde Islands*, Christopher Fyfe, trans., Hurst & Co. (London, 1962).

Carreiras, Helena, Diego Bussola, Maria Xavier, Beatriz Padilla and Andrés Malamud, 'Portuguese *Gauchos*: Associations, Social Integration and Collective Identity in Twenty-first Century Argentina, Uruguay and Southern Brazil', *Portuguese Studies Review*, 14, no. 2 (2006–7), 263–91.

Carvalho, Francisco, *A Emigração Portuguesa nos anos 60 do século XX. Porque não revisitá-la hoje?* CPES Centro de Pesquisa e Estudos Sociais (Lisbon, 2011).

Carvalho, Marcus, 'O Antilusitanismo e a questão social em Pernambuco, 1822–1848', in *Emigração/Imigração em Portugal*, Actas do Colóquio Internacional sobre Emigração e Imigração em Portugal (sec. xix-xx), Fragmentos (Alges 1993), 145–60.

Castelo, Cláudia, *Passagens para África. O Povoamento de Angola e Moçambique com Naturais da Metrópole (1920–1974)*, Edições Afrontamento (Porto, 2007).

——— 'Colonial Migration to Angola and Mozambque: Constraints and Illusions', in Eric Morier-Genoud and Michel Cahen, *Imperial Migrations. Colonial Communities and Diaspora in the Portuguese World*, Palgrave Macmillan (Basingstoke, 2012), 107–28.

Cenival, Pierre, ed., *Les sources inédites de l'histoire du Maroc: archives et bibliothèques de Portugal*, Tome 1 (1486–1516), Geuthner (Paris, 1934).

César, Guilhermino, *O 'Brasileiro' na Ficção Portuguesa*, Parceria A. M. Pereira (Lisbon, 1969).

Chanda, Rupa and Sriparna Ghosh, 'Goans in Portugal: Role of History and Identity in Shaping Diaspora Linkages', Working Paper 368, Indian Institute of Management (Bangalore, July 2012): http://www.iimb.ernet.in/research/working-papers/goans-portugal-role-history-and-identity-shaping-diaspora-linkages.

Chatwin, Bruce, *The Viceroy of Ouidah*, Picador Pan (London, 1982).

Clarence-Smith, W. G., *Slaves, Peasants and Capitalists in Southern Angola 1840–1926*, Cambridge University Press (Cambridge, 1979).

—— *The Third Portuguese Empire 1825–1975*, Manchester University Press (Manchester, 1985).

Coates, Timothy J., *Convicts and Orphans. Forced and State-Sponsored Colonizers in the Portuguese Empire, 1550–1755*, Stanford University Press (Stanford, CA, 2001).

Coelho, Adolfo, *Os Ciganos de Portugal*, Publicações Dom Quixote (Lisbon, 1995).

Colley, Linda, *Britons. Forging the Nation 1707–1837*, 2nd edn, Yale University Press (New Haven and London, 2005).

Collis, Maurice, *The Land of the Great Image*, New Directions (New York, 1985) (originally published by Alfred Knopf, 1943).

Conrad, Joseph, *An Outcast of the Islands*, first published 1896, Collins Classics (London, 1955).

Cooper, Afua, *The Hanging of Angélique*, University of Georgia Press (Athens, 2006).

Corkill, David, *The Development of the Portuguese Economy*, Routledge (London, 1999).

Costa Pinto, António, 'Elites, Single Parties and Political Decision-making in Fascist-era Dictatorships', *Contemporary European History*, II (2002), 429–54.

Cunha, Euclides da, *Rebellion in the Backlands*, Samuel Putnam, trans., University of Chicago Press (Chicago, 1964).

Cunha, Maria do Ceu, *Portugais de France*, CIEMI L'Harmattan (Paris, 1988).

Curtin, Philip, *The Atlantic Slave Trade: a Census*, University of Wisconsin Press (Madison, WI, 1969).

Dampier, William, *A Voyage to New Holland in the Year 1699*, Argonaut Press (London, 1939).

Darwin, John, 'Decolonisation and Diaspora', in Eric Morier-Genoud and Michel Cahen, *Imperial Migrations. Colonial Communities and Diaspora in the Portuguese World*, Palgrave Macmillan (Basingstoke, 2012), 316–26.

Defoe, Daniel, *The Life and Strange Surprizing Adventures of Robinson Crusoe of York, Mariner*, first published 1719, Oxford University Press (Oxford, 1999).

Disney, A. R., *A History of Portugal and the Portuguese Empire*, 2 vols., Cambridge University Press (Cambridge, 2009).

Doel, Priscilla, 'The White Fleet and the Iconography of Control', in Carlos Teixeira and Victor Pereira da Rosa, *The Portuguese in Canada*, University of Toronto Press (Toronto, 2000), 37–52.

Dubin, Lois C., '"Wings on their Feet…and Wings on their Head": Reflections on the Study of Port Jews', in David Cesarini and Gemma Romain, eds, *Jews and Port Cities 1590–1990*, Vallentine Mitchell (London, 2006), 16–30.

Duncan, T. Bentley, *Atlantic Islands. Madeira, the Azores and the Cape Verdes in*

Seventeenth-Century Commerce and Navigation, Chicago University Press (Chicago, 1972).

——— 'Navigation between Portugal and Asia in the Sixteenth and Seventeenth Centuries', in C. K. Pullapilly and E. J. Van Kley, eds, *Asia and the West. Encounters and Exchanges from the Age of Explorations*, Cross Cultural Publications (Notre Dame, IN, 1986), 3–25.

Eaton, Martin, 'Portuguese Migrant Worker Experiences in Northern Ireland's Market Town Economy', *Portuguese Studies*, 26, no. 1 (2010), 10–26.

Encyclopedia of Immigration: http://immigration-online.org/55-cape-verdean-immigration.html.

Endelman, Todd M., *The Jews of Georgian England 1714–1830*, University of Michigan Press (Ann Arbor, MI, 1999).

Engerman, Stanley L. and João César da Neves, 'The Bricks of Empire 1415–1999: 585 Years of Portuguese Emigration', *European Journal of Economics*, 26 (1997), 471–509.

Fagundes, Francisco Cota, *Hard Knocks: An Azorean-American Odyssey*, Gávea-Brown (Providence, RI, 2000).

Fedrici, Cesar, 'The Voyage and Travell of M. Caesar Fredericke, Marchant of Venice, into the East India and beyond the Indies', in Richard Hakluyt, ed., *The Principal Navigations Voyages, Traffiques & Discoveries of the English Nation*, 8 vols., Dent (London, 1927), vol. 3, 198–269.

Ferreira, João Pedro Rosa, *O Jornalismo na Emigração*, Instituto Nacional de Investigação Científica (Lisbon, 1992).

Ferreira, Jo-Anne S., *The Portuguese of Trinidad and Tobago*, University of the West Indies (St Augustine, 1994).

——— 'Madeiran Portuguese Migration to Guyana, St Vincent Antigua and Trinidad: A Comparative View', *Portuguese Studies Review*, 14, 2 (2009), 63–85.

Ferreira de Castro, José Maria, *Emigrantes*, first published 1928, Guimarães (Lisbon, 1946).

França, António Pinto da, *A Influência Portuguesa na Indonésia*, 3rd edn, Prefácio (Lisbon, 2003).

Frenz, Margret, 'Representing the Portuguese Empire: Goan Consuls in British Africa, c.1910–1963', in Eric Morier-Genoud and Michel Cahen, *Imperial Migrations. Colonial Communities and Diaspora in the Portuguese World*, Palgrave Macmillan (Basingstoke, 2012), 193–212.

Freyre, Gilberto, *Casa Grande e Senzala* (1933); translated as *The Masters and the Slaves*, Alfred Knopf (New York, 1946).

Garcia, José Carlos, *O Museu dos Baleeiros e a Cultura da Baleação*, O Museu do Ilha do Pico (Lajes do Pico, 2002), 13.

Gaspar, Frank X., *Leaving Pico*, University Press of New England (Hanover, NH, 1999).

Giles, Wenona, 'The Gender Relations of Nationalism, Remittance, and Return among Portuguese Immigrants Women in Canada: an Era of Transformation—the 1960s-1980s', *Portuguese Studies Review*, 11, no. 2 (2003–4), 25–40.

Glaser, Clive, 'The Making of a Portuguese Community in South Africa, 1900–1994', in Eric Morier-Genoud and Michel Cahen, *Imperial Migrations. Colonial Communities and Diaspora in the Portuguese World*, Palgrave Macmillan (Basingstoke, 2012), 213–38.

Godinho, Jacinto, *História da Emigração Portuguesa: Primeiros Emigrantes, Episódio 1* on YouTube.

Gomes, Nancy, 'Os portugueses na Venezuela', *Relações Internacionais*, 24 (2009) http://www.scielo.oces.mctes.pt/scielo.php?pid=S1645–91992009000400010& script=sci_arttext.

Goonatilleka, M. H., 'A Portuguese Creole in Sri Lanka. A Brief Socio-linguistic Survey', in Teotonio R. de Souza, ed., *Indo-Portuguese History. Old Issues, New Questions*, Concept Publishing Company (New Delhi, 1984), 147–80.

Graham, Helen, 'Money and Migration in Modern Portugal: an Economist's View', in David Higgs, ed., *Portuguese Migration in Global Perspective*, Multicultural History Society of Ontario (Toronto, 1990), 81–98.

Green, Toby, *The Rise of the Trans-Atlantic Slave Trade in Western Africa, 1300–1589*, Cambridge University Press (Cambridge, 2012).

Greenfield, Sidney, 'The Cape Verde Islands: Their Settlement, the Emergence of their Creole Culture, and the Subsequent Migrations of their People', in David Higgs, ed., *Portuguese Migration in Global Perspective*, Multicultural History Society of Ontario (Toronto, 1990), 158–81.

Haggard, H. Rider, *King Solomon's Mines*, first published 1885, Cassell and Co. (London, 1893).

Halikowski-Smith, Stefan, *Creolization and Diaspora in the Portuguese Indies. The Social World of Ayutthaya 1640–1720*, Brill (Leiden, 2011).

Halter, Marilyn, 'Cape Verdians in the United States', in Luís Batalha and Jørgen Carling, *Transnational Archipelago. Perspectives on Cape Verdean Migration and Diaspora*, Amsterdam University Press (Amsterdam, 2008), 35–46.

Harney, Robert F., '"Portygees and Other Caucasians": Portuguese Migrants and the Racialism of the English-speaking World', in David Higgs, ed., *Portuguese Migration in Global Perspective*, Multicultural History Society of Ontario (Toronto, 1990), 113–35.

Havik, Philip, 'Sócias, Intermediárias e Empresárias: o Género e a Expansão Colonial na Guiné', in *O Rosto Feminino da Expansão Portuguesa*, 2 vols., Comissão para a Igualdade e para os Direitos das Mulheres (Lisbon, 1995), vol. 2, 87–90.

Higgs, David, 'Portuguese Migration before 1800', in David Higgs and Grace M. Anderson, *A Future to Inherit. The Portuguese Communities of Canada*, McClelland and Stewart (Toronto, 1976), 8–28.

Higgs, David and Grace M. Anderson, *A Future to Inherit. The Portuguese Communities of Canada*, McClelland and Stewart (Toronto, 1976).

Januário, Ilda and Manuela Marujo, 'Voices of Portuguese Immigrant Women', in Carlos Teixeira and Victor M. P. Da Rosa, eds, *The Portuguese in Canada*, University of Toronto Press (Toronto, 2000), 97–111.

Jayasuriya, Shihan de Silva, *The Portuguese in the East*, Tauris Academic Studies (London, 2008).

Kaplan, Yosef, 'The Self-definition of the Sephardic Jews of Western Europe and their Relation to the Alien and the Stranger', in Benjamin Gampel, ed., *Crisis and Creativity in the Sephardic World 1391–1648*, Columbia University Press (New York, 1992),121–45.

Keese, Alexander, 'Managing the Prospect of Famine. Cape Verdean Officials, Subsistence Emergencies, and the Change of Elite Attitudes during Portugal's Late Colonial Phase, 1939–1961', *Itinerario*, 36, no. 1 (2012).

Kipling, Rudyard, *Captains Courageous*, first published 1897, Macmillan (London, 1932).

Klawe, Janina, 'O Papel das Mulheres nos Descobrimentos e na Expansão Portuguesa', in *O Rosto Feminino da Expansão Portuguesa*, 2 vols., Comissão para a Igualdade e para os Direitos das Mulheres (Lisbon, 1995), vol. 1, 253–68.

Klein, Herbert S., 'The Social and Economic Integration of Portuguese Immigrants in Brazil in the Late Nineteenth and Twentieth Centuries', *Journal of Latin American Studies*, 23 (1991), 309–37.

Klimt, Andrea, 'Divergent Trajectories: Identity and Community among Portuguese in Germany and the United States', *Portuguese Studies Review*, 14, no. 2 (2006–7), 211–40.

Lacerda Machado, Francisco Soares de, *História do Concelho das Lages*, Tipografia Popular (Figueira da Foz, 1936).

Laidler, John, 'Many Portuguese still chasing the American dream', *Boston Sunday Globe*, 4 December 1991.

Laurence, K. O., *Immigration into the West Indies in the 19th Century*, Caribbean Universities Press (St Lawrence, Barbados, 1971).

Law, Robin, 'The Evolution of the Brazilian Community in Ouidah', in Kristin Mann and Edna G. Bay, *Rethinking the African Diaspora*, Cass (London, 2001), 22–41.

Lewis, Alfred, *Home is an Island*, first published 1951, Tagus Press (Dartmouth, MA, 2012).

Linhas Gerais da História do Desenvolvimento Urbano da Cidade de Mindelo, República de Cabo Verde (Lisbon, 1984).

Linschoten, Jan Huyghen van, *The Voyage of Jan Huyghen van Linschoten to the East Indies*, A. C. Burnell, ed., 2 vols., Hakluyt Society (London, 1885).

Lockhart, James and Stuart Schwartz, *Early Latin America: a Short History of Spanish America and Brazil*, Cambridge University Press (Cambridge, 1983).

London, Jack, *Martin Eden*, first published 1909, Penguin Books (London, 1993).

———— *The Valley of the Moon*, first published 1913, The Echo Library (Teddington, 2008).

Macdonald, N. P., *The Making of Brazil: Portuguese Roots 1500–1822*, Book Guild (Lewes, 1996).

Machado, Augusto Reis, ed., *Viagem de Lisboa à Ilha de S.Tomé. Escrita por um pilôto Português (século XVI)*, Portugália (Lisbon, n.d.).

BIBLIOGRAPHY

Machado, Pedro, 'Without Scales and Balances. Gujerati Merchants in Mozambique, *c.*1680–1800', *Portuguese Studies Review*, 9, nos. 1–2 (2001), 254–80.

Maffia, Marta, 'Cape Verdeans in Argentina', in Luís Batalha and Jørgen Carling, *Transnational Archipelago. Perspectives on Cape Verdean Migration and Diaspora*, Amsterdam University Press (Amsterdam, 2008).

Magahlães Godinho, Vitorino, 'L'Emigration portugaise (XVᵉ-XXᵉ siècles), une constante structurale et les réponses aux changements du monde', *Revista de História Económica e Social*, 1, Jan.-June (1978), 5–32.

Mar-Molinero, Vanessa, 'Family and Transmission: Collective Memory in Identification Practices of Madeirans on Jersey', *Portuguese Studies*, 26, no. 1 (2010), 94–110.

Mark, Peter, *'Portuguese Style' and Luso-African Identity*, Indiana University Press (Bloomington, 2002).

Mauro, Fréderic, *O Império Luso-Brasilero 1620–1750*, Estampa (Lisbon, 1991).

McDermott, John D., 'The Famous Ride of John "Portuguese" Phillips, http://www.philkearny.vcn.com/phillips.htm.

McNeill, William H., 'Human Migration: A Historical Overview', in W. H. McNeill and Ruth S. Adams, *Human Migration Patterns and Policies*, Indiana University Press (Bloomington, 1978), 3–19.

Mendonça, Luís and José Ávila, *Emigração Açoriana (sécs. XVIII a XX)* (Lisbon, 2002).

Menezes, Mary Noel, *The Portuguese of Guyana: a Study in Culture and Conflict*, self-published (1993).

Merrick, Thomas and Douglas Graham, *Population and Economic Development in Brazil 1800 to the Present*, Johns Hopkins University Press (Baltimore and London, 1979).

Mira, Manuel, *The Forgotten Portuguese. The Melungeons and other Groups. The Portuguese Making of America*, Portuguese American Historical Research Foundation (Franklin, NC, 1998).

Monteiro, J. G., *A Guerra em Portugal nos Finais da Idade Média*, Editorial Notícias (Lisbon, 1998).

Monteiro, Vladimir Nobre, *Portugal/Crioulo*, ICL Estudos e Ensaios (Mindelo, 1995), 129–34.

Moore, Brian L. 'The Social Impact of Portuguese Immigration into British Guiana after Emancipation', *Boletin de Estudios Latinoamericanos e Caribe*, 19 (1975), 3–15.

Morier-Genoud, Eric and Michel Cahen, *Imperial Migrations. Colonial Communities and Diaspora in the Portuguese World*, Palgrave Macmillan (Basingstoke, 2012).

Morris, John N., *Alone at Sea: Gloucester in the Age of the Dorymen (1623–1939)*, Commonwealth Editions (Beverly, MA, 2010).

Moser, Robert Henry and Antonio Luciano de Andrade Tosta, *Luso-American Literature. Writings by Portuguese-speaking Authors in North America*, Rutgers University Press (New Brunswick, NJ, 2011).

Mundell de Calado, Kathleen J., 'At Odds and against all Odds: a Glimpse into the

BIBLIOGRAPHY

Portuguese Experience in British Guiana, through the Eyes of Edward Jenkins', *Revista de Estudos Anglo-Portugueses*, 19 (2010), 235–50.

Myett, Marilyn, 'Men from Azores marched into heart of Gloucester', *Gloucester Daily Times*, 12 February 1967.

Nafafé, José Lingna, *Colonial Encounters: Issues of Culture, Hybridity and Creolisation. Portuguese Mercantile Settlers in West Africa*, Peter Lang (Frankfurt am Main, 2007).

Nascimento, Augusto, 'Cape Verdeans in São Tomé and Príncipe', in Luís Batalha and Jørgen Carling, *Transnational Archipelago. Perspectives on Cape Verdean Migration and Diaspora*, Amsterdam University Press (Amsterdam, 2008), 55–60.

Newitt, Malyn, *History of Mozambique*, Hurst & Co. (London, 1995).

——— 'British Travellers' Accounts of Portuguese Africa in the Nineteenth Century', *Revista de Estudos Anglo-Portugueses*, 11 (2002), 102–29.

——— 'The Portuguese Nobility and the Rise and Decline of Portuguese Military Power 1400–1650', in D. J. B. Trim, ed., *The Chivalric Ethos and the Development of Military Professionalism*, Brill (Leiden, 2003), 89–116.

——— 'Portugal in European and World History*, Reaktion Books (London, 2009).

——— *The Portuguese in West Africa 1415–1670*, Cambridge University Press (New York, 2010).

——— 'The Portuguese African Colonies during the Second World War', in Judith Byfield, ed., *Africa in World War Two*, Cambridge University Press forthcoming.

Nunes, Ana Bela, Eugénia Mata and Nuno Valério, 'Portuguese Economic Growth 1833–1985', *Journal of European Economic History*, 18 (1989).

Nunes, Fernando, 'Portuguese-Canadian Youth and their Academic Under-achievement: a Literature Review', *Portuguese Studies Review*, 11, no. 2 (2003–4), 41–87.

Nunes, Rosana Barbosa, 'Portuguese Immigrants in Brazil: an Overview', *Portuguese Studies Review*, 8, no. 2 (2000), 27–44.

'Observatório da Emigração', produced by CIES Centro de Investigação de Estudos de Sociologia, http://www.observatorioemigracao.secomunidades.pt/np4/paises.html?id=14.

Oliel-Grausz, Evelyne, 'Networks and Communication in the Sephardi Diaspora: An Added Dimension to the Concept of Port Jews and Port Jewries', in David Cesarini and Gemma Romain, eds, *Jews and Port Cities 1590–1990*, Vallentine Mitchell (London, 2006), 61–76.

Oliveira Marques, A. H. de, *History of Portugal*, 2 vols., Columbia University Press (New York, 1972).

——— *A Expansão Quatrocentista*, vol. 2 of *Nova História da Expansão Portuguesa*, Joel Serrão and A. H. de Oliveira Marques, eds, Editorial Estampa (Lisbon, 1998).

Pap, Leo, *The Portuguese-Americans*, Twayne Publishers (Boston, MA, 1981).

Pearson, M. N., *The New Cambridge History of India. I.1. The Portuguese in India*, Cambridge University Press (Cambridge, 1967).

BIBLIOGRAPHY

Peixoto, João, 'A Emigração', in Francisco Bethencourt and Kirti Chaudhuri, eds, *História da Expansão Portuguesa*, 5 vols., Temas e Debates (Lisbon, 2000), vol. 5, 152–81.

Pellerin, Agnès, *Les Portugais à Paris au fil des siècles et des arrondissements*, Chandeigne (Paris, 2009).

Pelúcia, Alexandra, *Corsários e Piratas Portugueses*, A Esfera dos Livros (Lisbon, 2010).

Pereira da Rosa, Victor and Salvato Trigo, 'Islands in a Segregated Land: Portuguese in South Africa', in David Higgs, ed., *Portuguese Migration in Global Perspective*, Multicultural History Society of Ontario (Toronto, 1990), 182–202.

—— *Azorean Emigration. A Preliminary Overview*, Fernando Pessoa University Press (Porto, 1994).

Pereira, Miriam Halpern, *A Política Portuguesa de Emigração 1850–1930*, Editora A Regra do Jogo (Lisboa, 1981).

Pina Almeida, José Carlos, 'Citizens of the World: Migration and Citizenship of the Portuguese in the UK', *Portuguese Studies*, 23 (2007), 208–29.

Pina Almeida, José Carlos and David Corkill, 'Portuguese Migrant Workers in the UK: A Case Study of Thetford, Norfolk', *Portuguese Studies*, 26, no. 1 (2010), 27–40.

Pinto da França, António, *Portuguese Influence in Indonesia*, Calouste Gulbenkian Foundation (Lisbon, 1985).

Pyrard, François, *The Voyage of François Pyrard*, A. Gray, ed., 2 vols., Hakluyt Society (London, 1887–90).

Raynal, Guillaume-Thomas, *Histoire Philosophique et Politique des Etablissements et du Commerce des Européens dans les deux Indes*, first published 1770, 10 vols., Jean-Leonard Pellet (Geneva, 1782).

Robinson, Richard, *Contemporary Portugal*, George Allen and Unwin (London, 1979).

Rocha-Trindade, Maria Beatriz, 'The Portuguese Diaspora', in Carlos Teixeira and Victor M. P. Da Rosa, eds, *The Portuguese in Canada*, University of Toronto Press (Toronto, 2000), 15–43.

Rodrigues, Vitor Luís Pinto Gaspar da Conceição, 'A Guiné nas Cartas de Perdão (1463–1500)', in *Congresso Internacional Bartolomeu Dias e a sua Época*, Comissão Nacional para as Comemorações dos Descobrimentos Portugueses (Porto, 1989), vol. IV, 397–412.

Rogers, Francis M., *Atlantic Islanders of the Azores and Madeira*, Christopher Publishing House (North Quincy, MA, 1979).

Rogers, Meg, *The Portuguese in San Jose*, Arcadia Publishing (San Francisco, 2007).

—— *The Portuguese in San Leandro*, Arcadia Publishing (San Francisco, 2008).

Ross, Edward Alsworth, *The Old World and the New*, T. Fisher Unwin (London, 1914).

Rupert, Linda, 'Trading Globally, Speaking Locally: Curaçao's Sephardim in the

BIBLIOGRAPHY

Making of a Caribbean Creole', in David Cesarini and Gemma Romain, eds, *Jews and Port Cities 1590–1990*, Vallentine Mitchell (London, 2006), 109–22.

Russell-Wood, A. J. R., *A World on the Move*, Carcanet (Manchester, 1992).

Santos, Maria Emília Madeira, *História Geral de Cabo Verde*, 3 vols., Centro de Estudos de História e Cartografia Antiga and Instituto de Investigação Científica Tropical (Lisbon, 1991–2002).

Santos-Stubbe, Chirly dos, 'Abade Faria (1756–1819) in Scientific and Fine Arts Literature', in Charles Borges, Óscar Pereira and Hannes Stubbe, *Goa and Portugal: History and Development*, Concept Publishing (New Delhi, 2000), 336–45.

Saraiva, António José, *A Inquisição Portuguesa*, 3rd edn, Europa-América (Lisboa, 1964).

———— *A Inquisição e Cristãos-Novos*, Editorial Nova (Porto, 1969).

Segre, Renata, 'Sephardic Refugees in Ferrara: Two Notable Families', in Benjamin Gampel, ed., *Crisis and Creativity in the Sephardic World 1391–1648*, Columbia University Press (New York, 1992), 164–85.

Serrão, Joel, *A Emigração Portuguesa. Sondagem Histórica*, 2nd edn, Livros Horizonte (Lisbon, 1974).

Shils, Edward, 'Roots—The Sense of Place and Past: The Cultural Gains and Losses of Migration', in W. H. McNeill and Ruth S. Adams, *Human Migration Patterns and Policies*, Indiana University Press (Bloomington, 1978), 404–26.

Southey, Robert, *History of Brazil*, 1st edn 1817, Longman, Hurst, Rees and Orme (London, 1910).

Steinbeck, John, 'Tortilla Flat', in *The Steinbeck Omnibus*, Heinemann (London, 1950), 93–136.

Studnicki-Gizbert, Daviken, *A Nation upon the Open Sea. Portugal's Atlantic Diaspora and the Crisis of the Spanish Empire, 1492–1640*, Oxford University Press (Oxford, 2007).

Sutcliffe, Adam, 'Identity, Space and Intercultural Contact in the Urban Entrepôt: The Sephardic Bounding of Community in Early Modern Amsterdam and London', in David Cesarini and Gemma Romain, eds, *Jews and Port Cities 1590–1990*, Vallentine Mitchell (London, 2006).

Sweet, James H., *Recreating Africa*, University of North Carolina Press (Chapel Hill, NC, 2003).

Swetschinski, Daniel, *Reluctant Cosmopolitans. The Portuguese Jews of Seventeenth Century Amsterdam*, Littman Library of Jewish Civilization (Oxford, 2000).

Syrett, Stephen, *Contemporary Portugal. Dimensions of Economic and Political Change*, Ashgate (Aldershot, 2002).

Taft, Donald R., *Two Portuguese Communities in New England*, Columbia University Press (New York, 1923).

Tavernier, Jean Baptiste, *Travels in India by Jean Baptiste Tavernier*, V. Ball, ed., 2 vols., Macmillan (London, 1889).

Teixeira, Carlos, 'On the Move: Portuguese in Toronto', in Carlos Teixeira and

Victor M. P. Da Rosa, eds, *The Portuguese in Canada*, University of Toronto Press (Toronto, 2000), 207–20.

Teixeira, Carlos and Victor M. P. Da Rosa, eds, *The Portuguese in Canada*, University of Toronto Press (Toronto, 2000).

Tenreiro, Francisco, *A Ilha de São Tomé*, Junta de Investigações do Ultramar (Lisbon, 1961).

'The Voyage of M. George Fenner to Guinie, and the Islands of Cape Verde, in the yeere of 1566...', in Richard Hakluyt, *The Principal Navigations, Voyage Traffiques & Discoveries of the English Nation*, 8 vols., J. M. Dent (London, 1907), vol. 4, 139–55.

Thomas, Arnold, 'Portuguese and Indian Immigration to St Vincent (1885–1890)', *Journal of Caribbean Studies*, 14, 1&2 (1999–2000), 41–59.

Thomas, Gordon, 'The Portuguese "Gloucesterman"', *Gloucester, the Magazine of the New England Coast*, 2, no. 3 (1978), 4–7.

Trivellato, Francesca, 'The Port Jews of Livorno and their Global Networks of Trade in the Early Modern Period', in David Cesarini and Gemma Romain, eds, *Jews and Port Cities 1590–1990*, Vallentine Mitchell (London, 2006), 31–48.

Venturini, Alessandra, *Postwar Migration in Southern Europe 1950–2000*, Cambridge University Press (Cambridge, 2004).

Vieira, Alberto, 'Emigration from the Portuguese Islands in the Second Half of the Nineteenth Century: the Case of Madeira', in David Higgs, ed., *Portuguese Migration in Global Perspective*, Multicultural History Society of Ontario (Toronto, 1990), 42–60.

——— 'A Emigração portuguesa nos Descobrimentos: Do Littoral às Ilhas', *Portuguese Studies Review*, 15, nos. 1–2 (2007), 63–101.

Vilas-Boas e Alvim, Maria Helena, 'A Mulher e a Expansão na Perspectiva de alguns Cronistas e Historiadores seus Coevos', in *O Rosto Feminino da Expansão Portuguesa*, 2 vols, Comissão para a Igualdade e para os Direitos das Mulheres (Lisbon, 1995), vol. 1, 261–8.

Villiers, Alan, *The Quest of the Schooner Argus*, Hodder and Stoughton (London, 1951).

Villiers, John, 'The Estado da India in Southeast Asia', in Malyn Newitt, ed., *The First Portuguese Colonial Empire*, University of Exeter Press (Exeter, 1986).

Weber, Klaus, 'Were Merchants more Tolerant? "Godless Patrons of the Jews" and the Decline of the Sephardi Community in Late Seventeenth Century Hamburg', in David Cesarini and Gemma Romain, eds, *Jews and Port Cities 1590–1990*, Vallentine Mitchell (London, 2006), 77–92.

Westphalen, Cecilia Maria and Altiva Pilatti Balhana, 'Politica Legislação Imigratórias Brasileiras e a Imigração Portuguesa', in *Emigração/Imigração em Portugal*, Actas do Colóquio Internacional sobre Emigração e Imigração em Portugal (sec xix-xx), Fragmentos (Alges 1993), 17–27.

Whiteway, R. S., *The Rise of Portuguese Power in India, 1497–1550*, 1st edn 1899, reprinted Susil Gupta, Augustus Kelley (New York, 1967).

Williams, Jerry, 'Azorean Migration Patterns in the United States', in David Higgs,

BIBLIOGRAPHY

ed., *Portuguese Migration in Global Perspective*, Multicultural History Society of Ontario, (Toronto, 1990), 145–57.

Wolforth, Sandra, *The Portuguese in America*, R&E Research Associates (San Francisco, 1978).

Yerushalmi, Yosef, 'Exile and Expulsion in Jewish History', in Benjamin R. Gampel, *Crisis and Creativity in the Sephardic World 1391–1648*, Columbia University Press (New York, 1997), 3–22.

Websites

Slave trade database: http://slavevoyages.org/tast/assessment/estimates.faces

'The story of Portuguese Bermudans': http://www.rootsweb.ancestry.com/~bmuwgw/portuguese.htm

'The Portuguese of the West Indies': http://freepages.genealogy.rootsweb.ancestry.com/~portwestind/general/index.htm

swissinfo.ch 'Why Portuguese Seek Work in Switzerland' http://www.swissinfo.ch/eng/swiss_news/Why_Portuguese_seek_work_in_Switzerland.html?cid=342628 48. Interview with Rosita Fibbi.

Observatório da Emigração, http://www.observatorioemigracao.secomunidades.pt/np4/paises.html?id=244

Further Recommended Reading

Almeida, Onésimo T. and Alice Clemente, *George Monteiro: The Discreet Charm of a Portuguese American*, Gávea-Brown Publications (Providence RI, 2005).

Almeida, Onésimo T., *O Peso do Hifen. Ensaios sobre a Experiência Luso-America*, Imprensa das Ciências Sociais (Lisbon, 2010).

Ames, Glenn, *Renascent Empire? The House of Braganza and the Quest for Stability in Portuguese Monsoon Asia, ca 1640–1683*, Amsterdam University Press (Amsterdam, 2000).

Childs, Gladwyn, *Kinship and Character of the Ovimbundu*, Dawsons (London, 1949).

Davies, Richard Beale, *The Abbé Corrêa in America, 1812-1820—The Contributions of the Diplomat and Natural Philosopher to the Foundations of Our National Life*, Gávea-Brown Publications (Providence RI, 1993).

Duffy, James, *Portuguese Africa*, Harvard University Press (Cambridge, 1959).

Gann, L.H. and Peter Duignan eds., *Colonialism in Africa*, 3 vols, Cambridge University Press (Cambridge, 1969–75).

Goulart, Tony, ed., *Capelinhos: A Volcano of Synergies—Azorean Immigration to America*, The Portuguese Heritage Publications of California, (San Jose, 2008).

Hanson, Carl, *Economy and Society in Baroque Portugal, 1668–1703*, University of Minnesota Press, (Minneapolis, 1980).

Holton, K. da Costa and Andrea Klimt eds. *Community, Culture and the Making of Identity: Portuguese Americans along the Eastern Seaboard*, University of Massachusetts Press (Amherst, 2009).

BIBLIOGRAPHY

Marcos, Daniel, *The Capelinhos Eruption: Window of Opportunity for Azorean Emigration*, Gávea-Brown Publications (Providence RI, 2008).

Torga, Miguel, *Portugal* (Coimbra, 1950).

Warrin, Donald, *So Ends the Day*, University of Massachusetts Press (Amherst, 2010).

————— *Land as Far as the Eye can see*, University of Massachusetts Press (Amherst, 2013).

Wheeler, Douglas, *The Empire Time Forgot: writing a History of the Portuguese Overseas Empire*, Universidade Fernando Pessoa (Porto, 1998).

INDEX

INDEX

285